IN A SCENE FROM HER FILM *THE SUBJECTIVE FACTOR*, HELKE SANDER APPEARS
IN SILHOUETTE AGAINST PROJECTED DOCUMENTARY FOOTAGE THAT DEPICTS
SANDER HERSELF GIVING A SPEECH TO THE WEST GERMAN SDS IN 1968.

Politics of the Self

RICHARD W. MCCORMICK

Politics of the Self

FEMINISM

AND THE POSTMODERN IN

WEST GERMAN LITERATURE AND FILM

PRINCETON UNIVERSITY PRESS

COPYRIGHT © 1991 BY PRINCETON UNIVERSITY PRESS

PUBLISHED BY PRINCETON UNIVERSITY PRESS, 41 WILLIAM STREET,

PRINCETON, NEW JERSEY 08540

IN THE UNITED KINGDOM: PRINCETON UNIVERSITY PRESS, OXFORD

LIBRARY OF CONGRESS CATALOGING-IN-PUBLICATION DATA

McCORMICK, RICHARD W., 1951–

POLITICS OF THE SELF : FEMINISM AND THE POSTMODERN IN WEST GERMAN

LITERATURE AND FILM / RICHARD W. McCORMICK.

P. CM.

INCLUDES BIBLIOGRAPHICAL REFERENCES AND INDEX.

ISBN 0-691-06851-8. — ISBN 0-691-01483-3 (PBK.)

1. FEMINISM AND THE ARTS—GERMANY (WEST)

2. POSTMODERNISM—GERMANY (WEST) I. TITLE.

NX180.F4M37 1991

830.9′1′09045—DC20   90-47160 CIP

THE LYRICS QUOTED FROM "PINBALL WIZARD" BY PETE TOWNSHEND

FROM THE WHO'S ROCK OPERA TOMMY ARE REPRINTED BY PERMISSION

OF TOWSER TUNES, INC. COPYRIGHT 1969 BY FABULOUS MUSIC LTD.

ALL RIGHTS IN THE UNITED STATES, ITS TERRITORIES AND POSSESSIONS,

CANADA, MEXICO, AND THE PHILIPPINES ARE CONTROLLED BY

TOWSER TUNES, INC. ALL RIGHTS RESERVED.

INTERNATIONAL COPYRIGHT SECURED.

THIS BOOK HAS BEEN COMPOSED IN LINOTRON MELIOR

PRINCETON UNIVERSITY PRESS BOOKS ARE PRINTED ON ACID-FREE

PAPER AND MEET THE GUIDELINES FOR PERMANENCE AND DURABILITY

OF THE COMMITTEE ON PRODUCTION GUIDELINES FOR BOOK LONGEVITY

OF THE COUNCIL ON LIBRARY RESOURCES

PRINTED IN THE UNITED STATES OF AMERICA BY

PRINCETON UNIVERSITY PRESS, PRINCETON, NEW JERSEY

1 2 3 4 5 6 7 8 9 10

(Pbk.) 10 9 8 7 6 5 4 3 2 1

For Laura and Bob,
for Rita, and
for Joan

———

Contents

Acknowledgments

$\mathbf{M}$ANY FRIENDS, teachers, colleagues, and institutions have provided me with vital support—intellectually, materially, morally, emotionally—through the many stages of the long process that resulted in this book. The first person I want to thank is a scholar who offered invaluable guidance from the very beginning of the project through its every phase: Anton Kaes at the University of California, Berkeley. It is hard to express adequately my gratitude for his insight, encouragement, and friendship.

Early stages of the research for the project were supported by the German Academic Exchange Service, which funded the Interdisciplinary Summer Seminars in German Studies at Berkeley that I was able to attend, and the Fulbright Commission, which provided me with a grant for research in West Berlin in 1983–1984. My discussions with Karl Heinz Stahl at the Technical University of Berlin were very helpful, as were the seminars there on "New Subjectivity" led by Wolfgang Trautwein. I am also grateful to the staff at the library of the Deutsche Film- und Fernsehakademie Berlin (DFFB; German Film and Television Academy) in West Berlin and the staff at the library of the Deutsches Filmmuseum (German Film Museum) in Frankfurt. Thomas Stäcker's insights were valuable. Other friends in Germany who deserve thanks for their advice and support are Anne Lalk, Roland Ladage, Angela Waskow, Susanne Stoye, and Volker Groß.

In the United States there have been many scholars who provided help at various stages of the project. Hinrich Seeba and Paul Thomas assisted me at early stages of the manuscript. Leslie Adelson deserves special thanks for her willingness on short notice to read an earlier version of the manuscript and to make helpful comments. Among other scholars who have been kind enough to read this study or parts thereof (in various versions), I would like to thank Mark Anderson, Susan Bordo, Andreas Huyssen, Anna Kuhn, Eric Rentschler, Volkmar Sander, Margaret Herzfeld-Sander, and Jochen Schulte-Sasse. Sandra Frieden, Vibeke Petersen, and Melissa Vogelsang assisted me with the revision of the fourth chapter. I also want to thank Karen Ruoff Kramer for providing me with a copy of her dissertation, from which I learned a great deal. Others who were kind enough to share with me their work on similar topics include Roger Cook, Barbara Kosta, and Kathryn Strachota.

I want to thank the Department of German at Berkeley in general for its support of my graduate work there. Some of the people at Berkeley whose ideas and guidance contributed ultimately to this book include Bluma Goldstein, Gerd Hillen, Robert Holub, Susanne Loewenthal, and Frederic Tubach. By the same token, the Department of German at the University of Minnesota, where I now teach, has provided assistance toward the completion of this book; in this regard I want to thank especially my colleagues Frank Hirschbach, Ruth-Ellen Joeres, and Gerhard Weiss. I am also indebted to Angelika Rauch and Peter Mühle, who have worked for me as research assistants.

The filmmaker Helke Sander must also be warmly thanked for her willingness practically on the spur of the moment to provide footage from the working copy of *The Subjective Factor* so that a still could be made and used here as the frontispiece. For permission to quote the lyrics from Laurie Anderson's "It Tango," published by Difficult Music 1982, I thank Ms. Anderson and Beldock, Levine, & Hoffman. I am also grateful to Cathie Brettschneider, who edited the manuscript with great care and sensitivity.

Two friends whose assistance at a crucial stage of the research on this book deserves mention are Miriam Hayward and Rick Herbert. The great debt I owe my family and friends in general must also be acknowledged. Above all I want to thank Joan Clarkson, without whose constant friendship and encouragement this book and so much else would have been impossible.

Richard W. McCormick
Minneapolis, Minnesota
July 1990

Acronyms

APO   "Außerparlamentarische Opposition" ("extraparliamentary opposition"): leftist opposition organized outside of West Germany's parliament in the 1960s; the student protest movement was a part of it.

CDU   "Christlich-Demokratische Union" ("Christian Democratic Union"): founded after the second world war, it has been, in coalition with its Bavarian sister-party, the "Christlich-Soziale Union" (CSU; "Christian Social Union"), the major conservative party in West Germany.

DFFB   "Deutsche Film- und Fernsehakademie Berlin," the German Film and Television Academy in West Berlin, opened in 1966.

DKP   "Deutsche Kommunistische Partei" ("German Communist Party"): West German leftist party founded in 1968 that was rigidly aligned with the GDR and with Moscow (until Gorbachev and the opening of the Berlin Wall).

FDP   "Freie Demokratische Partei" ("Free Democratic Party"; also known as the "Liberals"): a small but influential centrist party in West Germany characterized by a strong belief in "liberal capitalism."

GDR   "German Democratic Republic" (in German: "Deutsche Demokratische Republik," or DDR): the East German state, which was founded in 1949 and closely aligned with the Soviet Union for most of its history.

HFF   "Hochschule für Fernsehen und Film": Munich's Academy for Television and Film, opened in 1967.

KPD   "Kommunistische Partei Deutschlands" ("Communist Party of Germany"): Marxist party founded by leftist Social Democrats Rosa Luxemburg and Karl Liebknecht at the end of 1918. It competed with its rival, the SPD, for leftist and working-class votes during the Weimar Republic (1918–1933). It was outlawed by the Nazis in 1933, and again in West Germany in 1956 at the height of the Cold War.

K-Parteien and K-Gruppen: "K-parties and K-groups" ("K" stands for "kommunistisch," i.e., "communist"): leftist splinter groups and small fledgling parties, mostly Maoist, that sprang up as the larger West German student movement began disintegrating at the end of the 1960s.

RAF   "Rote Armee Fraktion" ("Red Army Faction," also known as the "Baader-Meinhof group"): small group of activists who became terrorists. Their first "actions" were in 1968, and they grew ever more violent and sensational during the 1970s.

SDS   "Sozialistischer Deutscher Studentenbund" ("League of Socialist German Students"): originally a student group associated with the SPD, it moved further to the left during the 1960s. It was the leading organization within the West German student movement through 1968; in 1970 it dissolved. (Not to be confused with the SDS in the United States, the "Students for a Democratic Society," which played a similar role in the U.S. protest movement.)

SPD   "Sozialdemokratische Partei Deutschlands" ("Social Democratic Party of Germany"): Germany's first Marxist, working-class party, founded in the nineteenth century. Outlawed during the Third Reich. After the war, it again became influential in West Germany; when the KPD was banned in 1956, the SPD became the only left-wing West German party. In 1959 it distanced itself somewhat from its Marxist origins.

Politics of the Self

Introduction

West German
Literature and Film
Since 1968—Modern,
Antimodern, Postmodern?

ART SINCE 1968 has been undergoing what Thomas Kuhn,
writing about the history of science, described as a
"paradigm crisis": a moment in history when
the accepted belief system becomes
inadequate and the possibility
of a new belief system
is only vaguely
perceived.[1]

Loaded Terms

What, then, is the postmodern?[2]

Because of the debate in the early 1980s between Jean-François Lyotard and Jürgen Habermas, the international discussion of postmodernism has at times been characterized as a battle between Paris and Frankfurt.[3] When attempts are made to place the German side of this debate into some kind of historical context, they usually involve a discussion of the history of European, and specifically German, philosophical thinking. For example, in a 1986 article by Peter U. Hohendahl, there is a focus on such historical conflicts as that between the project of the Enlightenment as seen by the Left Hegelians and Nietzsche's critique of rationalism, a conflict that of course already anticipates the one between Habermas and Lyotard.[4] An approach based on the study of intellectual history is of obvious value, but it needs to be supplemented by an examination of cultural developments in Germany, including very recent ones that have in part shaped the society in which Habermas operates.

These recent developments provide the context for this study, in which literary and cinematic texts are examined against the background of cultural and political events since the late 1960s in the Federal Republic of Germany, that is, West Germany. Such events include the rise of the so-called New Subjectivity in literature; the increasing cultural influence of feminism and of literary works by women, as well as films by women; and politically, the shift among activists from orthodox socialism in the 1960s to ecological, feminist, and pacifist orientations by the early 1980s. But besides focusing on the specifically West German context of these events, I attempt to place them within the broader context of the "postmodernity."

One of the political and cultural projects most emblematic of the

---

[1] Kim Levin, *Beyond Modernism: Essays on Art from the 70s and the 80s* (New York: Harper and Row, 1988), p. xii.

[2] Jean-François Lyotard, "Answering the Question: What is Postmodernism?" trans. Regis Durand, in Lyotard, *The Postmodern Condition* (Minneapolis: University of Minnesota Press, 1984), p. 79.

[3] Lyotard's "Answering the Question" is a response to a paper by Jürgen Habermas, one version of which appears as "Modernity—An Incomplete Project," trans. Seyla Ben-Habib, in Hal Foster, ed., *The Anti-Aesthetic: Essays on Postmodern Culture* (Port Townsend, WA: Bay Press, 1983), pp. 3–15. The original version was a talk given by Habermas in Frankfurt in 1980.

[4] Peter U. Hohendahl, "Habermas' Philosophical Discourse on Modernity," *Telos*, no. 69 (1986), pp. 49–65.

upheavals of the late 1960s in Western Europe and the United States was the attempt to attack certain boundaries based on binary oppositions integral to the dominant worldview of Western society since the eighteenth century: the separations between a public and a private sphere, between the "personal" and the "political," between politics and art, and indeed between life and art. This endeavor was similar to the project of avant-garde movements earlier in the twentieth century such as Dada and surrealism. Habermas describes that project as the surrealist attempt to destroy the autonomous sphere of art in order to "force a reconciliation of art and life."[5]

As was the case with the efforts of the small but influential avant-garde of the 1920s, the more broadly based attempts of the 1960s "failed," for the most part, but their cultural legacy was lasting. Many West German novels and films of the next decade can be interpreted as ambivalent explorations of the experience of the 1960s, of the failures as well as the enduring influences. In this book, works by the authors Peter Schneider, Karin Struck, Peter Handke, and Botho Strauss, and by the filmmakers Wim Wenders, Helma Sanders-Brahms, and Helke Sander are examined in detail. My discussion of these texts includes a consideration of them as "postmodern" critiques and revisions of the roles played by modernism and the avant-garde in the politics and art of the twentieth century.

But it is not only that the interpretation of recent West German literature and film can benefit from the international discussion of postmodernity and postmodernism; the international debate, in turn, can be broadened by consideration of West German developments. One question explored in this study is just what "postmodern culture" might mean in the German context. This brings us back to Habermas.

From his somewhat controversial debates with the West German student movement—for instance, his polemical description of the young activists as "Left fascists" in 1967—through his interpretation of the cultural trends that characterized West Germany in the 1970s, Habermas maintained a generally critical stance toward the political and artistic developments of the West German generation that came of age in the late 1960s. This stance was not only typical of many of the more established leftist intellectuals within West Germany but also similar in tone to attitudes they held toward developments in France in the aftermath of 1968—developments that in France took place primarily in intellectual and critical circles rather than in terms of new political or artistic trends. Poststructur-

---

[5] Habermas, "Modernity," p. 11.

alism and the "Nouvelle Philosophie" in France were often equated with each other by these critics and attacked as an outbreak of "antimodern" irrationalism—in much the same way as the "New Subjectivity" in West German literature was attacked.

The adjective "antimodern" has a very specific historical meaning in Germany, implying a connection to National Socialism. That connection is made explicit in orthodox leftist explanations of German fascism, of which the most famous is associated with Georg Lukács: the idea that fascism was ultimately the result of a German tradition of irrationalism with roots in German Romanticism, an irrationalism further articulated by Nietzsche.[6] The more renegade leftist Ernst Bloch explained the success of the fascists in Germany in a quite different manner, however, arguing that the fetishization of reason by the Left in the Weimar Republic ignored real, "irrational" needs of the masses that the Nazis were able to manipulate.[7] Then, under the cover of an "antimodern" ideology, the Nazis went on to modernize Germany as no one before had succeeded in doing. (They accomplished this mainly by invigorating the industrial sector through a massive arms build-up.)

The use to which concepts like "antimodern" and the "irrational" have been put testifies to a specific German conception of a rational and progressive modernism. Outside Germany, however, modernism was by no means exclusively associated with "rationalism," or with the Left, as examples such as the Italian futurists, or Ezra Pound and T. S. Eliot, amply illustrate. Even within Germany, someone like Gottfried Benn provides a similar example; Germany was by no means immune to "reactionary modernism."[8] In West Germany the conflict around this constellation of issues erupted again in 1968, when those tendencies reflecting the more "irrational" influences within the international student movement—French existentialism and surrealism, the American "Beat" movement and rock and roll—were overshadowed and then suppressed by a sort of revival of the worst aspects of the rationalistic tradition of the Weimar Left, resulting in a phase of dogmatic Marxist-Leninism.

The dogmatic phase led in turn to its repudiation in the next twist

[6] See Georg Lukács's *Die Zerstörung der Vernunft: Der Weg des Irrationalismus von Schelling bis Hitler* (East Berlin: Aufbau, 1954). In English: *The Destruction of Reason*, trans. Peter Palmer (Atlantic Highlands, NJ: Humanities Press, 1981).

[7] Ernst Bloch, *Erbschaft dieser Zeit* [*Heritage of Our Times*] (1935; Frankfurt: Suhrkamp, 1973), p. 153.

[8] See the book with this title by Jeffrey Herf: *Reactionary modernism: Technology, culture, and politics in Weimar and the Third Reich* (Cambridge: Cambridge University Press, 1984).

of the dialectic, a "New Subjectivity" that rejected rationalistic objectivity—a "politics of the self" that gloried in personal expression and anarchistic spontaneity—and influenced West German literary and cinematic output of the 1970s. This subjective phase represents a change in outlook that must also be seen in some connection with new types of political activism: above all, the ecology, peace, and women's movements. Rather than "antimodern" I would term these phenomena "postmodern" responses—in some cases naive, in others more sophisticated—both to the various crises of modernization in the late twentieth century and to the excesses of the rationalistic modernism the traditional German Left still wants to defend. Taken together, these and other postmodern phenomena are no less ambivalent than "high modernism" was, having both reactionary and progressive aspects. Furthermore, the complexity of these phenomena cannot be understood solely in political terms.

Definitions?

At this point I want to try to define the adjective "postmodern" more precisely—or at any rate my use of the term, since the term has been used to mean many different things. I do not share Habermas's basic position that postmodern culture is inherently "antimodern" and negative; he is wrong simply to equate it with neoconservatism.[9] Nor do I agree with Lyotard's somewhat ahistorical use of the term "postmodern" to imply a condition of being somehow always ahead of the modern: "A work can become modern only if it is first postmodern."[10] This sounds rather like the modernist aesthetic of novelty, and in its implication of perpetual artistic progress it seems curiously modern.[11]

[9] Neoconservatism is of course one ideological trend (but only one) in an era I define as "postmodern." It tends, however, to champion a conservative version of "high modernism" against any "postmodernisms," at least in the United States—Hilton Kramer's The New Criterion would be the best example. Habermas has written about the differences between American and West German neoconservatism; see his essay "Die Kulturkritik der Neokonservativen in den USA und in der Bundesrepublik," in Habermas, Die neue Unübersichtlichkeit (Frankfurt: Suhrkamp, 1985), pp. 30–56. (I support him in his criticism of West German neoconservatism, especially in regard to the Historikerstreit—the "historians' debate"—about the Third Reich. On the historians' debate, see, e.g., the special issue of New German Critique, no. 44 [1988].)

[10] Lyotard, "Answering the Question," p. 79.

[11] Meaghan Morris refers to Lyotard's program for the future of art as "frontiersmanship." See Morris, The Pirate's Fiancée: Feminism, reading, postmodernism (London: Verso, 1988), p. 215.

The most popular conception of postmodernism has to do with architecture, the basis (but not the limit) of Charles Jencks's writings on the issue.[12] In that field, however, there are indications that those styles labeled "postmodernist" may already be passé.[13] Kim Levin, discussing the visual arts, writes: "The perspective has shifted: the prefix of choice in the '70s was *post*; in the '80s it's been *neo*."[14] It seems necessary to get beyond identifying postmodernism too narrowly in relation to individual movements within certain of the arts. Fredric Jameson's point seems valid: there are at least as many "postmodernisms" as there were modernisms, the former being reactions to the latter, which were themselves by no means parts of a single, monolithic movement.

Jameson tries to make a more encompassing analysis by specifying one of the underlying causes of the shift from the modernist movements in the arts to postmodern ones: he asserts that there has been a fundamental change in conceptions of the self, or the subject, over the course of this century. And, as one would expect from a critic who stands in the Marxist tradition, Jameson speculates that this change has something to do with recent economic developments in capitalist society.[15] This emphasis on the subject and on a historical approach is valuable in spite of the fact that Jameson, like Habermas (although not exactly for the same reasons), views postmodern culture in generally negative terms, seeing it more or less as a reflection of "late capitalism."

This Lukácsian "aesthetics of reflection" seems somewhat dated and related to Jameson's faith in some "master narrative" of history, which has been criticized by Craig Owens (following Lyotard).[16] The master narrative is a metanarrative and is thus *outside* history. As Linda Hutcheon writes, postmodern culture "cannot escape implication in the economic (late capitalist) and ideological (liberal humanist) dominants of its time. There is no outside. All it can do is question from within."[17] The idea of a place outside from where

[12] See, for example, Jencks's books *The Language of Post-Modern Architecture* (New York: Rizzoli, 1977) and *What is Post-Modernism?* (London: Academy, 1987).

[13] See Moshe Safdie, "Skyscrapers Shouldn't Look Down on Humanity," *New York Times*, 29 May 1988, "Arts and Leisure," p. 30.

[14] Levin, *Beyond Modernism*, p. xii.

[15] Fredric Jameson, "Postmodernism and Consumer Society," in Foster, *The Anti-Aesthetic*, pp. 111–25.

[16] Craig Owens, "The Discourse of Others: Feminists and Postmodernism," in Foster, *The Anti-Aesthetic*, p. 65.

[17] Linda Hutcheon, *A Poetics of Postmodernism: History, Theory, Fiction* (New York: Routledge, 1988), pp. xiii.

"pure critique" can originate is a modern one. Where indeed is that place of objective certainty in which any totalizing critique (Marxist or otherwise) pretends to stand "uncontaminated" by subjectivity, ideology, late capitalism, or postmodernity?[18] Theresa de Lauretis, in her criticism of Althusser, calls this (mythical) position "science," the place outside ideology—and history—upon which his writing seems to base its authority.[19] A historical approach is undoubtedly necessary, but not one anchored in any transhistorical "scientific" certainty.

It might also be charged that Jameson's attempt to subsume under the category postmodern the complex interrelationship of economic change, the undermining of traditional social, psychological, and ideological concepts of the subject, and a variety of artistic trends confuses rather than elucidates the term "postmodern." In this context, a distinction drawn by Jochen Schulte-Sasse is helpful: he maintains that one should distinguish "postmodernity"—as a historical condition with economic, political, and social determinations—from "postmodernism," which represents artistic and cultural forms of response to postmodernity.[20]

This distinction between a postmodernist cultural/ideological "superstructure" and the postmodern/postindustrial economic "base" is a useful one, and I shall use it, with some modifications. But the situation is more complicated, since socio-economic "modernity" (or the "modern") on the one hand does not correspond so neatly with cultural/artistic "modernism" on the other. "Modernity," after all, begins at the latest with the Enlightenment and the Industrial Revolution in the eighteenth century, if not with Descartes in the seventeenth (as the French tend to date it), or even, as Jencks maintains, with the rise of capitalism in Italy and France af-

[18] Hutcheon, A Poetics of Postmodernism, pp. xiii, 7, 216–17. See also Peter Sloterdijk's discussion of ideology critique in the first chapter of his Critique of Cynical Reason, which is arguably the best West German example of a "postmodernist" philosophical treatment of the legacy of the enlightenment. Sloterdijk finds that Marxist ideology critique has provided examples of the "most humorless reification of every opposing consciousness." He considers neoconservatism, however, much more cynical. Sloterdijk, "Cynicism—The Twilight of False Consciousness," trans. Michael Eldred and Leslie A. Adelson, New German Critique, no. 33 (1984), pp. 205–6. Sloterdijk's entire work, Kritik der zynischen Vernunft, 2 vols. (Frankfurt: Suhrkamp, 1983), has been published in English: Critique of Cynical Reason, trans. Michael Eldred (Minneapolis: University of Minnesota Press, 1987).

[19] Theresa de Lauretis, Technologies of Gender: Essays on Theory, Film, and Fiction (Bloomington: Indiana University Press, 1987), p. 9.

[20] Jochen Schulte-Sasse, "Modernity and Modernism, Postmodernity and Postmodernism: Framing the Issue," Cultural Critique 5 (1986–1987), p. 6.

ter 1450.[21] Modernism—since its beginnings cannot be dated much earlier than with Impressionism in the 1860s—can thus represent only one group of cultural responses to modernity, and a relatively late one at that. Furthermore, as has been noted, modernism itself was hardly monolithic: at the start, movements like Naturalism and Impressionism were basically affirmative of nineteenth-century science; subsequently, however, the various tendencies now grouped under "high modernism" were in many ways "antimodern," in terms of their disdain for modernization and mass culture and their embrace of myth. The avant-garde, however, especially in its German and Soviet varieties, embraced technology and innovation and considered its worst enemy precisely that elitist, pseudo-religious cult of art we associate with "high modernism" (and into which, ironically enough, the works of the avant-garde would be subsumed by the middle of the twentieth century, grouped together in the same museums).

Defining the "postmodern" and "postmodernism" is also no easy task, nor is distinguishing between the two. For my purposes, I will be using the term "postmodern" to refer to artistic, cultural, social, and political aspects of the current historical epoch, a "postindustrial" age in Europe, North America, and Japan. Globally it is an age in which rampant modernization has by no means halted but is perceived at least as much in threatening terms as it is in hopeful ones.[22] In any case, the West's unqualified faith in the "project of modernity" has been shaken, and that ideological insecurity is evident in all sorts of cultural phenomena. Thus all art today is in some sense or another "postmodern" (i.e., it can be placed in relation to this larger historical context). I shall try to restrict the use of "postmodernism" to refer to certain movements in the arts (and specific works of art) with actual agendas for moving "beyond" modernist programs. There are many "postmodernisms," and they must be understood in terms of historical developments both within the arts (e.g., with regard to modernist and premodernist traditions) and in

[21] Jencks, *What is Post-Modernism?*, pp. 46–47.

[22] On the concept of "postindustrial" society, Jameson, in his "Foreword" to Lyotard's *Postmodern Condition*, makes a valid point, citing Ernest Mandel's concept of a "third stage" of capitalism. Globally speaking, industrialization is by no means over; rather, the world is being industrialized at an unprecedented pace (pp. xiv–xv). Nonetheless, "postindustrial" is an accurate description of the situation in the older industrial nations, where heavy industry is in decline mainly because corporations based in those nations have shifted so much heavy industry to the Third World. And this does represent a new stage for international capitalism.

a broader social and political context. This general principle informs the approach taken here.

But in defining relations to modernism, we are once again in an area of major dispute. The situation in architecture is relatively clear, but in literature "postmodernism" referred to experimental "surfiction," at least in the 1970s. Both Jencks and Hutcheon (who, in contrast to Jencks, focuses primarily, though not exclusively, on literature) consider "surfiction" not postmodernist at all but rather late modernist.[23] Jencks, indeed, places "deconstruction" within "late modernism," which he separates from postmodernism with a suspiciously fixed boundary. For it is just such binary, "either/or" logic that most critics see as having been surpassed in the postmodern era, where instead one finds a logic of "both/and."[24] Deconstruction, and poststructuralism in general, is certainly postmodern if not postmodernist (as is late modernism); there is much to be said for viewing poststructuralism as a postmodernist "theory" (e.g., as a postmodernist problematization of the boundary between theoretical and literary writing). On the other hand, it is problematic simply to *equate* poststructuralism with postmodernism and thus ignore the significance of other perspectives—Marxist, feminist, and "New Historicist"—in the current theoretical landscape.[25]

E. Ann Kaplan cites "the end of binarisms" in her definition of postmodernism, and she asserts that there thus can be no postmodernism of "transgression" in order to show that Hal Foster's concept of a "postmodernism of resistance" is actually modernist/Brechtian.[26] It seems that she uses the end of binarisms to establish another fixed boundary. Whereas "transgression" does imply fixed boundaries (although not necessarily "binary" ones), "resistance" does not. Postmodernism can be political in an active, positive sense; its politics have lost that faith in the "ultimate truth" that binary thinking depends on, but this implies no uncritical acceptance of the status quo (or anything else). With regard to Kaplan's mention of Brecht, I would assert that the leftist avant-garde to which he belonged actually practiced the critique of binarism in

[23] Jencks, *What is Post-Modernism?*, pp. 8–9; Hutcheon, *A Poetics of Postmodernism*, p. 52.

[24] Hutcheon, *A Poetics of Postmodernism*, p. 49.

[25] Ibid., pp. 53–55, 90–91; see also Andreas Huyssen, "Mapping the Postmodern," *New German Critique*, no. 33 (1984), pp. 36–47. This article (pp. 5–52) also appears in Huyssen's book *After the Great Divide: Modernism, Mass Culture, Postmodernism* (Bloomington: Indiana University Press, 1986), pp. 179–221.

[26] E. Ann Kaplan, "Introduction," in Kaplan, ed., *Postmodernism and Its Discontents* (London: Verso, 1988), pp. 3, 5; Hal Foster, "Postmodernism: A Preface," in Foster, *The Anti-Aesthetic*, pp. xi–xii.

some ways, most specifically in its refusal to accept the bourgeois separation of art from life. What is "modernist" (and "modern") about Brecht is his nineteenth-century belief in the master narrative "science" (for other, less progressive modernists it was "myth" or "art"), the position outside of language, history, and ideology that guaranteed him the "truth" (the category that sets up the ultimate binary opposition). What was already in a sense postmodernist, however, was the emphasis in his texts on the involvement of the spectator in the production of meaning, the open admission of Brecht's own position, the interruption—but not elimination—of narrative illusion. There is in Brecht a rejection of what Peter Bürger calls the modernist passion for purity.[27] Instead, his plays are mixed forms, fragmentary, episodic, and open: "the work of Brecht, like that of postmodernism, values process ('the course') over product ('the finish')."[28]

Hutcheon, whose book *A Poetics of Postmodernism* is one of the most sustained and convincing attempts to define the term, considers contradiction, paradox, and especially irony and parody essential to postmodernism. "Parody" is for Hutcheon a concept quite similar to Jencks's "double coding";[29] she defines it as "repetition with critical distance that allows ironic signalling of difference at the very heart of similarity." (*Difference* is the postmodernist category that fragments the basic binary scheme of self/other.) She rejects Jameson's assertion that a neutral, blank "pastiche" replaces parody in postmodern art, writing the following in reference to his discussion of architecture:

> But the looking to both the aesthetic and historical past in postmodernist architecture is anything but what Jameson describes as pastiche. . . . There is absolutely nothing random or "without principle" in the parodic recall and re-examination of the past by architects like Charles Moore or Ricardo Bofill. To include irony and play is *never* necessarily to exclude seriousness and purpose in postmodernist art.[30]

Andreas Huyssen's discussion of postmodernism has also been important for this study, both in general and because of its relevance

---

[27] Peter Bürger, "Vorbemerkung," Foreword to *Postmoderne: Alltag, Allegorie und Avantgarde*, ed. Christa and Peter Bürger (Frankfurt: Suhrkamp, 1987), p. 10. On Bürger's concept of the avant-garde, see his *Theory of the Avant-Garde*, trans. Michael Shaw (Minneapolis: University of Minnesota Press, 1984); orig. *Theorie der Avantgarde* (Frankfurt: Suhrkamp, 1974).

[28] Hutcheon, *A Poetics of Postmodernism*, p. 220.

[29] Jencks, *What is Post-Modernism?*, p. 14.

[30] Hutcheon, *A Poetics of Postmodernism*, pp. 26–27.

for understanding the specific situation of West German culture since the 1960s. Huyssen emphasizes the revival of the project of the European avant-garde and its attack on "high modernism" in the 1950s and 1960s, and he considers the specifically American manifestations of this revival—pop art, the Beat movement—as the genesis of postmodernism.[31] When one examines West German literature and cinema of the 1970s, it is obvious that artists were reacting to the previous decade, but a larger historical context becomes clear when one begins to look at the West German experience of the 1960s in terms of the intersection of the influence of those American cultural developments with the revival of German avant-garde traditions from the 1920s in both art and politics.

Huyssen also stresses the dialectical relationship between "high modernism" and mass culture in modernity. Obviously, both are consequences of the modern industrial age, and modernism especially is inextricably linked to mass culture precisely in its attempt to define itself in opposition to the latter. But it is this strictly defined boundary between the two that has been increasingly undermined in postmodern culture: "The boundaries between high art and mass culture have become increasingly blurred, and we should begin to see that process as one of opportunity rather than lamenting loss of quality or failure of nerve."[32]

There are few better examples of just such a boundary and its increasing effacement than in the relationship between the two dominant narrative forms of the twentieth century, the novel and the film. Certainly this is one explanation for the increasing importance of film in West Germany during the 1970s. Some might even assert that, in the 1970s, the "New German Cinema" was much more vital—and indeed more sophisticated—than most West German novels were.[33] In any case, the historical discourses in the aftermath of

[31] Huyssen, "Mapping the Postmodern," esp. pp. 16–24.

[32] Huyssen, *After the Great Divide*, p. ix.

[33] Actually, of course, the situation is much more complex. It could be maintained that the dominance of the cinema in the 1970s had to do with the longing for sensual or visual "immediacy" and thus was a reaction against literary sophistication (and modernism). This is close to the argument of Michael Rutschky in his book on West German culture in the 1970s, *Erfahrungshunger: Ein Essay über die siebziger Jahre* [*Hunger for Experience*] (1980; Frankfurt: Fischer, 1982), which I will cite at various points in this study. On the other hand, often the films that satisfied such needs were not German films, and one could characterize much of the New German Cinema, with its stress on the director as *auteur* and its rejection of "entertainment," as a last bastion of modernism. Precisely this proudly inaccessible side of West German cinema has been disappearing in the 1980s, with the rise of directors of comedies like Percy Adlon and Doris Dörrie. The latter, who could arguably be labeled a "postfeminist"

the 1960s that I am exploring manifest themselves in both types of narrative text. While looking at the texts in relation to social and political history, however, I have attempted as well to contextualize them in terms of formal and institutional considerations specific to literature and to film.

Another important aspect of Huyssen's conception of postmodernism is the inclusion of feminism as a significant factor in the eclipse of modernism. Beginning in the 1970s, the feminist critique of modernism and the avant-garde has exposed the gendered nature of those artistic movements (i.e., their male bias). And feminism has of course played a crucial role in political and cultural developments since the 1970s, in West Germany and elsewhere. Feminism is not merely a "symptom" of postmodern culture; it has made an active contribution to the postmodern debate. As Meaghan Morris points out, while the "official" debate around postmodernism for a long time seemed to be waged almost exclusively by men, a bibliography of theoretical works by women on issues of obvious relevance to any such debate (subjectivity, language, psychoanalysis, semiotics, literary and film theory, and of course gender) can easily fill seven pages.[34]

The influence of feminism, of the women's movement, and of literary and cinematic production by women was—and is—of great significance for the developments examined here. It is an influence that represents one of the most positive aspects of postmodern culture. Feminism is also a site of obvious interaction between developments within art and criticism and larger social and political trends. The conscious attempt of feminist theorists to maintain the connection to the political and social struggle of women is in turn one of their greatest strengths. It is a strength also typical of intellectuals who are African-American, who are gay or lesbian, or who belong to other groups traditionally marginalized by the dominant culture of the West (for reasons of racial, ethnic, or sexual identity), and who maintain the connection between their work and the political struggles of their groups. This connection is often fraught with tension—between what de Lauretis calls the "critical negativity" of the-

---

director, makes very different films from those of Helke Sander, whose work is called "feminist modernism" by B. Ruby Rich. See Rich, "She Says, He Says: The Power of the Narrator in Modernist Film Politics," *Discourse*, no. 6 (1983), pp. 31–46.

[34] Morris, *The Pirate's Fiancée*, pp. 12–16; the bibliography is on pp. 17–23. A number of essays specifically examining the relationship of feminism to postmodernism are collected in Linda J. Nicholson, ed., *Feminism/Postmodernism* (London: Routledge, 1990).

ory and the "affirmative positivity" of politics—but it is a productive tension, indeed, a "double-coded," postmodern one.[35]

There is in fact much to welcome in the passing of modernism and the ideology of modernity: among other things, the exposure of underlying gender politics, the end of unqualified faith in technology and instrumental reason, and the questioning of the elitist dichotomy between "high art" and mass culture. In any case, for better or worse, modernism has passed, or rather, most "modernisms" have been eclipsed by newer movements. More important, the age that shaped modernist art has changed fundamentally. An ominous new era was glimpsed first at Auschwitz and Hiroshima; and now, after the Challenger and Chernobyl disasters, after oil spills in Alaska, acid rain in Europe, and the rising awareness of the threat of global warming, unqualified faith in the project of modernity is hard to revive. The (male-dominated) culture of the West has been deeply shaken in its understanding of progress, in its own self-image, and in its belief in its own goodness. It has obviously been shaken in its primacy as well. It is against such developments that contemporary art must be interpreted.

Three Trends

Many of those who have written on postmodernism locate its origins in the 1960s.[36] The first chapter of this book is titled "All Power to the Imagination!"—my translation of a slogan of the European student movement.[37] In that chapter, the late 1960s and the transition to the 1970s in West Germany are examined, with special focus on the political and cultural upheaval of those years. The origins of the movements for change during that turbulent period are also explored—the political, artistic, and intellectual influences in Germany, Europe, North America, and beyond that helped shape the West German attempt at "cultural revolution" at the end of the 1960s. In the following chapters, I analyze three trends amidst the various literary and cinematic responses to the demise of that "revolution" in the years that followed it.

The first trend represents the initial reaction against the final, sectarian phase of the student movement, a reaction characterized by its stress on the famous proclamation that the "personal is politi-

[35] See de Lauretis, *Technologies of Gender*, p. 26.

[36] Among others: Huyssen, "Mapping the Postmodern," pp. 16–24; Hutcheon, *A Poetics of Postmodernism*, p. 8; Kaplan, *Postmodernism and Its Discontents*, p. 5; Habermas, "Modernity," p. 6.

[37] All translations in this book are my own, unless otherwise noted.

cal." The literary manifestation of this reaction, usually called the "New Subjectivity," was heralded by the appearance of two novels in 1973: Peter Schneider's *Lenz* and Karin Struck's *Class Love* (*Klassenliebe*), which are discussed in the second chapter, "The Body, the Self." These two texts are characterized by a weariness with the cerebral and a longing for the sensual, and they champion personal needs over the schematic abstractions that had typified the student movement in its decline. They can be related to what Huyssen calls the optimistic, populist, "celebratory" strain of 1960s postmodernism, rejecting the austerity of high modernism (although their optimism is tempered by the melancholy of the early 1970s).[38] Formally, *Lenz* is an example of what might be called a consciously "naive" neorealism (and at the same time a loose adaptation of Georg Büchner's unfinished novella of the same name begun in 1835); Struck's text is an example of a new, almost radically autobiographical, realism that anticipated much subsequent writing by West German women.

The second trend I want to discuss is a more radical turn toward "inwardness" or interiority; it is much more pessimistic with regard to politics and the possibility of unmediated literary subjectivity. In a sense it continues the other strain of 1960s postmodernism, the "apocalyptic desperate strain."[39] In the third chapter, "Writing and the 'Erotic Gaze,'" I discuss Botho Strauss's short novel *Devotion* (*Die Widmung*) and the film *Wrong Move* (*Falsche Bewegung*), a collaboration by the writer Peter Handke and the filmmaker Wim Wenders (loosely based on Goethe's *Wilhelm Meister*). These two texts are characterized by an ironic self-reflexivity bordering almost on despair about the efficacy of language and by a fascination with specularity and the possibility of an "erotic gaze."

Hutcheon argues forcefully against the common notion that postmodern culture is dehistoricized or ahistorical: "History is not made obsolete: it is, however, being rethought—as a human construct."[40] In the West German context, I would assert that this is definitely true, and it has everything to do with twentieth-century German history. In the fourth chapter, "The Politics of Memory," I examine a tendency that emerged at about the same time as the notorious "German autumn" of 1977. At that time, the political resignation and relative quietism of the mid-1970s was disturbed by new, more desperate acts of terrorism and a correspondingly more repressive re-

[38] Huyssen cites Gerald Graff as having identified these two strains. "Mapping the Postmodern," p. 17.

[39] Ibid.

[40] Hutcheon, *A Poetics of Postmodernism*, p. 16.

action on the part of the West German state. Dangerous parallels with earlier periods of German history—the Third Reich, especially—were perceived by leftist artists and intellectuals, and in both literature and film a new confrontation with German history was noted in the late 1970s and early 1980s.

This "return to history" did not negate the emphasis on subjectivity of the early and mid-1970s but rather was merged with it, a fusion that paralleled much formal experimentation, especially on the part of filmmakers (e.g., Helke Sander, Helma Sanders-Brahms, Rainer Werner Fassbinder, and of course Alexander Kluge).[41] In Sanders-Brahms's *Germany, Pale Mother* (*Deutschland, bleiche Mutter*) and Sander's *The Subjective Factor*, the attempt to merge personal memory and historical discourse is seen in the mixture of fictional narrative and documentary footage, as well as in a postmodernist fusion of Brechtian distantiation with feminist autobiography. It is indeed in these films, more than in the novels I discuss, that one finds something closest to the "historiographic metafiction" Hutcheon considers exemplary of postmodernist literature: that is, not just a self-reflexive metafiction but one that examines the representation of history as well.[42]

[41] Anton Kaes's book *Deutschlandbilder: Die Wiederkehr der Geschichte als Film* (Munich: edition text + kritik, 1987) is devoted specifically to the phenomenon of the "history film" in West Germany in the late 1970s and early 1980s; a revised version has now appeared in English as *From Hitler to Heimat: The Return of History as Film* (Cambridge, MA: Harvard University Press, 1989).

[42] Cf. Hutcheon, *A Poetics of Postmodernism*, pp. ix, 5–6, 105–23, and passim. Of course, Schneider's *Lenz* and Handke's screenplay for *Wrong Move*, as loose adaptations of Büchner and Goethe, respectively, also bear some relation to Hutcheon's concept of "historiographic metafiction."

CHAPTER ONE

"All Power
to the Imagination!"
From the 1960s to the 1970s

THE CONTEMPORARY relevance of surrealism has become obvious, at the very latest since the events of May 1968. Not because the slogans of the surrealists were on the walls of public buildings during that period, but rather because aspirations that surrealism had proclaimed since the 1920s now found expression on a mass level: the revolt against a social order perceived to be repressive, the will to restructure interpersonal relationships totally, and the struggle to reunite art and life.[1]

CONTRASTS AND CONTINUITIES

Here, in this book, [workers] . . . speak for themselves. Whoever reads these interviews and stories will wish that Erika Runge gets going again soon with her tape recorder, in order to record more Bottrops, to record more personal testimony intensified by bitter experience, to record more sighs, curses, statements and contradictions—more documentation of a class that still does not live under equal justice.[2]

But what motivates an author to choose a subject (e.g., the depiction of the problems of wage-earners) to which the author cannot bring her own experience, or to use a language that is not her own (as is the case, for example, when one uses tape-recorded material)—in short, what motivates an author to seek recognition overall as a "nonauthor"?
    . . . [W]hy then didn't I bring in my own experiences and the things I had learned, my own imagination and my own language? I was not capable of it, although I had the need to do it. I wanted to write, but I didn't have the words. I wanted to speak of myself, my own wishes and difficulties, but I was afraid to expose myself.[3]

The attitudinal distance between the late 1960s and the mid-1970s in West Germany is underscored by the above juxtaposition of Martin Walser's praise for the *Bottrop Transcripts* with Erika Runge's questioning of her own motivation for compiling the *Transcripts*. Eight years after the book's publication, Runge questions the very quality Walser praises: that it does not deal with her own "bourgeois" experiences, that through it the working class speaks, or at least workers do—but she herself does not (at least openly). Her comments in 1976 testify to the validation of authorial subjectivity so much in vogue then, to the recognized value of a type of writing that is based on what was called *sich einbringen*—bringing one's self, one's own, personal experience, into discourse.[4]
    Neither quote—Walser's praise of Runge for effacing herself and

[1] Peter Bürger, cited in Hans Burkhard Schlichting, "Das Ungenügen der poetischen Strategien: Literatur im *Kursbuch* 1968–1976," in W. Martin Lüdke, ed., *Literatur und Studentenbewegung. Eine Zwischenbilanz* (Opladen: Westdeutscher, 1977), note 2, p. 57.

[2] Martin Walser, "Berichte aus der Klassengesellschaft," foreword to Erika Runge, *Bottroper Protokolle* (Frankfurt: Suhrkamp, 1968), pp. 9–10.

[3] Erika Runge, "Überlegungen beim Abschied von der Dokumentarliteratur," *Kontext* 1 (1976), pp. 99, 105.

[4] Karen Ruoff Kramer discusses *sich einbringen* and its relation to the rise of the new "subjective" politics during the 1970s in her dissertation, "/New Subjectivity/: Third Thoughts on a Literary Discourse" (Stanford University, 1984), pp. 149–50.

thwarting the ordinary expectations of bourgeois literature in order
to grant workers access to the public sphere, nor Runge's later critique of this denial of her own voice and experience—can be understood without reference to the process of politicization among West
German artists, intellectuals, and students during the late 1960s.
Runge was slightly older than the students who were coming of age
at that time, and Walser was definitely of another generation, but
both participated in that process of politicization, as did many other
literary figures.[5]

The relationship of that political movement to literature—and to
art in general—was especially crucial, and it would affect art for at
least another decade. Indeed, I would assert that West German literature and film since the 1960s cannot be understood without reference to the political and cultural uprising of that decade, in all its
contradictory impulses: toward social commitment and narcissistic
self-indulgence, toward existential liberation and political dogmatism, toward engagement in international politics and concern with
issues of personal "life-style," toward sexual emancipation and leftist asceticism. These contradictions contributed to the dissolution
and fragmentation of the movement by the early 1970s, and the traumatic nature of this experience shaped much political and artistic
discourse into the 1980s, especially for that generation which had
been most involved in the student protest movement.

But the significance of these contradictions is not limited to the
socio-historical context of West Germany in the 1970s. In their illumination of the problematic relationship of political commitment
and personal experience, these contradictions are closely related to
dichotomies integral to the dominant worldview of Western society
since the eighteenth century—the conflicts between a public and a

---

[5] David Roberts lists Walser among what he calls the "generation of 1960," the gen-
eration of—mostly left-wing—authors that by about 1960 had become dominant in
West Germany. Besides Walser he lists Günter Grass, Rolf Hochhuth, Siegfried Lenz,
Alexander Kluge, Dieter Wellershoff, Hans Magnus Enzensberger, Heinar Kipphardt,
Thomas Bernhard, Uwe Johnson, and Peter Weiss. See Roberts, "Tendenzwenden.
Die sechziger und siebziger Jahre in literaturhistorischer Perspektive," Deutsche
Vierteljahresschrift 56 (1982), p. 291.

Jost Hermand, arguing that the politicization of the 1960s in West Germany began
around 1961, cites as evidence (among other events) Walser's publication in that year
of the booklet Die Alternative oder Brauchen wir eine neue Regierung? just before the
1961 elections. It contained statements in favor of the SPD by many authors, including
Peter Rühmkorf, Enzensberger, Grass, Hans Werner Richter, Walser himself, and
Siegfried Lenz. Hermand, "Fortschritt im Rückschritt. Zur politischen Polarisierung
der westdeutschen Literatur seit 1961," in Manfred Durzak, ed., Deutsche Gegenwartsliteratur: Ausgangspositionen und aktuelle Entwicklungen (Stuttgart: Reclam,
1981), p. 301.

private sphere, and between art and politics—as well as older dichotomies renegotiated along similar lines: mind/body, male/female. One of the "revolutionary" projects of the late 1960s in Western Europe and the United States was the attempt to rethink, even eliminate, these dichotomies—a project that had also characterized earlier avant-garde movements such as Dada and surrealism. Jürgen Habermas describes the surrealist project as the "attempt to blow up the autarkical sphere of art and to force a reconciliation of art and life." Habermas connects this project with that of the late 1960s, citing Octavio Paz: "the avant-garde of 1967 repeats the deeds and gestures of 1917."[6]

The political protest movement in West Germany during the late 1960s dissolved in large part because of the failure to resolve the personal/political split adequately. Many of the novels and films of the next decade continue to explore that split, conducting—directly or indirectly—a critique of the late 1960s. The texts that emerge from this exploration can in turn be understood in part as postmodern reactions to or critiques of the roles played by modernism and the avant-garde in the art and politics of the twentieth century. The texts are simultaneously discontinuous and continuous with the traditions and experiences they explore.

The *Bottrop Transcripts* is clearly exemplary of a type of text consistent with the program of the West German Left in 1968 at the height of the student movement, as suggested by the following characteristics: its rejection of "art" and the literary, its attempt to document "objective reality," the apparent authenticity of its collected statements, its selfless commitment to the working class, and its opposition to traditional "bourgeois" literature. It is thus a text that can be used to mark one pole of the division commonly seen to exist between the "politicized 1960s" and the "subjective 1970s." To represent the other pole, I use Helke Sander's film *The Subjective Factor*, setting up this contrast in order to provide an overview of the artistic, cultural, and political changes in West Germany between the late 1960s and the early 1980s, the context necessary for understanding the texts examined in detail in this book.

The contrasts between the two texts, *Bottrop Transcripts* of 1968 and *The Subjective Factor* of 1980, can readily illustrate the transition between those two dates in accord with standard interpretations based on the split between the "political/objective" and the "personal/subjective."[7] Runge collected evidence about the situa-

[6] Habermas, "Modernity," pp. 11, 6.

[7] See, for example, Evelyne Keitel, "Verständigungstexte—Form, Funktion, Wir-

tion of workers in West Germany, "authentic" evidence that "spoke for itself"—literally, in that she tape-recorded workers telling their stories in their own words. Her role was to transcribe their words and get them published. All "personal" or "subjective" input on her part was avoided, or rather effaced;[8] even her own (obvious) commitment to the working class remains invisible and must be inferred from her willingness to put such a work together. In Sander's film, on the other hand, such self-effacement for political ends is specifically attacked within the narrative, as well as in the way the narrative itself is composed. Sander herself provides the voice-over commentary to the autobiographically based narrative; she also actually appears briefly in the film, and when she does, it is to watch an old film clip of herself giving a speech. (See the frontispiece.)

Another contrast is of course that Runge's text is a book and Sander's is a film. My choice of the latter reflects another trend: the increasing role film would play over the course of the 1970s, as a medium considered by many to be better suited to communicating subjective "immediacy." In his essay on literary trends of the 1970s, Helmut Kreuzer mentions the new appeal of film versus that of literature during that decade. After discussing the writers Peter Handke, Wolfgang Bauer, Thomas Bernhard, and Botho Strauss, he asserts that it was hard for these authors to compete with the new cinema of Herzog, Wenders, and Fassbinder, which appealed to the senses and emotions without being didactic.[9] Certainly a preference for "direct" visual experience over mediation by language can be ascertained among the younger generation in West Germany during the 1970s, in part because language had been so devalued by its function in the dogmatic jargon and grand, abstract systems used by some political groups in the late 1960s.[10]

Runge and Sander are both women, but in her book Runge seems to have subordinated herself to the working class, in apparent alignment with male-oriented and male-dominated views of socialism blind to the plight of women except as a *Nebenwiderspruch*, a "sec-

kung," *German Quarterly* 56 (1983), pp. 431–55. While the article is in many ways insightful, she seems to accept this standard, somewhat schematic division of the 1960s and the 1970s. (See, e.g., pp. 440–41, and note 3, p. 453.)

[8] For as Runge admitted in her 1976 article, her questions and editing had been guided by what she thought most effective for her political agenda, without any intention of presenting a statistical cross-section of worker attitudes. Runge, "Überlegungen," pp. 100–101.

[9] Helmut Kreuzer, "Neue Subjektivität. Zur Literatur der siebziger Jahre in der Bundesrepublik Deutschland," in Durzak, *Deutsche Gegenwartsliteratur*, p. 90.

[10] In this connection, see Michael Rutschky's book on the 1970s, *Erfahrungshunger*, especially the section "Allegorese des Kinos," pp. 167–92.

ondary contradiction" that would resolve itself only after the "primary" contradiction—that between labor and capital—is resolved. Her first book, containing hardly a visible trace of her authorship, thus in a sense did not really add to the small number of works by women that had by then gained some public exposure. Sander, on the other hand, was a veteran of the West German women's movement by the time she made *The Subjective Factor*, a film that in turn examines the origins of the women's movement within the larger student movement of the 1960s. It depicts that very blindness of male activists to the position of women, and the silence to which women were generally relegated—two of the factors that motivated the women to begin organizing on their own.

The comparison between the two texts thus demonstrates some of the most obvious shifts on the West German cultural and political scene from the 1960s to the 1970s: from politically motivated documentary "objectivity" to autobiographical "subjectivity"; from self-effacing transcription of others' words to self-reflexive filmmaking; from a successful leftist book by a "nonauthor" to the *Autorenfilm* (a film characterized by the total control of the *auteur* or director, a condition often considered typical of the New German Cinema); from male-determined socialism based on the subordination of subjective needs to political goals, to a feminism asserting that the "personal is political." But in comparing the *Bottrop Transcripts* and *The Subjective Factor*, one must also take into account certain continuities between the two texts—continuities that also are emblematic of the period they demarcate, and which to some extent undermine the standard interpretive dichotomies separating the 1960s from the 1970s.

First of all, one notes again that both texts were produced by women. In spite of the differences in levels of feminist consciousness and authorial self-confidence evident in the texts, the two women themselves are contemporaries, and their experiences in the late 1960s were similar in certain ways. In 1976 Runge admitted that she had been afraid to speak in her own voice eight years earlier; Sander depicts the protagonist of her autobiographical film going through the same type of insecurities in her dealings with the articulate male theoreticians of the student movement. And even in 1968, Runge chose to include interviews with three women (one of whom was a homemaker) among the eight titled interviews in the *Transcripts*.[11]

[11] In addition to the eight titled interviews, there is an excerpt of the "Betriebsversammlung 'Möller/Rheinbaben,' " in which only men speak, and an epilogue consist-

Furthermore, Runge had had no experience as a writer when she put together the *Bottrop Transcripts*; she had, however, worked on documentary films for the "third channel" (*Das dritte Programm*) of Bavarian State Television.[12] Sander, too, began her filmmaking career with documentary films.[13] Beyond this coincidental biographical similarity between the two women is the formal influence of documentary filmmaking, which is evident in the composition of both the texts. Runge explained in 1976 that her method of editing and arranging the tape-recorded statements had been a process similar to her work in editing documentary films, in which the footage was first divided up into thematic areas, and then selected shots were spliced into a new order.[14] As for Sander, one of the most striking formal characteristics of *The Subjective Factor* is her editing of pieces of documentary footage from the late 1960s into the autobiographically based fictional narrative she has constructed.

The documentary approach had been favored in West Germany as a form of political art in the mid- and late 1960s, beginning in the theater with Rolf Hochhuth's *The Deputy* (*Der Stellvertreter*, 1963), Heinar Kipphardt's *In the Matter of J. Robert Oppenheimer* (1964), and Peter Weiss's *The Investigation* (*Die Ermittlung*, 1965). The approach was then taken outside the theater into the workplace and corporate headquarters by Günther Wallraff with his exposés or "Reportagen"; Erika Runge, meanwhile, went with her tape recorder to the workers themselves. In the 1970s, "objective" documentary literature declined (although Walraff's work has continued to be successful through the 1980s).[15] The documentary approach, how-

---

ing of a conversation between two men and two women. Also, in the first titled interview, "Betriebsratsvorsitzender Clemens K.," the latter's wife and eldest daughter are quoted. Runge in fact treated women specifically in her next book: *Frauen. Versuche zur Emanzipation* (Frankfurt: Suhrkamp, 1969).

[12] Runge, "Überlegungen," p. 99.

[13] Helke Sander was one of only two women in the first class to begin studying at the DFFB in 1966, the year of the school's opening. She was also one of the first few women to begin film school anywhere in the Federal Republic. Her early films were primarily documentaries; from as early as 1969 her work dealt with issues of concern to the nascent women's movement of that time. See Renate Möhrmann, *Die Frau mit der Kamera. Filmemacherinnen in der Bundesrepublik Deutschland. Situationen, Perspektiven. Zehn exemplarische Lebensläufe* (Munich: Hanser, 1980), pp. 83–101.

[14] Runge, "Überlegungen," p. 101.

[15] Wallraff's unorthodox journalistic methods (e.g., using disguise and impersonation) can perhaps be compared with American "New Journalism." They are certainly departures from "objectivity," in that his method of exposing political conditions is highly individualistic and adventuristic. See Rainer Nägele's discussion of him, "Geschichten und Geschichte. Reflexionen zum westdeutschen Roman seit 1965," in Durzak, *Deutsche Gegenwartsliteratur*, p. 243. Some of Wallraff's most famous

ever—as a shift in emphasis away from the fictional and toward "authentic" reality—lived on during the "subjective" 1970s in the trend to autobiography.[16]

The depature from "objective documentary" is indeed already evident in the *Transcripts*, since of course it is not really one of the "factographies" that Hans Magnus Enzensberger found a hopeful trend in his famous 1968 essay in the edition of *Kursbuch* devoted to the "Death of Literature."[17] Runge did not collect "facts," she collected the subjective statements made by individuals about their own lives and working conditions. "And instead of speaking of my own desires and anxieties, I identified with the painful abundance of anxieties and desires of a whole class, gave them a voice."[18] What she permitted a group of workers—the chance to address a national audience on how they felt about their lives—would soon be demanded by many individuals, a number of whom came from more bourgeois backgrounds. They would aspire to authorship by writing autobiographies or autobiographical fiction.[19]

---

books: *Wir brauchen dich*, 1966; *13 unerwünschte Reportagen*, 1969; *Der Aufmacher*, 1977 (in which he reports his experiences working incognito at Springer's *Bildzeitung*); and *Ganz Unten*, 1985, which appears in English as *Lowest of the Low* (in it he reports on his experiences disguised as a foreign guest worker).

[16] Schlichting, "Das Ungenügen," p. 35.

[17] Hans Magnus Enzensberger, "Gemeinplätze, die Neueste Literature betreffend," *Kursbuch*, no. 15 (1968), p. 189. An English version of the essay is "Commonplaces on the Newest Literature," in Enzensberger, *The Consciousness Industry: On Literature, Politics and the Media*, trans. Michael Roloff (New York: Seabury Press, 1974), pp. 83–94.

[18] Runge, "Überlegungen," p. 106.

[19] To mention only a few autobiographical novels: Karin Struck's *Class Love* (*Klassenliebe*, 1973) and *Die Mutter* (1975); Verena Stefan's *Shedding* (*Häutungen*, 1975); Peter Schneider's *Lenz* (1973) and . . . *schon bist du ein Verfassungsfeind* (1975); Elisabeth Plessen's *Mitteilungen an den Adel* (1976); Brigitte Schwaiger's *Wie kommt das Salz ins Meer* (1977); Maria Erlenberger's *Der Hunger nach Wahnsinn* (1977); Fritz Zorn's *Mars* (1977); and Svende Merian's *Der Tod des Märchenprinzen* (1980). The discourse of the autobiography in the 1970s had to do with a blurring of the boundary between the autobiographical and the fictional: what Rutschky calls "this autobiographical writing, or, conversely, this reading of texts as autobiography" (*Erfahrungshunger*, p. 209). But it was not only the younger generation who participated in this discourse; autobiographies and autobiographical novels were written by older, and/or more established writers, which influenced the newer writers in many instances: Max Frisch's *Sketchbook 1966–1971* (*Tagebuch 1966–1971*, 1972) and *Montauk* (1976); Christa Wolf's *Patterns of Childhood* (*Kindheitsmuster*, 1976); Peter Handke's *A Sorrow Beyond Dreams* (*Wunschloses Unglück*, 1972) and *The Weight of the World* (*Das Gewicht der Welt. Ein Journal*, 1977); Günter Grass's *From the Diary of a Snail* (*Aus dem Tagebuch einer Schnecke*, 1972); Gerhard Zwerenz's *Kopf und Bauch* (1971); Hubert Fichte's *Versuch über die Pubertät* (1974); and Wolfgang Koeppen's *Jugend* (1976).

In addition, the concept of providing a voice for social groups that were traditionally silent would be of great importance to the women's movement. Rather than becoming the instrument for other groups to overcome silence, however, women who became writers would encourage members of their own sex to do so—by making public their own individual stories. Two best-sellers of the 1970s in West Germany, Karin Struck's *Class Love* and Verena Stefan's *Shedding*, must be seen in this context.

While the trend toward autobiography and autobiographical fiction was running its course in West German literature of the 1970s, certain filmmakers were experimenting with the mixture of documentary footage with fictional sequences, most notably Alexander Kluge, Helma Sanders-Brahms, Jutta Brückner, and of course Helke Sander. The films by the three women—Sanders-Brahms, Brückner, and Sander—were also very autobiographical. This continuity of interest in the documentary between 1968 and 1980 is one perspective that can contribute to a more differentiated understanding of the changes that did occur in that period.

Based on her experience with documentary filmmaking, the editing Runge did in assembing the *Bottrop Transcripts* was called "deconstruction and reconstruction" by Rainer Nägele, comparing it in some ways to Kluge's style.[20] Nonetheless, it differs from the type of montage used by Kluge and Sander at the end of the 1970s by virtue of its *invisibility*. In hiding herself behind "objectivity,"[21] Runge hoped to make her editing work disappear, thus giving an increased appearance of unmediated "authenticity" to her collection of statements.

The type of montage done by Kluge and Sander, on the other hand, draws attention to itself, to the discursive mediation of the filmmaker; their films work to undermine any apparent "immediacy," which is associated with dominant narrative cinema. Their styles are thus reminiscent of much work done by Jean-Luc Godard and were clearly influenced (as Godard's films were) by Bertolt Brecht's theories of distantiation and defamiliarization (*Verfremdung*).[22] One notes in Kluge and Sander an obvious dissatisfaction with conventional fiction, combined with disillusionment in the apparent "objectivity" of the documentary approach as well. Instead of merely moving into the "subjective" side of documentary authen-

[20] Nägele, "Geschichten," p. 243.

[21] Runge, "Überlegungen," p. 110.

[22] On Godard and Brecht see, for example, James Monaco, *The New Wave: Truffaut, Godard, Chabrol, Rohmer, Rivette* (New York: Oxford University Press, 1976), pp. 129–30, 206–7.

ticity (i.e., toward autobiography and autobiographical fiction), as was so common in the 1970s, films by Sander and Kluge employ fiction and documentary together, to relativize the claims of each. In Sander's *The Subjective Factor* especially one sees the autobiographical discourse of the 1970s tempered by documentary footage, as well as by other distantiation techniques.

The continuities between Runge's text and Sander's may be summarized as follows: authorship by women; the interest in the documentary approach—and in documenting the subjective side of political realities; the use of filmic montage as a working method, or at least as an influence on working method; and finally a certain commitment to politics, although politics conceived differently (from a relatively orthodox socialism to a feminist and pacifist socialism). I would not assert that these particular continuities can necessarily be found in each of the texts I will examine in depth, let alone throughout the vast literary and cinematic output of West Germany during the years in question. But they are nonetheless representative of the kind of continuities that do exist, especially in the texts produced by that generation most marked by the events of 1968. Thus they help to problematize the more simplisitc views of these years: the "political" 1960s and the "subjective" 1970s.

Helmut Kreuzer has written that the two decades actually belong together.[23] The common historical epoch to which he alludes, however, does not begin in 1960, according to most literary critics, nor does it end in 1979. Rather, the beginning is set usually between 1965 and 1968.[24] A process of politicization in West Germany had begun in the early 1960s, a process joined by a generation of writers like Martin Walser, Hans Magnus Enzensberger, Peter Weiss, Rolf Hochhuth, Heinrich Böll, and Günther Grass. Between 1965 and 1968 these authors were in turn joined—and largely overtaken—by a new generation that was influenced by new politcal and cultural developments that were national and international in scope. David Roberts uses 1968 to mark the end of the postwar era in West German literature because of the arrival of this new generation on the

[23] Kreuzer, "Neue Subjektivität," p. 97.

[24] Kreuzer sets the beginning at 1966 ("Neue Subjektivität," p. 77); Roberts uses 1968 ("Tendenzwenden," p. 312). The year 1968 is also used in Michael Zeller, ed., *Aufbrüche: Abschiede. Studien zur deutschen Literatur seit 1968* (Stuttgart: Ernst Klett, 1979), as well as in W. Martin Lüdke, ed., *Nach dem Protest. Literatur im Umbruch* (Frankfurt: Suhrkamp, 1979). The year 1965 is used in Paul Michael Lützeler and Egon Schwarz, eds., *Deutsche Literatur in der Bundesrepublik seit 1965* (Königstein/Ts.: Athenäum, 1980). As cited above in note 5, Hermand ("Fortschritt") is an exception here.

scene, arguing that its "existential" and "ecological" outlook would
determine new approaches to politics and art after the transition period of 1968–1972 (i.e., after the student movement), a period in
which older and newer approaches fused—and clashed.[25]

Roberts's use of the label "ecological" places this generational
shift in the international context of a "postindustrial" critique of industrial progress. Two developments cited by Andreas Huyssen as
significant aspects for a critique of high modernism are the emer-
gence of feminism and the ecological tendency from the New Left.[26]
Besides this shift in political emphasis, including the feminist attention to gender, I would also mention the following developments in
the same postmodern context: the reevaluation of subjectivity as
against the traditional leftist cult of reason and abstraction (which
Leslie A. Adelson has called "idolatry of the concept"[27]); the exploration of subjectivity with regard to gender; the related interest in
the relation between writing and experience; the continued deterioration of the dichotomy between art and life as well as "high" art
and "low" art; and the increasing importance of filmmaking in relation to literature.

To explore these developments further in their specifically West
German manifestations, let us examine the social and cultural uprising of the 1960s in West Germany in its specific political and intellectual origins, in its various and somewhat contradictory attitudes
to art, and in its effect on subsequent political and artistic trends
after its demise.

THE WEST GERMAN STUDENT MOVEMENT

Compelled to sacrifice their lives in meaningless labor producing meaningless goods, millions are being robbed of their right to self-realization;
each one who is born into existing relations [is] from birth on hemmed
in, demoralized, broken, mutilated, discouraged, cut off forever from

[25] Roberts, "Tendenzwenden," p. 312.

[26] Huyssen, "Mapping the Postmodern," pp. 27, 51. David Roberts, in the introduction to a new book in English on West German literature of the 1970s, now explicitly
connects the "ecological" shift mentioned in his 1982 article to the rise of the wom-
en's movement and the peace movement, to a new concern with "the problematic of
modernity and modernization," and to the debate around postmodernism. Roberts,
"From the 1960s to the 1970s: The Changing Contexts of German Literature," Introduction to Keith Bullivant, ed., *After the Death of Literature: West German Writing
of the 1970s* (Oxford: Berg Publishers, 1989), pp. xv–xvii.

[27] Leslie A. Adelson, *Crisis of Subjectivity: Botho Strauss's Challenge to West German Prose of the 1970s* (Amsterdam: Rodopi, 1984), p. 12.

possibilities for self-development that for the first time in human history could be available, based on the high level of productive forces.[28]

The above passage by the West German writer Bernward Vesper expresses the essence of the New Left's basic analysis of Western capitalism, with its depiction of the alienated working masses cut off from their potential for self-realization by an unjust system of economic relations, in spite of the existence of the technological means to achieve this utopian goal for the first time in history. This analysis obviously owes much to Herbert Marcuse, who had written, for example, in *One-Dimensional Man* (1964):

> The technological processes of mechanization and standardization might release individual energy into a yet uncharted realm of freedom beyond necessity. The very structure of human existence would be altered; the individual would be liberated from the work world's imposing upon him alien needs and alien possibilities. The individual would be free to exert autonomy over a life that would be his own.[29]

Marcuse's critique—that technology's liberating potential for all human beings had been perverted by capitalism—was highly influential on the international student movement in the 1960s, including its West German branch, as soon as *One-Dimensional Man* appeared in German translation in 1967. The sentiment that technology had the potential to unleash—rather than suppress—creativity and imagination on the part of even the most oppressed and alienated individuals was echoed in one of the slogans of the Parisian students of May 1968: "L'imagination au pouvoir!" In German this was "Die Phantasie an die Macht!" and in English, "Power"— or "All power"—"to the imagination!"

"Three Phases"

The emphasis in Marcuse's formulation is on the *individual's* potential for growth and creativity, a potential frustrated by technocratic administration of the means of production; the antiauthoritarian and individualistic nature of this position clearly differs from the perspective of more orthodox socialism, such as that from which

[28] Bernward Vesper's autobiographical essay *Die Reise* (*The Journey*), unfinished at the time of his suicide in 1971, was first published in 1977. According to dates made by Vesper on the original manuscript, the passage quoted here was written on 15 July 1970. Vesper, *Die Reise. Romanessay* (1977; Reinbek: Rowohlt, 1983), p. 250; see also p. 596, note 48.

[29] Herbert Marcuse, *One-Dimensional Man: Studies in the Ideology of Advanced Industrial Society* (Boston: Beacon Press, 1964), p. 2.

Rolf Hosfeld and Helmut Peitsch criticize Marcuse's "existentialist" influence on what they and others refer to as the "antiauthoritarian" phase of the West German student movement.[30]

This first phase of the movement is usually dated from 1966 until some point in 1968. There is some validity to its being characterized as individualistic and existentialist in nature. Its politics were based largely on the ideal of personal refusal: each committed individual would refuse to cooperate with a system seen as authoritarian and immoral.[31] Political activity consisted of symbolic demonstrations of resistance, inspired by moral commitment to the emancipation of each individual from the alienation of a deadening technocratic order. Personal emancipation—including sexual liberation and the enjoyment of pop culture, from rock music to Louis Malle's film *Viva Maria!*—was not considered separate from political struggle. The personal and the subjective were an integral part of the movement during this phase; as Dieter Kunzelmann of West Berlin's Kommune I ("Commune No. 1," founded in 1967) stated: "I have orgasm problems and I demand that society take notice!"[32] The emphasis that would be placed on personal experience a few years later, in the mid-1970s, was by no means new, although it was somewhat altered.

Hosfeld and Peitsch's critique of this early phase as individualistic and existentialist, based in part on their examination of Heidegger's influence upon Marcuse, is an analysis typical of the movement's "second" phase, which Hosfeld and Peitsch call its "organized" phase. This latter phase is also referred to as the Marxist-Leninist or "dogmatic" phase, depending on the perspective of the critic.[33] Wolf Biermann, for instance—at that time still an East

[30] Rolf Hosfeld and Helmut Peitsch, " 'Weil uns diese Aktionen innerlich verändern, sind sie politisch.' Bemerkungen zu vier Romanen über die Studentenbewegung," *Basis* 8 (1978), pp. 92–126; see esp. pp. 95–102.

[31] Hosfeld and Peitsch, " 'Weil uns diese Aktionen . . . ,' " pp. 96–97.

[32] Cited in Vesper, *Die Reise*, p. 285. This personal and subjective tendency was perhaps best represented within the protest movement in the United States by Abbie Hoffman and the "Yippies"—the Youth International Party.

[33] Leslie A. Adelson calls the "second phase" "a dogmatic, Marxist-Leninist phase" in her book *Crisis of Subjectivity*, p. 4. See also Klaus Hartung's "Versuch, die Krise der antiautoritären Bewegung wieder zur Sprache zu bringen," *Kursbuch*, no. 48 (1977), pp. 15, 31, 41. For more discussion of the "three phases" see Hosfeld and Peitsch, " 'Weil uns diese Aktionen . . . ,' " pp. 92–93; and Leslie A. Adelson's "Subjectivity Reconsidered: Botho Strauss and Contemporary West German Prose," *New German Critique*, no. 30 (1983), pp. 3–7. Other discussions of the student movement include Horst Denkler's "Langer Marsch und kurzer Prozeß. Oppositionelle Studentenbewegung und streitbarer Staat im westdeutschen Roman der siebziger Jahre," in Wolfgang Paulsen, ed., *Der deutsche Roman und seine historischen und politischen*

German dissident, not yet a West German one—summarized the transition from the "first" to the "second" phase in the West German movement as follows: "Following the antiauthoritarian phase comes, with thick-headed logic, the dogmatic, authoritarian hangover: the rebels trot off the bourgeois playing-field and then march, ordered in sects, into the barracks of dogmatism."[34]

The second phase is usually dated from 1968 or 1969; it lasted into the early 1970s. This was the period of splintering Marxist-Leninist groups, mostly Maoist-oriented, especially the so-called K-Gruppen, each of which asserted that it held the true line on Marxist-Leninism.[35] "Subjectivity" was suspect, replaced by an inflexible party line based on a supposedly "objective" analysis of material conditions, a submission to a dogmatic use of theory (once again, the "idolatry of the concept").

In the "third" phase, subjectivity enjoyed a renaissance; the dominant political style that survived can be designated as that associated with the "Spontis," an older faction of the movement. The Spontis were named by their "organized" opponents for what was considered an affinity for spontaneous, unplanned actions; their antidogmatic and nonaligned stance would be very influential in the ecological and antinuclear protests of the 1970s. These protest movements, however, were no longer dominated by students and indeed based much of their politics on a reaction against the dogmatic, sectarian excesses that typified the decline of the student movement.

Bedingungen (Bern: Francke, 1977), pp. 124–44; Michael Schneider's "Von der alten Radikalität zur neuen Sensibilität," *Kursbuch*, no. 49 (1977), pp. 174–87; Peter Mosler's *Was wir wollten, was wir wurden: Studentenrevolte—zehn Jahre danach* (Reinbek: Rowohlt, 1977); Frank Wolff and Eberhard Windaus, eds., *Studentenbewegung 1967–1969. Protokolle und Materialien* (Frankfurt: Verlag Roter Stern, 1977); and Lüdke, *Literatur und Studentenbewegung.*

[34] Wolf Biermann, "Das gute Wort 'Dableiben,' " rev. of *Lenz* by Peter Schneider, *Spiegel*, 10 December 1973, p. 142. At that time, Biermann, although writing for *Spiegel*, was still in the GDR. In 1976, when the East German government revoked his passport while he was on a concert tour in the West, he involuntarily became a resident of West Germany. There he also functioned as a leftist dissident.

[35] In the terms "K-Parteien" and "K-Gruppen" ("K-Parties" and "K-Groups"), the letter K stands for Kommunistisch- ("communist"), which was an essential part of the names—and acronyms—of almost all the Maoist-oriented splinter organizations that developed in the late 1960s and early 1970s in West Germany and West Berlin. In Ulrike Kolneder-Zecher, ed., *Eine linke Geschichte. Ein Lesebuch zum Stück* (West Berlin: GRIPS Theater, 1980) there is information on the continuing fragmentation that spawned all the groups; most helpful is the "flow chart" on pp. 204–5. The following poem is cited on p. 205: "Kinder tun die KP lieben / Einst gabs eine / Heut' gibts sieben." (A loose translation: "Kids think the KP's just heaven / Once there was one / Now there are seven.")

By returning to Vesper's remarks, however, which express so well the antiauthoritarian position, one gets a feeling for the inadequacies of the neat division of the student movement into three phases as sketched above. His remarks date from 1970, in the midst of the "dogmatic phase"; their specific context is a passage in which Vesper criticizes a denunciation of Ulrike Meinhof and her "Red Army" in the leftist magazine *Konkret*.[36] In 1970 Vesper's antiauthoritarianism is sympathetic to a terrorist group and negative toward a writer whose position Vesper derides as covertly pacifistic. The confusion of positions here cannot be ascribed merely to Vesper's state of mind. The fact is that of course the "second" phase contained many tendencies; while the dogmatic Marxist-Leninist groups may have been "dominant," at least two other factions existed: the Spontis and of course the terrorists, who are not mentioned at all in the "three-phase" scheme. The largest group of all during this phase, however, may well have been made up of those who had withdrawn from these squabbling factions while maintaining some connections to—and sympathy for—various ones among them; this would include those withdrawing from the larger "political" struggle into experimentation with "life-styles." And it included Vesper, whose writings attack not only dogmatic leftists (whose support for the workers meant affirmation of the work ethic, not emancipation from it) but also the monomania of the terrorists, whose analyses Vesper nonetheless often seemed to share.[37]

This amorphous "second phase" was actually a phase of disintegration. The West German Sozialistischer Deutscher Studentenbund (League of Socialist German Students), known as the SDS, split apart in a fashion similar to the American SDS (Students for a Democratic Society). In 1969, the American organization ruptured into two factions, one Maoist and one proterrorist.[38] In West Germany, the vari-

[36] The writer whom Vesper attacks is Wallraff; *Die Reise*, p. 249.

[37] Vesper, *Die Reise*, pp. 251, 290; the latter reference is to a remark about Andreas Baader. Gudrun Ensslin, Vesper's lover (and the mother of his son Felix), left Vesper for Baader. Ensslin and Baader were instrumental in forming the Rote Armee Fraktion (Red Army Faction; RAF), also called the "Baader-Meinhof Group," after Baader and the leftist journalist, Ulrike Meinhof, who also joined the RAF.

[38] The West German SDS began as the socialist student group associated with the SPD; in 1960, in conjunction with the acceptance of the "Godesberger Programm," the SPD broke off all ties to the SDS. Through the course of the 1960s, the SDS drifted leftward, becoming the principal organization of the student protest movement from 1966 to 1968; then it fragmented. In 1968, RAF was formed and began its first terrorist activities. In 1969, Moscow-aligned members of the SDS were expelled. Within a year, many of the remaining SDS members had joined the Maoists in the "K-Gruppen"; on 3 March 1970, the SDS formally disbanded.

The American SDS, formed around 1960 as a student group loosely connected to the Socialist Party, also moved left during the 1960s. At its convention in Chicago in

ous tendencies that had been loosely united in the first phase began to split apart as the initial successes of the student movement faded and the underlying strength and resilience of the "establishment" became clear for even the most euphoric activists to see. The Marxist-Leninists—the Maoists of the K-Gruppen, as well as the Moscow-aligned activists who in 1968 founded the Deutsche Kommunistische Partei (German Communist Party; DKP)—remained highly organized, unlike the anarchistic Spontis. To the extent that the Marxist-Leninist factions remained "above ground," unlike the terrorist cells that went "underground," they were dominant during this phase, but their concern with party lines and "party-building" (i.e., breaking into ever smaller sects) can be considered a retreat from active engagement in the political sphere. In any case, as a tendency it exhausted itself, and it was the Sponti tendency that survived (antidogmatic in all ways except perhaps in its enmity to theory, which had been so discredited by the dogmatists).

Thus it makes as much sense to stress the continuity of certain strands of the movement from its very beginnings as it does to determine the phases of its evolution. It is obvious that the various strands existed, however blurred, before 1968, in the "first phase": for example, already in 1967 the members of the "Commune No. 1" (including Dieter Kunzelmann) were expelled from the West Berlin SDS, an early sign of the growing split between more orthodox socialists and "life-style" anarchists.[39]

What is useful in the three-phase scheme are the dates, albeit vague, that mark the evolution of opposing tendencies and the eventual dissolution of the movement. Between 1968 and 1969, splits between groups that had formerly coexisted in a loosely unified, antiauthoritarian student movement became irreparable: between countercultural anarchists and socialists concerned with international imperialism; between nonaligned Spontis and organized socialists; between Marxist-Leninists of Soviet and of Maoist leanings, between both of these groups and the terrorists, and between all three groups and democratic socialists. Such splits in turn reflected an ongoing process of radicalization within each of the groups, especially within the Marxist-Leninist and terrorist camps, leading to

---

August 1969, it split into two factions, the (Maoist) Student-Worker Alliance/Progressive Labor group and the Revolutionary Youth Movement/"Weathermen," the faction oriented toward terrorism.

See Wolfgang Kraushaar's "Notizen zu einer Chronologie der Studentenbewegung," in Mosler, *Was wir wollten*, pp. 249–95; see esp. pp. 252, 277–78, 290, 292, 295; see also Todd Gitlin, *The Sixties: Years of Hope, Days of Rage* (Toronto: Bantam, 1987), esp. pp. 110–11, 380–91.

[39] See Kraushaar, "Chronologie," p. 268; the date of expulsion was 3 May 1967.

increasing social marginalization. The Marxist-Leninists became ever more involved in sectarian splintering among themselves, and the terrorists were criminalized and then imprisoned (often in solitary confinement). In part because of such internal dynamics, the West German student movement had largely run its course by 1972 or 1973.

But *only* in part. The three-phase scheme is useful but necessarily oversimplified; I have tried to problematize it somewhat in order to give some idea of the actual diversity of the student movement in West Germany, which was surely more heterogeneous than I can convey here. One cannot, however, analyze the movement in terms of internal dynamics alone; it did not arise nor did it decline in a vacuum; there were significant political and cultural developments on both national and international levels that determined much of the movement's history, and which remained largely outside the control of the movement.

National and International Determinants

One of the most important political factors on the national level during the 1960s was the growing dissatisfaction among leftists with the Sozialdemokratische Partei Deutschlands (the Social Democratic Party of Germany; SPD). The SPD was the only legal party on the left in West Germany after the Kommunistische Partei Deutschlands (the Communist Party of Germany; KPD) had been banned in 1956, during the height of the Cold War. At the end of 1959, with the approval of the Bad Godesberg program, the SPD had distanced itself from the party's Marxist origins, proclaiming itself to be no longer a party of the working class but rather a *Volkspartei*, a "people's party" appealing to all sectors of the population.

This weakening of the SPD's position as an alternative to the status quo made support for it somewhat problematic for leftist intellectuals; events after 1966 made it much more difficult, when the SPD was willing not only to enter the Große Koalition, the "Great Coalition," but also to support the adoption of the *Notstandsgesetze* (emergency laws).[40] The Great Coalition was formed in late 1966 when the SPD joined with the conservative Christlich-Demokratische Union (the Christian Democratic Union; CDU) in a coalition government with the Christian Democrat (and former Nazi) Kurt Kiesinger as Chan-

[40] Nägele, "Geschichten," pp. 235–36.

cellor.[41] This coalition meant that there was no longer any parliamentary opposition at all on the left. Dissident leftists began to organize outside parliament: this was the beginning of the "extraparliamentary opposition" (Außerparlamentarische Opposition) or APO. The students who joined this opposition swelled its numbers to the point that one could say the student movement and APO were largely synonymous; although there had been student protests before this point, the student movement became massive in size in response to the Great Coalition.

When large numbers of students began protesting in the streets, the government became more eager to draw up and pass laws that provided for the contingency of a state of emergency—the famous *Notstandsgesetze*. Leftist concern about such laws had to do with the use to which similar emergency measures had been put by the National Socialists: namely, to outlaw the Left and indefinitely suspend parliament. When these laws were finally passed in 1968 with the help of the SPD—a party that had itself been eliminated in the 1930s—leftists viewed it as another betrayal.[42] It also foreshadowed the marked lack of sympathy for the "extraparliamentary opposition" that the SPD would demonstrate once it came to power on its own, when Willy Brandt became Chancellor. (A coalition between the small West German liberal party—the Freie Demokratische Partei [Free Democratic Party, or FDP]—and the SPD defeated the CDU in the 1969 elections.)

In terms of national politics, then, the Great Coalition under Kiesinger provided one of the major catalysts for the student movement in West Germany; international politics provided others. Above all, U.S. policy, especially with regard to Vietnam, was the principal cause for much student protest. The West Berlin SDS had been organizing protests against U.S. intervention in Vietnam since at least the end of 1965 (in part influenced by similar protests in other nations, especially in the United States itself).[43] Easter protests against the nuclear arms race (and West Germany's role therein) dated back to the 1950s.

The critique of U.S. international policy led in 1967 to a protest that, because of ensuing police brutality, would have a momentous effect in radicalizing the movement (somewhat comparable to

[41] On the national level, the CDU actually functions in coalition with its sister party in Bavaria, the Christlich-Soziale Union (CSU; "Christian Social Union"). What I am labeling here (for brevity's sake) as the CDU is hence more accurately called the CDU-CSU.

[42] See Denkler, "Langer Marsch," p. 129.

[43] Kraushaar, "Chronologie," pp. 262–63.

events around the 1968 Democratic convention in Chicago). Leftist students in West Berlin saw the Shah of Iran as both a U.S. puppet and a flagrant violator of human rights; this impression was reinforced by a teach-in led by Bahman Nirumand, an Iranian, at the Free University, held just as the city of West Berlin was planning to welcome the Shah as an honored guest.[44] The students who came out en masse to protest the reception of the Shah and his wife at the opera on 2 June 1967, encountered an unexpected police attack that resulted in the death of one student, Benno Ohnesorg (he was shot from behind). As Klaus Hartung has written in his "insider's" analysis of the student movement, this tragedy represented, paradoxically enough, an enormous success for the protesters:

> The battle at the opera on 2 June 1967, actually had all the marks of a defeat. Backed into a corner, we took a beating. And to this day we haven't really been able to deal with the death of a comrade. But the very fact that the Senate had set itself the goal of destroying the student opposition, and that with every indication of military preparation—this made us realize our power for the first time. From then on there was something to defend that hadn't yet existed in postwar Germany: a radical opposition.[45]

The mobilizing effect of this event throughout West Germany cannot be underestimated. The movement grew ever larger in spite of, or rather because of, repressive tendencies demonstrated by West Berlin's Senate and the West German state—tendencies that the demonstrations openly exposed. The demonstrations created a media sensation as well. For awhile the movement seemed unstoppable, and it increased its demands accordingly. But even at this stage one could note an interesting dependency underlying the strategic confrontations with the state: the movement depended on the ugly reaction it brought forth from the "establishment"; it justified itself and began to define itself in terms of this reaction. As one commentator later wrote, in a social-psychological analysis of the movement: "The success of the student revolt demanded social conditions that corresponded to it. It needed an enemy that furthered its methods of interaction with complementary provocations. This enemy was at hand in the repressive and morally susceptible realm of public opin-

[44] On 1 June 1967, the day before the Shah was to be welcomed in West Berlin, Bahman Nirumand analyzed the dictatorial regime in Iran before more than 3,000 students in the "Audimax" of the Free University. Kraushaar, "Chronologie," p. 270.

[45] Hartung, "Versuch," p. 20.

ion. Without the public's completely narrow-minded reaction, the student movement would hardly have taken off."[46]

The generational conflict of the 1960s was of special import to student revolts in West Germany, since the generation that had built up the nation had done so largely by bracketing out the troublesome fascist past of so many of its leading contemporaries. The culpability of the older generation could not have been symbolized better than by the fact that Kiesinger, a man who had worked in Goebbels's Propaganda Ministry, was Chancellor. Any signs of impatience and repression on the part of the West German state with regard to the democratic rights of protesters were thus guaranteed to resonate with ugly historical overtones and to vindicate the feelings of moral righteousness of the younger generation.

The political success of the student movement was a surprise not only to officialdom but also to the students themselves.[47] And this unexpected success led to what could be called delusions of omnipotence, with a good deal of resultant misreading of social realities.[48] Just as in the United States, where, as Todd Gitlin has argued, the protest movement was ultimately damaged by naiveté with regard to the power of the media and to unforeseen effects of the news coverage that had seemed initially so empowering,[49] so too did West German media attention have a distorting effect on the student movement. In West Germany, however, it was especially clear that one large media concern, owned by the conservative Axel Springer and most famous for its national daily newspaper, a tabloid called the *"Bild"-Zeitung*, was an enemy of the students; there was no danger of liberal or social-democratic "co-optation" of the movement on that front. It was a leading voice of the most narrow-minded public reaction to the student movement, taking a very dim view of any sort of street demonstrations or any serious challenge to authority, and thus was the perfect foe for an antiauthoritarian movement protesting the inadequacies of West German democracy.

The Springer press, for its part, vilified the students from the beginning by labeling them as most archconservatives would label any protesters against a conservative status quo: as communists conspiring to overthrow the state. It used this label very early, at a point

---

[46] Johann August Schülein, "Von der Studentenrevolte zur Tendenzwende oder der Rückzug ins Private. Eine sozialpsychologische Analyse," *Kursbuch*, no. 48 (1977), p. 105.

[47] Hartung, "Versuch," p. 20.

[48] Schülein, "Von der Studentenrevolte," p. 106.

[49] Todd Gitlin, *The Whole World is Watching: Mass Media in the Making and Unmaking of the New Left* (Berkeley: University of California Press, 1980).

when, as Hartung has written, very few in the movement would have characterized themselves as "revolutionaries."

> On top of that, at our disposal, we had—to our dismay—an instrument of propaganda that screamed "Stop thief!" before we had even shoplifted. The *"Bild"-Zeitung* in particular defined us in terms of revolution at a point when this was only a historical concept for us; the newspaper depicted chaos while we still only wanted to make the formal right to demonstrate into a real one; it conjured up the overthrow of the system when we were still searching *within* that system for the opportunity of political self-determination.[50]

Implied in Hartung's description is a dynamic also evident in an American countercultural slogan of the 1960s: "We are the people our parents warned us against." It was a dynamic that worked in this fashion: for shock value, members of a younger generation would assume exactly those traits that embodied the worst fantasies their parents entertained for the future of their children. What was often overlooked (especially by rebellious youth) is that this type of rebellion is an *identification* with the parents, merely a reverse one, and that in this way it is the fears (or suppressed desires, for that matter) of the older generation that become the determinants of the "rebellious" behavior of the children. Springer's *"Bild"-Zeitung* defined what the protesters were doing in terms of a right-wing hysteria campaign, and the protesters unwittingly began in effect to accept such definitions.[51]

A less complicated phenomenon was the simple underestimation of the forces, including the media, to which the students were opposed. The campaign in the Springer press to defame Rudi Dutschke (whose leadership role in the movement was in part attained through such media attention) bore fruit, as it were, in the assassination attempt by a neofascist upon Dutschke's life on 11 April 1968; injuries from this shooting would continue to affect his health

[50] Hartung, "Versuch," p. 20. Compare the statement of Antje Krüger, one of the founding members of the "K1," the "Commune No. 1": "So I was glad to join the K1 because it was really theater. And the main thing for me was that the actions we planned were fun. The wildest fun was of course reading the paper the next morning to see how the press reacted to them." From an interview with Dieter Kunzelmann, another cofounder of the K1, at which Krüger was also present in the West Berlin magazine *Zitty* for the week of 14–27 September 1984, titled "Ohne uns läuft hier gar nichts mehr," p. 61.

[51] This dynamic has also been noted by Rutschky in his discussion of the terrorists in the 1970s; he asserts that they increasingly acted in accordance with West German society's ever more hysterical views of them, up to the point of tacitly accepting the idea that they must be exterminated. *Erfahrungshunger*, pp. 123–24.

until he finally died of related complications in 1980. As with the death of Ohnesorg, the attempt on Dutschke's life caused massive demonstrations all over West Germany. After Ohnesorg's murder, however, the goal had been to demonstrate in defiance of what students considered an illegal proscription of their right to do so. The goal after Dutschke was shot became a much more ambitious and difficult one: the anti-Springer campaign attempted to close down West Germany's largest newspaper publisher. This proved impossible. The student movement was also unable, in spite of massive demonstrations in May of 1968, to stop the passage of the *Notstandsgesetze*, the emergency laws.

The student movement did not have the organization, unity, numbers, and strength to effect its goals, which in the face of the disappointments of 1968 became, paradoxically enough, ever more ambitious. Ultimate social transformation was not likely, given an "establishment" by this point much less taken aback by the movement and ready to defuse it by both co-optative and repressive means. Various strategies were attempted by different groups of activists—ranging from trying to organize the working class in the factories to moving underground and forming terrorist cells. But none had the desired effect of winning over any sizable portion of the population to the goals of revolutionary socialism as envisioned by the ever more militant students.

The radicalization after 1968 can be seen—at least in part—as a reaction to frustration about the increasing sense of failure in the movement. The most radical elements of the movement, by going "underground" or joining Marxist-Leninist sects that fought primarily with each other about their ideological purity, were in effect pulling out of meaningful confrontation with the dominant forces in West German society, conforming more than they cared to admit to the marginalization into which right-wing stereotypes tried to place them.

Hartung maintains that the adoption of dogmatic stances was a smokescreen for justifying the impotence of the movement and its inability to attract support from the West German masses; this is indeed the essence of political sectarianism: "*disillusionment in the people became the principle that legitimated work for the party. Failure was the daily justification of the pursuit of the party line.*" Hartung calls this attitude the "Avantgardeanspruch," the claim that one's own group is the (political) avant-garde, or vanguard.[52] Its function is to turn failure to win support into proof of the purity of

---

[52] Hartung, "Versuch," p. 16; emphasis in the original.

one's party line: if the party line were popular, it would of course
be reformist or revisionist. And the more esoteric the theoretical debate on the fine points of Marxist-Leninist theory became, the less
energy was left for any realistic attempt to define an oppositional
praxis that had some chance of success within a complex industrial
society like West Germany in the latter half of the twentieth century.
The "blurring of political reality" began with the onset of the Marxist-Leninist phase: "The analysis of daily politics, which could have
exposed the weaknesses and contradictions of the enemy, disappeared. On the contrary, the strength of the enemy blended into the
propagandistic line of the leftist sects."[53]

The strength of the opponent, meanwhile, appeared increasingly
ominous. The SPD, with Willy Brandt at its head, won the national
elections in the fall of 1969 with its coalition partner, the FDP. A
program of reform was announced for West Germany, but the SPD
chose not to protect anyone to its left from the right-wing clamor to
do something about the protest movement. The SPD supported the
Radikalenerlaß, the "Radicalism Decree," of January 1972, which
sought to prevent radicals from getting government jobs and ushered
in an era of anxiety for anyone who had been an activist—not for the
terrorists, but rather for those reform-minded students who had
opted for changing the system from within (the long march "through
the institutions").

The *Radikalenerlaß* became known colloquially as the *Berufsver-
bot*, the "career prohibition," a sort of blacklisting of certain potential applicants for the many civil service positions in West Germany
(for instance, all teaching jobs). Again, it is doubtful that this measure deterred many practicing terrorists, which is all the more
ironic, since the measure was ostensibly passed in response to the
activities of a small (albeit ambitious) number of terrorists (mainly
in the "Red Army Faction" or RAF). The main purpose, or at any rate
the main result, of such legislation was to intimidate the "extraparliamentary" Left. Combined with the low morale due to the infight-
ing on the left during the student movement's dogmatic phase, this
intimidation had an especially chilling effect on political activism.

But in examining the turbulence of the late 1960s, and its decline
in the early 1970s, it is not enough to look at its specifically political
side. Cultural and artistic developments were also significant aspects of the "cultural revolution" of those years, as was aesthetics—
or rather, "antiaesthetics."

[53] Ibid. p. 31.

THE DEATH OF LITERATURE?

The International Avant-Garde

1961: 10/28. As Dieter Kunzelmann, member of Spur, a group of artists in Munich, is selling a newspaper with the text "The Cardinal, the Film, and the Orgy," a young woman reports him to the police. . . .

1964: . . . . 5/5. The annual conference of the Association of German Advertising Executives, meeting in Stuttgart's Liederhalle, is interrupted by the two members of the group Subversive Action, Dieter Kunzelmann and Frank Bröckelmann, who play loud recordings of the "Passion of St. Matthew" and the hit song "Surfing Bird." As leaflets with an "Appeal to Those Who Massage Souls" are simultaneously thrown from the gallery, they are arrested. . . .

1967: . . . . 1/1. After a long phase of preparation, the "*Viva Maria* Phase"—named after the Louis Malle film—Dieter Kunzelmann, Fritz Teufel, Rainer Langhans and others found the "Commune No. 1" in the Charlottenburg district of West Berlin. By 5/3 they are expelled from the SDS on account of "false immediacy," "self-overestimation," and "escapist tendencies." The specific cause was, among other things, a statement by Kunzelmann: "What do I care about Vietnam? I have orgasm problems."[54]

The above items from Wolfgang Kraushaar's chronology of the student protest movement deal with the beginnings of Dieter Kunzelmann's career, from the groups Spur and Subversive Action in Munich in the early 1960s to the Commune No. 1 in 1967.[55] They bring to light a significant influence upon the West German protest movement that is easy to ignore when describing its political development: namely, the influence of twentieth-century avant-garde art movements on the cultural experimentation and style of the student movement—not just in France or the United States, but also in West Germany. It is an influence that provides a context that explains such disparate phenomena of the 1960s as documentary theater, Pe-

[54] Kraushaar, "Chronologie," pp. 255, 257, 268.

[55] Dieter Kunzelmann was born in Bamberg in 1939, studied in Munich, and moved to West Berlin in 1966. His career is somewhat exemplary: after the days of the Commune No. 1, he spent time in prison on various charges from 1970 to 1975. A good deal of that period was spent in pretrial custody for charges of which he was eventually acquitted. In 1983 he was elected to the West Berlin Parliament as a delegate of the "Alternative Liste," a party aligned with the West German Greens, thus having gone all the way from the extraparliamentary movement (APO) into parliament (or West Berlin's Senate, at any rate).

ter Handke's play *Offending the Audience* (*Publikumsbeschimp-fung*, 1966), and the Commune No. 1.

Kraushaar's chronology of the international student movement is interesting because it does not ignore this influence; it begins, indeed, with an entry about the reading given by "Beat" writers Allen Ginsberg, Jack Kerouac, and Gary Snyder in San Francisco on 12 October 1955; its second entry discusses the founding on 28 July 1957, of the Situationist International by artists and intellectuals from France, Italy, Belgium, West Germany, the Netherlands, and Scandinavia. In the first issue of their journal, the situationists demanded the realization of communism by revolutionizing everyday life, a more or less anarchist position.[56] The roots of such a demand are clearly in surrealism—in the same way that Kunzelmann's pranks were similar to those of the dadaists. Such attitudes and actions express a desire to fuse the political with the personal through a destruction of the boundary between art and politics, and between art and everyday life.

A similar overlap of the political with the artistic is evident in Klaus Hartung's discussion (mentioned above) of West German political sects in the late 1960s, when he explains certain of their attitudes with the term *Avantgardeanspruch*—their pretension to being the avant-garde. It is precisely this fusion (and to a certain extent confusion) of artistic and political terminology—and goals—that characterizes both the political movements of the late 1960s and some of the intellectual influences named above: the situationists, the surrealists, the dadaists, even the "Beats." Parallels can be easily drawn between dominant tendencies within the student movement and Dada's attack on the elitism and auratic distance from life—and politics—of modernist art, and surrealism's antipathy to functionalized reason and science, as well as its simultaneous (and somewhat contradictory) commitment to Marxism. Demanding power for the imagination—"L'imagination au pouvoir"—is basically a surrealist position.[57] The proclamations of the death of art and literature—"L'art est mort," "Der Tod der Literatur," and somewhat more radically—"Die Kunst ist Scheiße" ("art is shit")—are clearly dadaist.[58]

[56] Kraushaar, "Chronologie," pp. 180–81.

[57] Cf. André Breton: "The imagination is perhaps on the point of reasserting itself, of reclaiming its rights. If the depths of our minds contain within it strange forces capable of augmenting those on the surface, or of waging a victorious battle against them, there is every reason to seize them." From Breton, *Manifestoes of Surrealism*, trans. Richard Seaver and Helen Lane (1924; Ann Arbor: University of Michigan Press, 1969).

[58] Once again, one notes the dadaist antipathy to the passion for "purity," which, as Peter Bürger writes, characterizes modernism. In C. and P. Bürger, *Postmoderne*, p. 10.

Kraushaar's citation of the situationists and the Beats is especially appropriate in this context, because they represent two postwar attempts—one European and the other American—at resurrecting the critique by those earlier movements of "high modernism." Both the Beats in the 1950s and the "pop" sensibility of the 1960s represent American versions of this revived avant-garde critique, the lineage being that which Huyssen calls "in shorthand the Duchamp-Cage-Warhol axis."[59] During the 1960s, American "pop" culture influenced Europe—and the European student movement; thus were "imported" surrealist and dadaist impulses returned to the continent of their origin in a recycled, more populist (and popularized) form. The influence of these tendencies upon the student movement illuminates an aspect of the latter that is arguably postmodernist. "What were the connotations of the term postmodernism in the 1960s? Roughly since the mid-1950s literature and the arts witnessed a rebellion of a new generation of artists such as Rauschenberg and Jasper Johns, Kerouac, Ginsberg and the Beats, Burroughs and Barthelme against the dominance of abstract expressionism, serial music and classical literary modernism."[60]

Huyssen goes on to describe other tendencies in this early postmodernism that he sees as an "American Avantgarde": "a powerful sense of . . . rupture and discontinuity" analogous to that which characterized surrealism and Dada; an iconoclastic attack on institutionalized art (which in America meant primarily European "high modernism"); "technological optimism" (e.g., the influence of Canadian Marshall McLuhan); and finally the "attempt to validate popular culture as a challenge to the canon of high art, modernist or traditional," a "populist" trend "with its celebration of rock n' roll and folk music, of the imagery of everyday life." These tendencies are part of his argument for what he terms the "specifically American character of postmodernism."[61] I would maintain that the European generation that came of age in the 1960s was very much influenced by these American currents of the 1950s and 1960s. Jean-Luc Godard, after all, alludes to the American "pop" influence in the student movement with the famous line about this generation as the "children of Marx and Coca-Cola."[62]

In West Germany aesthetic developments on the part of this (erstwhile) younger generation provide some evidence of this influence—in the late 1960s, one notes it in the work of Rolf Dieter

[59] Huyssen, "Mapping the Postmodern," p. 16.

[60] Ibid., pp. 16–17.

[61] Ibid., pp. 18–24.

[62] This is said in Godard's film Masculin/Féminin (1966).

Brinkmann[63] and in the use of rock and roll in the student films of
Wim Wenders. In the mid-1970s, the same influence is evident in
the general concern with "authenticity" and everyday experience
that one finds in the work of Jürgen Theobaldy and other "New Subjective" lyricists and in much similarly labeled prose of that era.
The direct legacy of surrealism and Dada within the student movement, unmediated by American pop art and pop culture, was of
course already recognized at the time.[64] In 1971 Peter Bürger wrote
that the aspirations of surrealists in the 1920s had become the program for the much more broadly based student movement: both the
surrealists and the movements of 1968 shared "the revolt against a
social order perceived to be repressive, the will to restructure interpersonal relationships totally, and the struggle to reunite art and
life."[65]

Another important intellectual influence on the movement, the
critical theory of the Frankfurt School, is of course quite distinct
from the impulses of surrealism, Dada, and pop art. To some extent
it was through the Frankfurt School that a new generation was introduced to the writings of Marx, more or less suppressed in (West)
Germany since the fascist era. (It was only later in the decade that
there was a widespread dedication to exclusive study of the "classic" writers themselves—Marx, Engels, Lenin, Mao.) As Hosfeld and
Peitsch point out in their analysis of the existentialist underpin-
nings of the antiauthoritarian phase, the influence of Jean-Paul Sar-
tre was also important with regard to the "style" of Marxism to
which students were first attracted.[66]

But in terms of the fusion of artistic and political discourse noted
above in the program of cultural anarchists like Kunzelmann and
even—unwittingly—in the style of dogmatic Marxist-Leninists of
the late 1960s, it must be added that the influence of the Frankfurt
School on the movement was hardly limited to the rediscovery of

[63] The most obvious acknowledgment of such American influences—specifically
the "Beat" and the "psychedelic" movements—can be seen in the anthology of North
American poetry and prose titled Acid. Neue amerikanische Szene (Darmstadt: März-
Verlag, 1969), collected and edited by Rolf Dieter Brinkmann and R. R. Rygulla. For
an introduction to the work of Brinkmann (1940–1975), see Michael Zeller's "Die
Zärtlichkeit der Gewalt. Zehn Bemerkungen zu Rolf Dieter Brinkmann," in Zeller,
Aufbrüche: Abschiede, pp. 47–59; see pp. 53–56 for a discussion of the influence of
the American "scene" of the 1960s on Brinkmann.

[64] See, e.g., Karl Markus Michel, "Ein Kranz für die Literatur. Fünf Variationen über
eine These," Kursbuch, no. 15 (1968), pp. 169–70, and Enzensberger, "Commonplaces," p. 88.

[65] Bürger, cited in Schlichting, "Das Ungenügen," note 2, p. 57.

[66] Hosfeld and Peitsch, " 'Weil uns diese Aktionen . . . ,' " pp. 95–96.

Marx, or to the more openly political pronouncements by members of the Frankfurt School such as Herbert Marcuse. *Aesthetic* theory had a very great influence, especially as formulated by Marcuse, Theodor W. Adorno, and Walter Benjamin, who infused art with political, indeed utopian, significance. Influenced by the writings of the early Marx, they conceived of art as containing utopian elements of a nonalienated praxis in the midst of, and in resistance to, reified industrial society. For Adorno only the most "autonomous" modernist art could possibly resist co-optation by socially dominant forces, and no political praxis (artistic or otherwise) could. But Marcuse (at least for awhile) believed that the boundaries between art and politics might be overcome in the here-and-now, with utopian consequences for everyday life.[67]

One area in which all these disparate influences on the cultural uprising of the 1960s are more or less unified is in the critique of both technocracy and Reason, a critique widely shared in that decade. It was an opposition to an "irrational" Reason that had been functionalized in the service of domination. This sentiment was behind the rebellion against what was considered a repressive social order. It was an indictment of the type of rationality Marcuse saw behind "the suppression of individuality in the mechanization of socially necessary but painful performances." This type of rationality was also behind what Marcuse saw as the victory of empiricism, behaviorism, and "value-free" analysis in the social sciences, a victory deadly for any hope for transcendence of the status quo, and for "negation of the prevailing modes."[68]

At the same time, in the 1960s there was still a faith that technology, under truly democratic control, and in the service of "Eros," not "Thanatos," could be liberating. Some technological optimism had survived—the legacy of various groups within the avant-garde of the 1920s, especially in Germany and the Soviet Union (e.g., Brecht, Benjamin, Heartfield, Vertov, and Tretyakov).[69]

The 1960s critique of reason is reflected more or less in Jean-Luc Godard's 1965 film *Alphaville*, in which a futuristic, techno-fascist state based on Logic, Mathematics, and Order is subverted by secret agent Lemmy Caution, in the name of those values suppressed there: poetry, love, conscience, the irrational. On the thematic level, the film is a bit closer to the privileging of art rather than a dadaist or Brechtian antiauratic stance. Formally, Godard's foregrounded use

---

[67] Ulrich Gmünder, *Kritische Theorie. Horkheimer, Adorno, Marcuse, Habermas* (Stuttgart: Metzler, 1985), p. 105.

[68] Marcuse, *One-Dimensional Man*, p. 4.

[69] Huyssen, "Mapping the Postmodern," p. 22.

of montage was highly influenced by Brecht's theories on distantiation. The origins of this style of montage can also be traced to dadaist photo-montage, another attempt somehow to reconnect art
"with the life of the times," as the dadaist Raoul Hausmann put it.[70]
Furthermore, the film's playful citation of popular film genres—spy
films (this was the era of James Bond films, it should be recalled)
and science fiction films—as well as its homage to Friedrich Mur-
nau's *Nosferatu* of 1922 (through the editing of negative footage into
the film at various points) make it a film that could arguably be labeled postmodernist.[71]

In West Germany during the mid-1960s, one of the few films with
a formal style comparable to the films of Godard was Alexander
Kluge's *Abschied von gestern* (1966), known in English as *Yesterday
Girl*, although a more literal translation would be "Farewell to Yesterday." The film's use of montage clearly shows the influence of the
French "New Wave" and especially of Godard. Kluge's film epito-
mizes that tendency at the very beginnings of the "New German Cinema" to search for a new film language, an alternative to the dominant conventional narrative of Hollywood.[72] The film depicts a cold,
technocratic state with some similarity to that in *Alphaville*, but this
is not a science fiction society. It is West Germany in the early
1960s, a "value-free" bureaucracy in which the "end of ideology"

[70] Raoul Hausmann, "Fotomontage," quoted in Anton Kaes, "Verfremdung als Verfahren: Film und Dada," in Wolfgang Paulsen and Helmut G. Hermann, eds., *Sinn
aus Unsinn. Dada International* (Bern: Francke, 1982), p. 73.

[71] The "villain" in *Alphaville*, "Dr. von Braun," also has the alias "Dr. Nosferatu."

[72] The "New German Cinema" is usually dated from the "Oberhausen Manifesto"
of 1962, a declaration by young German filmmakers proclaiming the birth of a new
cinema, an alternative to the West German commercial cinema, which had been to a
disturbing extent a continuation of the Nazi film industry. By the early 1960s the
artistic bankruptcy of the commercial industry was nearly complete. Claiming that
they were already developing a "new language of film," the young filmmakers at
Oberhausen declared: "The old film is dead. We believe in the new." A leader among
the original signers was Alexander Kluge. The manifesto appears in English in Pflaum
and Prinzler, *Cinema in the Federal Republic of Germany*, trans. Timothy Nevill
(Bonn: Internationes, 1983), p. 5, and in Eric Rentschler, *West German Filmmakers
on Film: Visions and Voices* (New York: Holmes and Meier, 1988), p. 2. Other English
sources on the New German Cinema include Thomas Elsaesser, *New German Cinema: A History* (New Brunswick, NJ: Rutgers University Press, 1989); Eric Rentschler,
*West German Film "in the Course of Time": Reflections on the Twenty Years since
Oberhausen* (Bedford Hills, NY: Redgrave, 1984); Timothy J. Corrigan, *New German
Film: The Displaced Image* (Austin: University of Texas Press, 1984); Klaus Phillips,
ed., *New German Filmmakers: From Oberhausen Through the 1970s* (New York:
Frederick Ungar, 1984); James Franklin, *The New German Cinema: From Oberhausen
to Hamburg* (Boston: Twayne, 1983); and John Sandford, *The New German Cinema*
(New York: Da Capo Press, 1980).

had to do with a suspiciously official disinterest in the past. It is this "farewell to yesterday" that Kluge's film investigates.

For both art and politics, the historical situation in West Germany in the 1960s had much to do with the revival of leftist and avant-garde traditions of the 1920s, which had been suppressed more or less since the National Socialists came to power in 1933. The Christian Democrats who governed West Germany in the 1950s were not interested in highlighting any continuities that may have existed between their conservative regime and the Third Reich, hence the official disinterest in the past; nonetheless, one obvious continuity was a strong anticommunist posture. The memory of leftist culture within the Weimar Republic seemed for this regime somehow more disturbing than the fascist legacy. As the Christian Democratic hegemony began to weaken in the 1960s, and with the international revival of radical avant-garde traditions from the 1920s, the conservative attempt to suppress the progressive legacy of the Weimar Republic was challenged, and a specifically West German revival began that was somewhat different from that in France or the United States.

The German Tradition

This continuity with leftist traditions of the Weimar Republic could not have been better symbolized than by the fact that it was Erwin Piscator who staged the first production of *The Deputy* (*Der Stellvertreter*) by Rolf Hochhuth on 20 March 1963.[73] Piscator himself had been one of the leading innovators of the leftist theater movements in the 1920s, having already experimented with "documentary" approaches in that decade. It was only fitting that he direct Hochhuth's play and thereby assist a new movement in the attempt to develop documentary theater.

The Deputy is based on extensive research into the relationship between the Vatican and the National Socialist regime in Germany; nonetheless the play conforms for the most part to conventional dramatic form. The documentary approach was then radicalized by Heinar Kipphardt and Peter Weiss, who moved away from the conventional techniques of dramatic fiction and toward a greater dependence on "objective" documents (for the most part court transcripts).

The trend toward "objectivity" was also a legacy of the Weimar

[73] Wolfgang Beutin et al., eds., *Deutsche Literaturgeschichte: von den Anfängen bis zur Gegenwart*, 2nd ed. (Stuttgart: Metzler, 1984), p. 530.

Republic, both in the mainstream artistic trend known as the "New Objectivity" (Neue Sachlichkeit) and in certain rationalistic tendencies on the left. After the demise of the republic, the Marxist philosopher Ernst Bloch criticized these tendencies for their part in the Left's failure to stop the National Socialists: in his famous formulation, "The Nazis speak deceptively, but talk to human beings; the Communists speak with complete truthfulness, but talk only about objects."[74] The Left's overly "objective" attitude took many forms, from an excessive dependence on statistics and fairly dry economic analyses, to the much more visionary (if also—in retrospect—somewhat naive) fascination with the revolutionary potential of technology and science. This fascination was found for the most part among leftist artists and intellectuals, most notably Piscator, Brecht, and Benjamin.

But of course the reference to Brecht and Benjamin makes it clear that no mere "scientific objectivity" can explain this tendency, and that it is not as unrelated to the "irrational" surrealists in France as it might appear. Common to both the French and the German avantgarde is the heritage of Dada: the attempt to destroy bourgeois art by destroying its aura and creating an "anti-art" that would not be cut off from life but indeed would become a collage of "objets trouvés," objects found in "life." The attempt to make art confront life subsequently took various forms—from the introduction into art of erotic and aggressive subconscious fantasies (as in the surrealist film Un chien andalou by Salvador Dali and Luis Buñuel) to the incorporation of social and historical documents (e.g., the use of newspaper articles in Alfred Döblin's novel Berlin Alexanderplatz and a similar montage in the film Kuhle Wampe, for which Brecht wrote the screenplay). Common to both the Brechtian and surrealist forms was also the assertion that this breakup of traditional art forms by reality (social or subconscious) was inherently political.

After writing The Investigation (1965) and then Vietnam-Discourse (1968), Peter Weiss was probably the leading "documentary" playwright of the late 1960s.[75] During this "objective" phase, he was nonetheless quite open about the political commitment, the Parteilichkeit (the necessity of taking sides), underlying his writing, as of

[74] Bloch, Erbschaft dieser Zeit, p. 153. For a discussion of Bloch's critique of fascism and the Left's inadequate response to it, see Anson Rabinbach, "Unclaimed Heritage: Ernst Bloch's Heritage of our Times and the Theory of Fascism," New German Critique, no. 11 (1977), pp. 5–21.

[75] Weiss was best known internationally in the 1960s for his play Marat/Sade (1964), written before his documentary plays for the theater.

course Brecht had been. Hans Magnus Enzensberger, as late as 1966, saw little value in Weiss's political—and aesthetic—stance:

> Since Peter Weiss and others are challenging me to show my colors, I shall respond in this way: the diverse souls in their breasts and in mine are not of interest at the level of global politics. This moral rearmament on the Left can leave me out. I prefer doubts to convictions. I find revolutionary babble odious. I don't need images of the world that are free of all contradiction. In case of doubt reality will decide.[76]

Enzensberger was at the time editor of the new *Kursbuch*, begun in 1965 and thereafter one of the leading Left-oriented cultural and political journals in West Germany; his 1966 statement is interesting from many perspectives. It is interesting to note the distaste for dogmatic political systems and for revolutionary "babble" in a man who within four years would go to Cuba out of commitment to its revolution and would write there a documentary piece for the theater, *The Havana Inquiry* (*Das Verhör von Habana*, 1970). Enzensberger was also the man whose name would become so associated with the concept of the "Death of Literature" because of his 1968 essay in *Kursbuch* no. 15.[77]

What is relevant here is the continuity between the 1966 statement and the 1968 essay, "Commonplaces on the Newest Literature," in which Enzensberger notes as hopeful signs the greater interest of the younger generation in agitational literature and "factographies" as opposed to experimental texts and fiction.[78] There is a shift with regard to his positive evaluation of "agit-prop" in 1968, perhaps, but there is definitely a continuity with regard to "factographies": "In case of doubt, reality will decide." It is the insistence on empirical "reality" that is continuous. While in the 1968 article the rejection of moral and political engagement has been somewhat altered, what is constant is the valuation of reality over art and the artist, an underlying belief in the "inadequacy of poetic strategies."[79] This empirical, antifictional stance would remain significant into the 1970s, even though by then many, like Enzensberger himself, would become disenchanted with the grand, schematic

---

[76] *Kursbuch*, no. 6 (1966), quoted in Schlichting, "Das Ungenügen," p. 33.

[77] Enzensberger's career is symptomatic of many cultural shifts over the years. Compare the positions cited here with his "Zwei Randbemerkungen zum Weltuntergang" in *Kursbuch*, no. 52 (1978), pp. 1–8.

[78] Enzensberger uses the word "Faktographien" in the original German essay, "Gemeinplätze, die Neueste Literatur betreffend," p. 189.

[79] This is the title of Schlichting's essay "Das Ungenügen der poetischen Strategien."

worldviews they had embraced, systems that explained reality so confidently—and reductively. "Authenticity" to reality, as I have discussed above, would survive the end of the 1960s as a goal for writers; indeed, given the shift toward the autobiographical, it would flourish.

The "Death of Literature" is a concept that *Kursbuch* no. 15 investigates, but in fact, Enzensberger's essay in that issue did not maintain that the concept was accurate. In this sense, among others, his essay can be compared with John Barth's 1967 essay on the "Literature of Exhaustion."[80] Both essays are attached to popular slogans with regard to literature that they do not uncritically accept—though Barth's essay does of course use the slogan for its title. Both essays (especially Enzensberger's) assert that literature is not dead but socially irrelevant.[81] Finally, both essays represent breaks with literary modernism that are of great relevance to any discussion of the postmodern.

For Barth, of course, this significance has been amply recognized, perhaps even overemphasized.[82] Enzensberger's position, in any case, differs from that of Barth in this regard. Whereas Barth makes a virtue of sorts out of literature's marginality and especially of the Sisyphean task of writing in the face of the "exhaustion" of modernism's aesthetic of novelty, all the while remaining reverent vis-à-vis the modernist legacy, Enzensberger rather viciously derides the futility of the projects of both the modernists and the avant-garde. In no small part, however, his bitterness has to do with his analysis of the function literature had played since the beginning of the West German state.

That "high modernism" became institutionalized as the official art in the postwar era by Western capitalism (the system against which much modernist art had originally been directed) is an insight shared by many critics.[83] The use to which modernism was put

[80] John Barth's "The Literature of Exhaustion" appeared first in the August 1967 issue of *The Atlantic*; it can also be found in Raymond Federman, ed., *Surfiction: Fiction Now . . . and Tomorrow* (Chicago: Swallow Press, 1975), pp. 19–33.

[81] Enzensberger, "Commonplaces," p. 92; "Gemeinplätze," p. 195.

[82] Barth himself has addressed his essay and its relation to postmodernism in an "update" of his 1967 article: "The Literature of Replenishment: Postmodernist Fiction," *The Atlantic* (July 1980), pp. 65–71.

[83] See, for example, Huyssen, "Mapping the Postmodern," pp. 16–18; Fredric Jameson, "The Politics of Theory: Ideological Positions in the Postmodernism Debate," *New German Critique*, no. 33 (1984), pp. 53–54; Charles Newman, *The Post-Modern Aura: The Act of Fiction in an Age of Inflation* (Evanston, IL: Northwestern University Press, 1985), pp. 27–35.

in West Germany in the same period was an especially sly form of
co-optation, in Enzensberger's formulation:

> The less thought was given to real social changes, to the rearrangements
> of power and ownership conditions, the more indispensable became for
> West German society an alibi in the superstructure. Very different mo-
> tives came together here in a new-fangled amalgamation:
>
> The wish to compensate, at least intellectually, for the complete bank-
> ruptcy of the Third Reich;
>
> The evidently urgent need, regardless of the great collective crime, to
> once again be regarded as a "cultured people";
>
> . . . A form of anti-fascism which satisfies itself with having better
> taste than the Nazis, and which manifested its democratic mentality by
> buying what the former called "degenerate": pictures on which nothing
> can be recognized and poems with nothing in them.
>
> The need to be at least esthetically "with it" in the world, the wish to
> be classy enough to make it in world cultural circles—this objective was
> most recently achieved with The Tin Drum.[84]

In its scathing indictment of modernism, Enzensberger's position
comes into an odd proximity with the Nazi denunciation of Expressionist art (a verdict shared also by some German leftists in the
1930s).[85] It seems to be motivated by anger at the futility of the proclaimed political "engagement" of a whole generation of West German literati. Not only was their activity futile, so the argument goes,
it was objectively in the service of the corrupt status quo to which
they proclaimed opposition.

Enzensberger did not pronounce literature dead, but useless;
therefore, for him, any self-styled revolutionaries wasting their energies in 1968 trying to "kill" such a marginal phenomenon were
fools. He gave precious little hope to those who hoped to affect political change through literature. Although he saw some—modest—

---

[84] Enzensberger, "Commonplaces," p. 86.

[85] In 1936, there was a Nazi exhibition of Expressionist art, titled "Entartete Kunst":
"Degenerate Art." By 1937, a debate among the (exiled) German Left arose about the
legacy of Expressionism, defended by some as utopian and visionary on the one hand
and attacked by others as a decadent formalism complicit in the rise of fascism. This
was the famous Expressionism debate. Georg Lukács was the most prominent expo-
nent of the (socialist-) realist camp; among those who defended Expressionism were
Ernst Bloch and, in a series of essays that were not published at the time, Bertolt
Brecht. See Die Expressionismusdebatte, ed. Hans Jürgen Schmitt (Frankfurt: Suhrkamp, 1973); Ernst Bloch, "Diskussionen über Expressionismus" and "Das Problem
des Expressionismus nochmals," in his book Die Kunst, Schiller zu sprechen (Frankfurt: Suhrkamp, 1969); and Bloch et al., Aesthetics and Politics (London: NLB,
1977)—see esp. Fredric Jameson's afterword, "Reflections in Conclusion."

political effectiveness in Günter Wallraff's reports and a few other examples of work that could be called political journalism, anything that was "literary" was inescapably bourgeois.[86]

Fiction-writing was thus not an appropriate activity for the politically committed; "factographies" might be of some value. As Michael Zeller has written of the late 1960s in West Germany, "In place of the poetic subject came the non-literary document"; he cites as examples the mountains of files used by Kipphardt, Weiss, and Enzensberger himself, the tape-recorded interviews by Erika Runge, the investigation of data on the corporations by F. C. Delius, the "Reportage" as practiced by Wallraff, and the incorporation of the *objet trouvé* he sees as characteristic of the poetry of Erich Fried[87] and the plays and poetry of Peter Handke. A generational difference, however, can be noted in the strategies Zeller names as responses to what he sees as a crisis of literary fiction and of the "poetic subject."[88]

The strategy of the older generation (i.e., Weiss, Enzensberger, and Kipphardt) was definitely a retreat behind "mountains of files," whereas the strategies of the younger writers depended more on leaving the writer's desk and experiencing personally, at least to some degree, the political realities being investigated, whether by interviewing workers, as Runge did, or actually becoming an employee in a factory or newspaper, as Wallraff did. At the time, they too were hiding behind the claim of objectivity, as Runge later complained. But by 1976, Wallraff admitted: "Certainly the decisive thing is the subjective experience."[89]

It is questionable how politically committed Peter Handke's experimental work in the 1960s was, but the mention of Handke, in any case, indicates that the retreat from "subjectivity" in West German literature was not confined to documentary literature or any other type of explicitly "politicized" literature. West German experimental literature was attacked by Enzensberger because of its "technocratic" ideology and for being "revolutionary" in form only.[90] Nonetheless, it was no more characterized by any traditional concept of a "poetic subject" than was documentary literature. A 1974 book called *The Execution of the Narrator* discussed West German

---

[86] Enzensberger, "Commonplaces," pp. 90, 93.

[87] Erich Fried's collection of poetry titled *und Vietnam und* appeared in 1966.

[88] Michael Zeller, "Einleitung: Versuch, zehn Jahre westdeutsche Literatur in den Blick zu nehmen," in Zeller, *Aufbrüche: Abschiede,"* pp. 6–9.

[89] Quoted in ibid., p. 9.

[90] Enzensberger, "Commonplaces," p. 88.

novels of the late 1960s in terms of the "liquidation of subjectivity" and the "destruction of the closed narrative context."[91]

Subjectivity in Crisis

The rise of a new "subjectivity" in literature by the mid-1970s is surely related to the "crisis of subjective agency" of which Adelson writes in her discussion of the student movement.[92] But of course the crisis of subjective agency was not simply a specific reaction by West German students to the deterministic abstractions of the dogmatic phase of the protest movement. Subjective agency—related as it is to the ideology of the "autonomous subject"—has been in crisis at least since the consolidation of industrial capitalism in the late nineteenth and early twentieth centuries.[93] The crisis of the subject in that era found its literary reflection in the crisis of narration explored in the novels of what now is called "high modernism": the novels of Joyce, Proust, and Musil, to name a few. The modernist response to the crisis—a depiction of the subject as hopelessly determined by political and/or subconscious forces beyond its control (following Marx and/or Freud), and as fragmented by the complexity of modern urban life—allowed no hint of hope save perhaps for a return of some kind of mythic consciousness, with artists as its priests. Various avant-garde movements attacked this elitism as itself a last vestige of bourgeois subjectivity and its auratic art. With the canonization of modernist art—and even much avant-garde "anti-art"—by mid-century, a radicalized avant-garde in Europe called for the end of any art that could be institutionalized. This new avant-garde demanded the revolutionization of everyday life itself. In America, meanwhile, the antielitist Beat and Pop movements validated subjective experience and devalued modernist "distance."[94]

[91] Kurt Batt, *Die Exekution des Erzählers*, cited in Peter Beicken, " 'Neue Subjektivität': Zur Prosa der siebziger Jahre," in Lützeler and Schwarz, *Deutsche Literatur*, p. 167.

[92] Adelson, *Crisis of Subjectivity*, p. 1.

[93] Indeed, one could argue that the very incorporation of the idea of the "autonomous subject" into Western ideology at the end of the *eighteenth century* was a sign of crisis, wishful thinking by the bourgeoisie in ever more rationally organized societies that entrepreneurial freedom would guarantee personal autonomy—and not contribute to the process of ongoing social organization and instrumentalization.

[94] The "Beat" validation of subjective experience should not, however, be connected necessarily to the ideology of the "autonomous" subject. The affinity of the Beats to Zen Buddhism and forms of Eastern mysticism is only one indication of their preference for fluid conceptions of identity.

For that generation of youth which was influenced by these tendencies in the 1960s, it was hoped that the experience of life itself could be reclaimed from a bureaucratic, technocratic order seen as stifling, repressive, and alienating. The idea of a revolutionary art was no longer tenable, as Enzensberger had argued, but neither did his scaling down of the writer's function to the organizer of "factographies" have much appeal. As implied in his argument, the real battle was not over literature but in "life" itself. And this was where most students wanted a revolution; the debate about revolutionary literature was not of much interest.

> At issue was more—in any case it didn't concern literature. A new immediacy of experience, unknown possibilities for influencing politics outside the omnivorous monopoly of the major parties, unexpected opportunities for freedom were at the top of the day's agenda. Questions about writing literature were now deemed insignificant, if not timid and escapist. The work of cultural sublimation was especially despised, since above all it was important to experience life to the full, and to experiment with one's own everyday existence, rather than with its symbolic transcendence.[95]

In the initial euphoric months of the student movement, these "unexpected opportunities for freedom" seemed within reach. This new generation of artists, intellectuals, and students began to entertain all sorts of utopian dreams: dreams of a nonalienated experience of life, of interpersonal and sexual relationships unencumbered by traditional social restrictions, of each individual truly participating in the political and economic decisions affecting his or her life. It was for the most part a privileged and idealistic group, inspired by all the revolutionary thinkers and movements of the last century. And while the demands of the late 1960s may have had a narcissistic aspect,[96] they also were based, it should be remembered, on fundamental democratic notions of self-determination.[97]

[95] Zeller, *Aufbrüche: Abschiede*, pp. 6–7.

[96] Many, most notably Christopher Lasch in *The Culture of Narcissism*, have argued that the cultural legacy of the 1960s is in many ways "narcissistic"; though there is much value in such analyses, their sweeping nature is somewhat problematic, as is the implication that the rise of a new "narcissistic" or even "oral" personality type is a completely negative development. For a discussion of positive, indeed utopian, elements within the complex of narcissism, see C. Fred Alford's "Nature and Narcissism: The Frankfurt School" in *New German Critique*, no. 36 (1985), pp. 174–92.

[97] Decentralized participatory democracy, especially the concept of *Basisdemokratie*, democracy of the base ("from the bottom up"), is a concept that has been central to those groups that have their roots in the West German student movement: the

I would argue that not only is much West German literature of the 1970s a response to a crisis of subjective agency within the student movement, as Adelson rightly argues, but that the student movement *itself* was a reaction to the larger, international crisis of the subject in this century and to the various modernist and avant-garde attempts to articulate it. The student movement represented in part an ambivalent critique of those attempts, a critique that is thus appropriately labeled postmodern, attacking much within modernism and at the same time borrowing much from it.[98]

In this sense, Zeller's bracketing out of the literary is only partially accurate; it is true that during the antiauthoritarian phase, the emphasis was on life in the streets, not in books or the theater or the museums. But even this attitude had its roots in earlier avant-garde movements, as I have discussed above; it represented—to be sure on an unprecedented mass scale—the carrying of certain avant-garde strategies outside the art world into life. Art and literature may have been eclipsed by politics in the late 1960s, but this was a new sort of politics, a politics that was itself a kind of street theater.[99]

This is, once again, a blurring of the boundaries between politics, art, and life—less charitably, following Habermas, one might call it a leveling.[100] The influence of earlier avant-garde movements in art upon this "leveling" suggests that what was happening was not the achievement of the old avant-garde goal, elitist art being undermined by the invasion of "life." Rather it was more an invasion of life by concepts from avant-garde art. This in turn suggests metaphors like "the textualizing of the world," a term used in Nägele's discussion of the blurring of the fictional and the documentary within modern West German novels.[101]

When the initial euphoria subsided, of course, and the world had not been transformed overnight, the crisis of subjective agency—which had seemed, for a brief moment of apparent omnipotence, to have been transcended—was experienced with a new severity by the generation that came of age in the 1960s. For a while, after all, it had been unusually influential, and thus perhaps somewhat intoxi-

women's movement, the ecology movement, the peace movement, the Greens. *Basisdemokratie* seems to have had no more spectacular success than in East Germany in 1989, where people in the streets toppled the party hierarchy nonviolently. (How much *Basisdemokratie* they will enjoy in a reunified Germany remains to be seen.)

[98] As Huyssen writes, the two main strains of 1960s postmodernism, "the apocalyptic desperate strain and the visionary celebratory strain," were already present within modernism. "Mapping the Postmodern," p. 17.

[99] Cf. the remarks of Antje Krüger, cited above, note 49.

[100] Habermas, "Modernity," p. 11.

[101] Nägele, "Geschichten," p. 246.

cated with confidence in its ability to control the world. Its influence was due to its relative wealth, education, and numbers, and by the growing importance of the news media. All these factors were dependent on postwar prosperity, consumer capitalism, and the ascendance of the electronic media—the beginnings of the "postindustrial" information industry.

As a result of this intoxicating hubris and privilege, the disillusionment came hard. The subordination of subjectivity to the rigid party line among those who became "dogmatic" among West German activists was only one of many responses to this traumatic realization of relative powerlessness. Other responses included more active forms of desperation—terrorism—for a very small group, but passive resignation was the most common response. Another was the rise of a "new subjectivity" in literature a few years later.

DOGMATIZATION AND RESIGNATION

In May of 1968, protests by French students at the Sorbonne led to a situation in which labor unions called a general strike, and more than a million protesters filled the streets of Paris in the largest demonstration in French history. Nationwide, workers took over factories all over France, and General de Gaulle's government came quite close to falling. But it did not fall and indeed managed forcibly to retake occupied factories and university buildings and to win an absolute majority in special national elections at the end of June. This was the closest to a revolution any group of activists in Western Europe or the United States came in the late 1960s, but it was closer perhaps than many people remember today. It also begins to explain the depths of the ensuing "postrevolutionary" syndrome of resignation among members of a student movement that was international in scope—a movement up until then encouraged by news of student revolts in Berkeley, Paris, and West Berlin; at Harvard and Columbia, and even in Prague, where students had much to do with the "Prague Spring" of 1968 (a peaceful revolution crushed only by Soviet tanks).

In May 1968, the student movement in West Germany was fresh from street battles with police, in the aftermath of the attempt on Rudi Dutschke's life in April—street battles that had been the most severe Germany had seen since the Weimar Republic. In May the issue that mobilized a broad group of progressives was the likelihood of imminent passage of the *Notstandsgesetze*—the emergency laws—by the West German Parliament. In the last two weeks of

May, over 80,000 people in more than fifty cities demonstrated against their passage—in vain. Progressive hopes were once again dashed by the SPD: a majority of SPD delegates voted with conservatives to pass the emergency laws. Just as in France, where the Communist Party was seen as having betrayed the May uprisings by distancing itself from the factory takeovers, in West Germany the disillusionment with the institutionalized parties in parliament grew. Since the Great Coalition, this disillusionment was already quite strong.[102]

Marxist-Leninists, Terrorists, "Sensibilists," and Others

One difference between the situation in France and that in West Germany was the response of the labor unions. On 11 May 1968, the day when 60,000 protesters from all over West Germany had gathered in Bonn, the SDS appealed to the unions to call a general strike in solidarity with the protest against the emergency laws; unlike what was happening in France, this appeal went unheard.[103] In the face of disappointment, the movement in West Germany, like so many other student movements in that year, underwent a radicalizing process, moving toward the espousal of various types of revolutionary socialism. There was a strong impulse to win the workers away from the established labor unions. That those unions were relatively conservative was certainly true; whether the strategies adopted by the students would win over many workers was another question.

Part of this radicalizing process led to increasing dissension within the movement as to the appropriate revolutionary strategy, a factionalizing that would lead to the gradual breakup of the SDS, the last remnants of which would completely disband by early 1970, only two years after the high-water mark of the movement.[104] This was also the period in which it became less accurate to speak of a

[102] Kraushaar, "Chronologie," pp. 278–82. This situation might be compared with the situation in the United States in 1968, where the protest movement against the war in Vietnam had succeeded in discouraging Lyndon Johnson from running for a second term and had fueled the Kennedy and McCarthy campaigns. All that the protesters ultimately got from the "liberal" Democratic party at its convention in Chicago that August was the prowar Hubert Humphrey (thus making it easier for the more conservative Richard Nixon, the Republican candidate, to win) and of course the brutality of Mayor Daley's police. The latter, besides wounding many of the thousands who protested in Lincoln and Grant Parks, tear-gassed McCarthy headquarters (no doubt radicalizing those students still committed to working within the "system").

[103] Kraushaar, "Chronologie," p. 281.

[104] Ibid., pp. 284–95.

"student movement"; with the "turning toward the proletariat," activists from the various Marxist-Leninist factions started taking jobs in the factories in order to organize the workers along the lines of more militant styles of socialism.

It was the beginning of *Basisarbeit*, work in the industrial "base" of the capitalist economy, to win over the working class to a truly revolutionary—not "revisionist" or "reformist"—socialism. More important than work in the factory was simultaneous *Betriebsgruppenarbeit*, the organization of cells within factory shops dedicated to enlightening the workers to a correct analysis of the contradictions between labor and capital. (In Peter Schneider's 1973 novel *Lenz*, the protagonist belongs to such a group, which meets to read the writings of Mao together.)

Such strategies were, however, by no means shared by everyone in the movement, and their adoption by some factions was part of the above-mentioned breakup of the movement in West Germany. Those groups interested in the maintenance of public protest against the Springer press or the Vietnam war, for instance, accused the groups in the factories of shirking the real struggle: "the comrades came under suspicion of disappearing into the proletariat."[105] For the groups in the factories, however, the real struggle was that of the working class; the only question was finding the right strategy, the correct theoretical line, the right party to guide that struggle. In the midst of these theoretical and factional debates, women in the movement began to raise their voices against the blindness of male activists to the position of women, as well as the male infatuation with abstractions and inability to understand concrete needs—like the need for child care, one of the first needs addressed by the newly founded "Aktionsrat zur Befreiung der Frauen," the "Action Committee for the Liberation of Women."[106]

Those who devoted themselves to organizing the working class (and arguing with each other over the correct party line) were not the only ones who could be accused of stealing away from the public confrontation with the "establishment." The retreat into dog-

[105] Hartung, "Versuch," p. 35.

[106] The women's "Action Committee" entered on the scene with its intervention at the 1968 Frankfurt sds Conference. Helke Sander, who spoke for the "Action Committee" at the conference, thematizes that speech in her film *The Subjective Factor* (1980). Ulrike Meinhof, at the time still a "legitimate" journalist, wrote in support of the "Action Committee," commenting on the Frankfurt affair in an article titled "Die Frauen im sds, oder: In eigener Sache," *Konkret* 12 (10 October 1968). See also Renny Harrigan, "The German Women's Movement and Ours," *Jump Cut*, no. 27 (1982), p. 43.

matic sects splitting hairs over the fine points of Marx, Lenin, and Mao was paralleled by another, more dramatic move away from public protest in the streets: the move underground into terrorist cells. The activists who chose this path also considered themselves revolutionary socialists but were not content with the patient study and preaching of revolutionary theory—they were the other side, as it were, of a (most undialectical) dichotomy between theory and praxis. Both groups can be seen as responses to the failure of the student movement to have the impact it desired on West German society—and to a crisis of subjective agency as well.

The dogmatists viewed their earlier antiauthoritarian strivings as mistaken bourgeois individualism and sought to correct this "subjectivist" error through subordination to a collective (dedicated to the correctness of its "objective" analysis of the interests of the only valid "subject" of history, the proletariat). The terrorists, on the other hand, instead of subordinating themselves to theory and dedicating themselves to the organization of the working class, romanticized their acts of violence against leading corporate and state institutions as inspiration for the oppressed masses, as an invitation to join them in revolt. Behind this romantic vision, of course, it is not difficult to see the desperate need of embittered idealists to strike back at the society they had been unable to change—to strike back regardless of the prospects of success, or the personal consequences.[107]

But the relationship between the terrorists and the dogmatic groups was more direct than merely that between alternate responses to the failures of the student movement. As Klaus Hartung writes, the evolution in the direction of terrorism by those who formed the RAF, and the West German state's increasingly harsh re-

---

[107] In this stance can be seen some of the ultimate consequences of what Rolf Hosfeld and Helmut Peitsch call the existentialist side of the student movement. The moral *Weigerung*—refusal, rejection—of existing conditions by individuals became active, violent "resistance" by small groups, in spite of the odds. See Hosfeld and Peitsch, "Weil uns diese Aktionen . . . ," p. 96.

In discussing the "terrorist" route, one ought not to forget that it evolved over a period of time. The initial strategy was quite different from later developments. The first action by those who formed the RAF was a department-store bombing in Frankfurt on 3 April 1968. The group considered it a protest "against the indifference of society to the murder in Vietnam" (Kraushaar, "Chronologie," pp. 277–78); it occurred at night, when no one was there, so that no one would be hurt. Of course, this immediately criminalized the group and caused the press to label it "terroristic," bringing a whole set of connotations to mind for the populace. This put into motion a process through which the population became ever more frightened of the RAF, which became ever more desperate, and did indeed conform ever more closely to the hysterical stereotype first propagated by the press.

sponse to the RAF, were developments that had a direct effect on the emerging sectarian groups. The terrorists claimed for themselves the tradition of active resistance and symbolic protest within the movement in a dramatic way that was alien to the sober work of the orthododox Marxist-Leninists and at the same time showed how dangerous anything vaguely approaching seriously "revolutionary" resistance would be in terms of state reaction.

It thus became much easier—and safer—for groups to distance themselves from the RAF on theoretical grounds than to work for any kind of united front that transcended the divisions of the protest movement. Theoretical activity in defining each group's separate identity and "line" was somehow much safer than any realistic analysis of the movement's prospects or of effective oppositional strategies—including serious organization of the working class (i.e., beyond competitive proselytizing). But a sense of powerlessness lay beneath all that feverish theoretical activity—its underside, as it were: "Abstract Marxism and real impotence had become inseparably bound."[108]

This insight is also found in Enzensberger's 1968 essay:

> If I am right, if no verdict is possible on writing, all the revolutionary haranguing, which looks for relief from its own impotence in the liquidation of literature, won't accomplish anything either. A political movement which, instead of attacking the power of the state, tangles with aging belletrists would only manifest its own cowardice in this manner. . . . Instead of shouting "Hands up!" to the producers of slim volumes, the militant groups should attack the cultural apparatuses whose social function—in contrast to that of poetry and prose—is only too clearly recognizable and without whose rule ruling has become inconceivable. However, these apparatuses aren't impotent opponents against whom the Left can turn its fear, its puritanism, and its philistinism into aggression without actually risking something.[109]

Enzensberger thus attacks dogmatic attitudes in the student movement associated with a concept of the "Death of Literature"—with which his essay has also (inaccurately) been associated. His point is, of course, well taken: such dogmatism bespeaks a misdirection of focus in "revolutionary" strategy, given the marginality of art by the 1960s, and it is tantamount to avoiding real enemies.

Michael Schneider used language similar to Enzensberger's, describing how the protest movement "to a certain extent stuck a pis-

[108] Hartung, "Versuch," p. 32.
[109] Enzensberger, "Commonplaces," pp. 92–93.

tol to the breasts of writers and artists."[110] He saw this as a consequence of the movement's simplistic negation of its own middle-class heritage. This negation led to a totally ahistorical perception of all aesthetic categories as well as, psychologically, a rigid repression of the activists' own (bourgeois) past—in other words, rigid self-denial.[111] Thus had avant-garde impulses against elitist, bourgeois art mutated with the rise of orthodox Marxist-Leninism into a complex of aesthetic and psychological repression similar perhaps to attitudes we associate with the Chinese "cultural revolution" of the 1960s—an odd transition given the anarchistic bent of those original surrealist and dadaist impulses.

But, again, by no means did all student activists embrace such a rigid political, aesthetic, and psychological program. Most of them belonged to factions other than the dogmatic and the terrorist groups. Common to most factions by 1969, however, was the same sense of powerlessness with regard to major political change that can be seen lurking behind the dogmatic and the terrorist stances. For these other activists, resignation was more openly admitted, and it often meant a "retreat" into the personal experimentation that had always been a part of the movement, but which was subsequently rejected by the dogmatic groups. In addition to the interest in "life-style" experimentation (e.g., communal living, experimentation with drugs), aesthetic activity also received renewed emphasis among those individuals disillusioned with politics. The same enmity to aesthetic tradition that Michael Schneider mentions with regard to the more dogmatic factions, however, can also be seen among those who opted to continue making art.

One such young man was Wim Wenders, who was attending film school in Munich in the late 1960s. In 1968 and 1969, he lived for awhile in a political commune; he was also arrested at a demonstration for allegedly hitting a policeman, a charge he denied. Later, still in film school, he would make an experimental documentary on the tactics of the Munich police, called *Police Film* (*Polizeifilm*, 1970), but by then he had become disenchanted with the activists among whom he lived. His place of refuge was the cinema: "I went to see westerns every night, and they [his housemates] were talking about imperialism and fighting this and fighting that."[112] As the student

---

[110] M. Schneider, "Von der alten Radikalität," p. 174.

[111] Michael Schneider, "Peter Schneider: Von der alten Radikalität zur Neuen Sensibilität," in *Die lange Wut zum langen Marsch. Aufsätze zur sozialistischen Politik und Literatur* (Reinbek: Rowohlt, 1975), p. 327.

[112] Wim Wenders, quoted in Kathe Geist, "Wenders in the Cities," in Phillips, *New German Filmmakers*, p. 382.

movement dissolved, many of the commune members went underground; Wenders experimented (temporarily) with drugs.[113] Both
choices were responses to the general disillusionment of the era. In
discussing his first feature film, *Summer in the City* (1970), Wenders
described the pervasive disappointment of the time:

> To me, now, *Summer in the City* is really a documentary about the end
> of the Sixties; it's much more of a documentary than any of my other
> films. It *is* a fiction film, but its length, as well as the black-and-white
> photography, and the wide-angle lenses and the fixed shots make it
> more like a documentary about the ideas people had in 1969 and 1970,
> the way people felt. . . . An enormous disappointment; and a feeling, as
> in a dream, of being completely powerless: that's what the film is about
> for me now. Not just powerless, but motionless; and emotionless.[114]

During this period of what one might call "postrevolutionary" resignation and depression, Wenders was writing articles for the journal *Filmkritik*. Both that journal and Munich's Academy for Televi-
son and Film (Hochschule für Fernsehen und Film, or HFF) were
associated by the end of the 1960s with a movement—or an attitude—known as "Sensibilismus" ("Sensibilism") that can be seen
to contain both some of the older avant-garde impulses so influential
early in the student movement and the pessimism and resignation
to which Wenders alludes with regard to this later stage of the movement. In his book on West German film, Eric Rentschler describes
the *Sensibilisten* ("Sensibilists") as follows:

> The *Sensibilisten* eschewed logical systems and political categories, in-
> sisting on the integrity of the subjective experience in all its immediacy
> and directness. One relied on the momentary uniqueness of lived en-
> counters. There existed an unspoken taboo against intellectualizing what
> one perceived: direct experience of the world was enough in and of it-
> self. Munich's *Sensibilisten* made films with extended travelling shots
> and long takes. They pointed their cameras out of apartment and car
> windows onto the streets. The works had a contemplative tenor and very
> little if any story line; they consisted of series of images meant to cap-
> ture the ineffable feel of things.[115]

What one notes in such a program is an openness to "reality" and
a rejection of the mediation of both traditional narrative and intellectual conceptualization, a rejection reminiscent in some ways of

[113] Geist, "Wenders in the Cities," pp. 381–82.
[114] Wenders, in an interview with Jan Dawson in her booklet, *Wim Wenders* (Toronto: Festival of Festivals, 1976), p. 19.
[115] Rentschler, *West German Film*, p. 174.

the program of many avant-garde and experimental film movements of this century, from the surrealists to the Italian neorealists. The formal program of the neorealists was similar to the Sensibilists' approach, but the Sensibilists lacked a political program. The stance against logic and for subjective experience is similar to the surrealist program, but the surrealists would find the Sensibilists too fixated on the surface of reality, with no interest in the subconscious. For the Sensibilists, such an interest would probably be rejected as part of another schematic system for intellectualizing experience.

The common stance they shared with other avant-garde movements of the century was the rejection of the traditional narrative as perfected in dominant Hollywood cinema. And, as Wenders's remark about *Summer in the City* suggests, his early work provides evidence of a blurring of the boundaries between the fictional and the documentary, a phenomenon that became a topic of debate and an experimental project in the cinema as well as in literature during the 1970s and early 1980s, influencing films as divergent as Kluge's *The Patriot* (*Die Patriotin*, 1979), Helke Sander's *The Subjective Factor* (1980), and Wenders's own *Nick's Film—Lightning over Water* (1980).

The specific influence of the experience of the student movement is also obvious in the attitudes of the Sensibilists: the rejection of political and theoretical categories that their more strident and dogmatic contemporaries were dragging into discredit. In the same context can be placed the resignation so typical of the end of a decade that had revived so many utopian hopes. This resigned, depressive state involved a withdrawal from social engagement so severe that only the object world seemed safe; as Kathe Geist writes, Wenders and his colleagues in film school made it "a point of style to exclude people from their films and deal primarily with objects."[116]

In spite of this "objective" side, Sensibilism has been considered "an early form of the tendency journalists would later designate as the 'New Subjectivity.' "[117] "New Subjectivity" would be pro-

[116] Geist, "Wenders in the Cities," p. 382. Geist also discusses Wenders's Sensibilist period in her book *The Cinema of Wim Wenders: From Paris, France to "Paris, Texas"* (Ann Arbor: UMI Research Press, 1988), pp. 14–17.

[117] Rentschler, *West German Film*, p. 174. To push the subjectivity/objectivity paradox a bit further, I would like to cite Siegfried Kracauer on "New Objectivity" (*Neue Sachlichkeit*) in Weimar Germany. His discussion of that artistic movement sounds very similar to much discussion of "New Subjectivity," at least in terms of resigned attitudes about political change. For "New Objectivity" the resignation was in response to the failed German revolution after World War I, as well as the demise in the arts of a rather utopian Expressionism. Kracauer quotes Gustav Hartlaub, who coined the term in 1924 with regard to a trend among painters: "It was related . . . to

claimed in the mid-1970s, and the Sensibilists were around at the end of the 1960s, and even then what was new about them was probably their pessimism. Similar groups of avant-garde, anarchist, and nondogmatic students had been associated with the larger counterculture of the 1960s from its beginning; in the early years, however, they had been as optimistic and as confident of the imminence of radical and revolutionary change in society as had the other students who thought of this revolution increasingly in terms of orthodox socialism.

It may be that it was not exclusively the failed utopian hopes of revolutionary socialism alone, or the dogmatic groups' overly "theoretical" bent, that led to the resignation and depression that accompanied the breakup of the student movement. Rather it was perhaps the confident belief in imminent, almost millennial, change that characterized all the various political and cultural tendencies. The adherents of all groups were left with a great void when their optimistic hopes were dashed. This included a disillusionment in all manifestos, whether political, cultural, or artistic; whether surrealist, Maoist, or Frankfurt-school. And the new feelings of powerlessness were as strong as the quite recent feelings of omnipotence had been.

The Tendenzwende: 1971–1974

> Sublimating the drives: that is, working for later enjoyment. . . . That's the kind of shit we are trained into, and we have to find our way back to total irresponsibility first, just to save ourselves. The "movement" only confuses the goal, but it's in no position to satisfy our needs. At the worst it will sacrifice our generation. But what's important now is to start here with freedom, that is, to develop the self. That's all that matters.[118]

Bernward Vesper criticized the movement for being unable to address the question of personal needs; it could not free the individual

---

the general contemporary feeling in Germany of resignation and cynicism after a period of exuberant hopes (which had found an outlet in expressionism). Cynicism and resignation are the negative side of the Neue Sachlichkeit; the positive side expresses itself in the enthusiasm for the immediate reality as a result of the desire to take things entirely objectively on a material basis without immediately investing them with ideal implications." Kracauer himself summarizes: "In other words, New Objectivity marks a state of paralysis. Cynicism, resignation, disillusionment: these tendencies point to a mentality disinclined to commit itself in any direction." Kracauer, From Caligari to Hitler: A Psychological History of the German Film (1947; Princeton, NJ: Princeton University Press, 1974), p. 165.

[118] Vesper, Die Reise, p. 45.

from the alienation and the delayed gratification of bourgeois social-ization. Vesper's critique seems, especially with its emphasis on the self, to be a call for the "new subjectivity" of the mid-1970s. Like Sensibilism, however, it too had an earlier origin; in Vesper's origi-nal manuscript for The Journey (Die Reise), this passage is dated 22 August 1969.[119]

There is a pessimism in Vesper's statement about the future of his own generation that, certainly for himself and others to whom he was close (his former lover Gudrun Ensslin, Andreas Baader, Jan-Karl Raspe, Ulrike Meinhof), turned out to be an accurate predic-tion. In 1971, after having been hospitalized for his mental condi-tion, Vesper committed suicide. By this point, the disillusionment within, and dissolution of, the movement (to which Vesper's state-ments—and life—are testimony) had progressed to the point where the sectarian Marxist-Leninist groups were dwindling in member-ship. In 1972, the year began, as mentioned above, with the passage of the Radicalism Decree, and by June the core of the RAF (its "first generation": Baader, Ensslin, Raspe, and Meinhof) had been cap-tured, never to leave prison alive.

In 1973, active U.S. involvement in Vietnam ended, thus elimi-nating one of the major international motivations for the protest movement. The paralysis on the left was accompanied by an inter-national recession in the wake of the 1973 oil crisis, which scrapped the last of the SPD's limited plans for reform; in 1974 a national "ten-dential shift" (the Tendenzwende) to the right was symbolized within the SPD at the highest level of government, when Willy Brandt resigned as Chancellor and was replaced by the more conser-vative, managerial Helmut Schmidt.

In this atmosphere, political change seemed unlikely, and politi-cal activism had in any case been discredited during the dogmatic phase through its "idolatry of the concept," its tendency toward re-liance upon various schematic models for interpreting the world, especially those based on dogmatic versions of Marxist theory. The reliance on dogmatic interpretations in the aftermath of the failures of the student movement had made a complex, frustrating global and national reality appear simple, but as the gap between these in-terpretations and reality widened, the dogmatic groups declined, and in the ensuing backlash, all theoretical activity was discred-ited.[120]

---

[119] Vesper, Die Reise, "Noten," p. 595. Also in the late 1960s, Rolf Dieter Brink-mann demanded the "disempowerment of the head through the body" in ACID. See Zeller, Aufbrüche: Abschiede, p. 58.

[120] As Hartung has noted, the rise of the dogmatic fetishization of Marxist theory within the student movement led to a reduction in the quality of theoretical analysis

Certain psychological processes that characterized the dogmatic phase could not go on forever: for example, the rigid repression of personal identity in sectarian groups, and the dogmatic avoidance of the personal needs and emancipatory impulses with which the student movement had begun. As some of the last of the dogmatic students gave up this regimen, a renewed emphasis on categories like personal experience, personal identity, and personal history— evident earlier among some groups—began to enjoy a general revival, and a broad backlash against the dogmatic concept of politics began to emerge.

It was too late for Bernward Vesper himself, and his autobiographical essay would have to wait a few years before it would be published. Rather it would be books by two students who had participated in Marxist-Leninist groups that would profit from, and give voice to, this wide sentiment which to a certain extent brought unity to former members of the various factions of the fragmented student movement. Appearing in 1973, Peter Schneider's *Lenz* and Karin Struck's *Class Love* (*Klassenliebe*) both became immediate best-sellers, proclaiming the validity of personal concerns and sensual experience and the absurdity of simplistic conceptual systems that denied or had no room for such categories. Rather than a simple retreat from politics, the two novels, each in its own way, asserted that the "personal is political"—not exactly a new sentiment, given the antiauthoritarian tendency within the New Left, but one that would be much more dominant in the 1970s, now that orthodox Marxist-Leninism had discredited itself. The significance of this attitude toward personal experience would be great. It became an essential part of the program of new political groupings like the ecology movement, the antinuclear movement, and, perhaps most important, the women's movement. It also had an aesthetic aspect, in terms of the implied new role for literature that the success of these two texts seemed to herald.

("Versuch," p. 34); it was not so much "theory" that became so all-powerful during the dogmatic phase but—obviously—dogma.

CHAPTER TWO

The
Body,
the Self

ISN'T THE FINAL GOAL of writing to articulate the body? . . .
Linguistic flesh has been puritanically repressed.
Abstraction has starved language. . . . In
order to reconnect the book with the
body and with pleasure, we must
disintellectualize
writing.[1]

AGAINST THE STRAITJACKET OF THEORY

During the *Tendenzwende*, the period following the demise of the student movement and the restoration of a more conservative climate in West Germany, one notes among the generation that came of age in the late 1960s a backlash against the dogmatic style of politics that had characterized the fading years of the student movement. Subjectivity had been a repressed category for those who had devoted themselves to the study of "scientific socialism"; personal experience had long been at odds with the neatly wrapped perceptions of the world belonging to the faithful in the various political sects. Now the personal became again the basis for political commitment, in keeping with the idea that the "personal is political." This principle guided a new wave of activists who were much more wary of any rigid theoretical orthodoxy (socialist or otherwise) than earlier antiauthoritarian activists had been.

Writers, too, began to champion subjective experience, which now was to be the fundament of writing. Rigid discipline in the cause of the class struggle was now seen as counterproductive, and a swing back to the mid-sixties critique of technocracy and rationalism was evident; poetry, love, and the irrational, just as in Godard's *Alphaville*, were once again to be defended. So literature, too, could be raised from the dead: "Jetzt dichten sie wieder"—"Now they compose literature again"—as some West German critics greeted this shift.[2]

But it was a question of more than just literature, even during the literary revival of the mid-1970s. If anything, questions of literary form were too easily dismissed, in keeping with the new antitheoretical sentiment. Nor was there any joyous return to poetry; one noted in both the prose and the poetry of the proclaimed New Subjectivity a rather desperate hunger for unhindered sensual enjoyment of the world and a troubled introspection, since the sensuality and immediacy so sought after remained elusive in the midst of ruined personal relationships and lost political faith. This tendency toward psychological self-examination was indeed a return to the subject, but the subject was still in crisis, still fragmented; mere dis-

[1] Chantal Chawaf, "Linguistic Flesh," trans. Yvonne Rochette-Ozzello, in Elaine Marks and Isabelle de Courtivron, eds., *New French Feminisms: An Anthology* (Amherst: University of Massachusetts Press, 1980), p. 177; orig. "La chair linguistique" in *Nouvelles littéraires*, 26 May 1976.

[2] This formulation was used in *Stern* magazine in October 1974. Cited in Michael Buselmeier, "Nach der Revolte. Die literarische Verarbeitung der Studentenbewegung," in Lüdke, *Literatur und Studentenbewegung*, p. 158.

missal of formal and theoretical questions would not re-create meaning and wholeness.

The new emphasis on *sich einbringen*, on personal involvement and experience, and especially the obsession with the body, is discussed by Michael Rutschky in his essay on West Germany during the 1970s, *The Hunger for Experience* (*Erfahrungshunger*). The individual, no longer comforted by utopian systems conferring hope, meaning, and collective identity, becomes more painfully aware of his or her alienation in, and conditioning by, a deadening and senseless social order; oppositional activism in the hostile external world seems futile, theoretical interpretations seem hollow, language inadequate. The last refuge for the embattled subject is the body: "The socialized individual dissolves in a swarm of threatening discourse, and that drives one to seek self-realization, self-determination beneath language, in perception, in the body, if necessary in fear and pain."[3]

There were of course many activists still interested in oppositional politics, but the goals of the politics that now became predominant reflected similar tendencies: theoretical and global perspectives were renounced in favor of attention to local and personal issues, to immediate and concrete problems, to concern with direct physical and sensual experience—and to sexual politics. These interests could be seen in new types of political organizing.

The concern with housing, of all needs one of the most concrete (and most essential to creation of a private or "intimate" sphere), led to the squatters' movement, whose strategy of occupying buildings was the essence of direct action to meet immediate needs. Through their emphasis on local environmental issues, ecological activists and those groups opposed to atomic power plants were able to attract support outside the standard ranks of student activists, forming *Bürgerinitiativen*, independent "citizens' initiatives." These were local coalitions of citizens dissatisfied with the insensitivity shown toward their concerns about their immediate environment by the national, institutionalized political parties.

Finally, the West German women's movement, which had been born during the student movement in the concrete struggle for daycare centers (an issue that the male activists had found irrelevant vis-à-vis the struggle against capitalism and imperialism), grew nationwide during the early 1970s with the campaign to repeal abortion laws. Rather than trying to organize a global revolution, the women's movement began organizing for control of that most spe-

---

[3] Rutschky, *Erfahrungshunger*, p. 225.

cific and personal reality: the body and its reproductive functions. Why, after all, should women wait for the proletariat to gain control of the means of production before they could gain control of their own bodies?

The strategies of these various groups were hardly homogeneous, ranging from the strong, anarchist "Sponti" influence in the housing movement and in some antinuclear groups to the more reformist and coalition-oriented influences in the *Bürgerinitiativen*, and from similar coalition-oriented women's groups to more separatist ones. This too reflected the distrust of "party lines," party discipline, and anything approaching global analysis or strategy. The preference for decentralization led to a certain amount of localism, perhaps even parochialism.

Squatters in Frankfurt rejected the offer of Alexander Kluge's film crew to document their struggle—they would allow it only if the crew would live with them and experience their struggle directly.[4] Women, however, did make documentaries about abortion and other issues for the women's movement—these films launched the careers of some of the women who would become successful filmmakers in the course of the 1970s.[5] The difference between Kluge's experience and that of the women is of course that he was, to the squatters, an established outsider, not a personal member of their group; the women making these films were not established, and they were part of the group engaged in struggle.

These political orientations of the 1970s are postmodern, in that they advance the critique of rationalism and technocracy one step farther than had been done in the 1960s. There is in them little faith at all left in technology or in Marx's "scientific socialism," and this distances the newer ideologies from the utopian dreams of the avant-garde earlier in the twentieth century. One similarity with Dada, surrealism, and pop art, however, would be the anti-intellec-

[4] This incident occurred during the filming of *In Gefahr und größter Not bringt der Mittelweg den Tod* (*In Danger and Dire Need, the Middle Way Brings Death*, 1974) by Kluge and Edgar Reitz. The film is, as Miriam Hansen writes, a "brilliant montage film which deals with the fragmentation of public events and private experience as observed during the Frankfurt 'Häuserkampf' ["housing battle"] of February 1974." Hansen, "Cooperative Auteur Cinema and Oppositional Public Sphere: Alexander Kluge's Contribution to *Germany in Autumn*," *New German Critique*, nos. 24–25 (1981–1982), note 38, p. 54. See also *Kursbuch*, no. 41 (1975), pp. 41–84.

[5] For example, important documentary films on women's issues were made by Helke Sander and Claudia von Alemann. Sander, for instance, made a documentary in 1972 called *Macht die Pille frei?* (*Does the Pill Liberate?*) on the birth control pill and its effects on the female body. See Möhrmann, *Die Frau mit der Kamera*, pp. 22–32, 86–87.

tual attitude that surfaced in some of the newer political orientations.

Feminism and the politics of gender have much to do with the newer perspectives: rationalism and technology began to be seen as elements of a system of domination of "man" over "nature" in a fashion integrally related to the domination of man over woman.[6] The feminist critique of modernization—and modernism—is one of the most significant factors within postmodern culture.[7]

Feminist criticism arose alongside the women's movement, as did a new burst of literary activity by women and—especially in West Germany—the new cinematic production by women mentioned above. It is important in looking at the "subjectivity" of the literature that appeared during the 1970s not to ignore the question of gender. Of two of the early texts that can be said to have heralded the "New Subjectivity" in West Germany, one was written by a woman. Karin Struck and Peter Schneider wrote books that became instant best-sellers in West Germany during 1973, first and foremost among that younger audience which had been politicized in the late 1960s, as the authors themselves had been.

The label "New Subjectivity" was to some extent the creation of literary critics of West Germany's *Feuilleton*. The label had an obvious relation to real developments, but it was also used in part to co-opt texts like those by Struck and Schneider.[8] Struck and Schneider were cited as evidence that the younger generation was turning its back on politics, an assertion at odds with both texts, I would argue. Thematically both books demand that the "personal is political"; formally, while perhaps problematic in certain ways (and def-

---

[6] Although rationalism was thus discredited, this did not mean that all feminists were willing to concede all theoretical activity to men. There has been much controversy within the women's movement between those espousing a "feminist" antiintellectualism and those opposed to tacit acceptance of what they see as the rational-male/irrational-female dichotomy in bourgeois ideology. See Evelyn Torton Beck and Biddy Martin, "Westdeutsche Frauenliteratur der siebziger Jahre," in Lützeler and Schwarz, *Deutsche Literatur*, esp. pp. 140–42; Renate Möhrmann in her article "Feministische Trends in der deutschen Gegenwartsliteratur," in Durzak, *Deutsche Gegenwartsliteratur*, pp. 344–48; Helke Sander's "Feminism and Film," a talk she gave in Graz in 1977, published in *Frauen und Film*, no. 15 (1978), then translated by Ramona Curry in *Jump Cut*, no. 27 (1982), pp. 49–50.

[7] Huyssen, "Mapping the Postmodern," p. 27. See also Barbara Ehrenreich, *The Hearts of Men: American Dreams and the Flight from Commitment* (Garden City, NY: Anchor, 1984), esp. pp. 52–67 for her critique of the "male determinations" of the "Beat movement," which Huyssen sees as so important to postmodernism in the 1960s (pp. 16–24).

[8] This point is made by Kramer in "/New Subjectivity/"; see esp. pp. 245–46.

initely distinct from each other), they anticipated much subsequent literature of the 1970s.

Lenz is Schneider's reworking of a nineteenth-century text, a return of sorts to (leftist) literary tradition, to Georg Büchner, for a validation of the attempt to depict personal alienation; at the same time it is a validation of literary tradition and of literature itself as a vehicle for expression of the subjective experience of reality. A similar revisiting of older literary texts and traditions became a trend in Germany during the 1970s; some other examples include Peter Handke's *Wrong Move* (*Falsche Bewegung*, 1973) in its reference to Goethe's *Wilhelm Meister*, and East German writer Ulrich Plenzdorf's *The New Sorrows of Young W.* (*Die neuen Leiden des jungen W.*, 1973) in its reference to Goethe's *The Sorrows of Young Werther.*[9]

In Schneider's novel, the validation of literature as a vehicle for expression of the subjective expression of reality was not only a rejection of the political repression of the personal but also a rejection of literary modernism, for the most part. The novel's "naive realism," as Russell Berman has called it,[10] almost bordering on the "trivial," represents an example of what Huyssen calls the "populist" strand within the postmodern tendencies of the 1960s—the enmity toward the elitism of modernism and the complementary positive valuation of popular culture and "accessibility."[11] *Lenz's* popularity, at any rate, certainly had much to do with the ability of those who had gone through the student movement to identify with the experiences in Schneider's text; many "insiders" of the movement, indeed, may well have recognized the autobiographical nature of the novel.[12]

Karin Struck's *Class Love* (*Klassenliebe*), on the other hand, is not a novel at all in a traditional sense, being at once much more openly autobiographical and much more formally "chaotic." Not having much of a plot, it is a collage of apparent diary entries, letters (both written and tape-recorded), and quotes from friends and famous authors (identified and unidentified). Furthermore, whereas both

[9] This trend obviously bears some relation to Hutcheon's concept of "historiographic metafiction." See Hutcheon, *A Poetics of Postmodernism*, pp. ix, 5–6, 105–23, and passim.

[10] Russell A. Berman, "Language and Image: Cinematic Aspects of Contemporary German Prose," in Sigrid Bauschinger, Susan L. Cocalis, and Henry A. Lea, eds., *Film und Literatur: Literarische Texte und der neue deutsche Film* (Bern: Francke, 1984), p. 219.

[11] Huyssen, "Mapping the Postmodern," p. 23.

[12] Hartung has critized precisely this—hidden—"authenticity" of *Lenz* as "the sanctimonious play between autobiography and novel." "Versuch," p. 22.

Schneider's *Lenz* and Struck's *Class Love* address sexuality and sexual relationships in their attempts to articulate longing and conflicts within the personal sphere, *Class Love* voices the question of gender more radically. Struck was often at odds with the West German women's movement and with feminist critics, but *Class Love* is considered "the first decisive breakthrough of a feminist literature."[13] The book refers to the plight of those who have been marginalized and silenced because of class and gender, and it suggests how they can learn to develop their own voices and thus begin to take control of their lives. Indeed, Struck's book appears to be a result of the same process, and the form in which she chose to do so served as a model for subsequent writing by women in West Germany.[14]

THE BODY VERSUS THE HEAD: PETER SCHNEIDER'S *LENZ*

> For some time he hadn't been able to stand the wise face of Marx above his bed. Once already he had hung it upside down. To let the intellect drip away, he explained to a friend. He looked Marx in the eyes. "What were your dreams, you old know-it-all? At night, I mean. Were you ever actually happy?"[15]

When Schneider's short novel *Lenz* first appeared in 1973, the above passage on the first page must have seemed quite heretical to the remaining orthodox leftists in West Germany and Berlin. This was probably one of the reasons the book enjoyed immense popularity among so many contemporaries who had also been politicized during the late 1960s but had since become disenchanted with the dogmatic sectarianism of much of the protest movement. Since about 1969, which is when Schneider sets his novel,[16] the move-

[13] Möhrmann, "Feministische Trends," p. 342. Möhrmann is very critical of Struck, especially in her discussion of interactions between West German women filmmakers and women writers in the early 1970s. See *Die Frau mit der Kamera*, p. 28.

[14] Struck can be seen to stand at the beginning of a trend that includes Verena Stefan's *Shedding* (1975), Elisabeth Alexander's *Die Frau die lachte* (1975), Margot Schroeder's *Ich stehe meine Frau* (1975), Brigitte Schwaiger's *Wie kommt das Salz ins Meer* (1977), Jutta Heinrich's *Das Geschlecht der Gedanken* (1977), Christa Reinig's *Entmannung* (1977), Karin Petersen's *Das Fette Jahr* (1978), Judith Offenbach's *Sonja* (1980), and Svende Merian's *Der Tod des Märchenprinzen* (1980).

[15] Peter Schneider, *Lenz. Eine Erzählung* (West Berlin: Rotbuch, 1973), p. 5. All further references to this work appear in the text.

[16] Nothing is explicitly stated within the story itself in terms of a specific date, but the text on the back cover of the Rotbuch paperback calls Lenz an intellectual at the end of the 1960s. Most critics place the story somewhere in the period between 1968

ment had fragmented into squabbling factions, many of which continued to subdivide. Indeed, Schneider's protagonist alludes to this process of fragmentation when, upon his return to Berlin after his stay in Italy, he notes that little has changed during his absence: "students were still founding new political parties" (p. 90).

Disillusionment with the sectarian groups was widespread by 1973 among those who had participated in the student movement. This audience could easily identify with Lenz's insistence that categories like happiness and dreams have a place in a discussion about—or "with"—Marx; it was so weary of the abstractions associated with dogmatic Marxist-Leninism that the idea of draining all the intellect out of the Master must have sounded quite liberating. The nondogmatic Left shared Lenz's aspiration toward a different kind of political activism, one that united theory with praxis and benefited from—instead of repressing—the struggle to come to terms with personal history.

To the extent, however, that the novel represented a backlash against a tendency associated with the Left, namely the tendency during the "dogmatic phase" to repress personal and artistic expression, it was used by critics to welcome—or bemoan—the *Tendenzwende*, the political shift they saw occurring in West Germany.[17] Certainly the text is marked by the conflict between political activism and personal life, abstract theory and concrete experience, socio-political and personal history. Nonetheless, the idea of the "flight into *Innerlichkeit*" ("inwardness") with which *Lenz* is so often associated is problematic. It seems more useful to view the novel in terms of the formulation Rutschky uses in discussing the 1970s: "the substitution of sense with sensuality," a rejection of rational meaning in favor of emotional and physical feeling (obviously based

---

and 1970, using passages in the text that seem to allude to actual events. Manfred Beller asserts that the bombings in Milan mentioned in the text (on p. 67) allow Lenz's stay in Italy to be dated fairly precisely in early summer, 1970; see Beller, "Lenz in Arkadien. Peter Schneiders Italienbild von Süden betrachtet," *Arcadia* 13 (1978-Sonderheft), p. 103. The text is dated 1970 by Hosfeld and Peitsch, " 'Weil uns diese Aktionen . . .' " (p. 109) and Malcolm Pender, "Historical Awareness and Peter Schneider's *Lenz*," *German Life and Letters*, n.s., 37 (1983–1984) (p. 156); 1969 is used by Buselmeier, "Nach der Revolte" (p. 166) and Oskar Sahlberg, "Peter Schneiders Lenz-Figur," in Ludwig Fischer, ed., *Zeitgenosse Büchner* (Stuttgart: Ernst Klett, 1979) (p. 150); and Wolfram Schütte writes "around 1968" in his review, *Frankfurter Rundschau*, 13 October 1973, p. xi.

[17] For a discussion of the term *Tendenzwende*, see above, Chapter 1. See also Roberts, "From the 1960s to the 1970s," pp. xi–xxiii and "Tendenzwenden," pp. 290–313.

on a rigid and somewhat unhealthy dichotomy between the rational and the emotional).[18]

Rutschky connects this phenomenon not only to the collapse of the protest movement but also to the historical experiences that had shaped West Germany since the rise of the National Socialists: fascism, the war, defeat, and the attempt to bury those disturbing memories during the conservative restoration of the Christian Democrats in the 1950s and early 1960s.[19] The same historical symptoms can be noted in Schneider's Lenz, as well as some indication of an attempt to come to terms with them. How well the novel confronts these problems is another issue—an issue that is itself equally symptomatic of literary politics in the wake of the student movement.

Abstraction versus Sensuality

Lenz's turning the poster of Marx "on its head" is amusing at one level for the allusion to the standard old saw about Marx having turned Hegel on his head. The humor marks the significance of the allusion as well: turning Hegel "on his head" refers to the replacement of dialectical idealism with dialectical materialism, the subordination, indeed, of the "head" (the realm of ideas, intellect, and ideology) to the "body" (the realm of production, of material reality, and material needs). Lenz is not interested in "reversing" Marx in order to return to Hegelian idealism; it is not intellect for which he longs, for he feels that intellect is rather oppressively dominant among his leftist friends. Lenz is more inclined to subordinate rationality to the realm of feelings: the subordination of the "head" to the "body" has his full support, although of course by the "body" he would mean a specific, individual body with its sensual needs and irrational dreams, and not an abstraction of the current global relationships of production and resources.

Standing the poster of Marx on its head also alludes directly to the famous quote from Georg Büchner's Lenz (1835) that opens Schneider's work: "he sometimes felt annoyed that he could not walk on his head."[20] In both texts, the dominant position of the "head"—and rationality—is placed into question; implied is a desire to overturn dominant modes of experiencing and understanding the world. The reference to two people upside down on the opening

[18] Rutschky, Erfahrungshunger, p. 150.

[19] Ibid., pp. 149–63.

[20] Georg Büchner, Lenz (1835), trans. Michael Patterson, in Büchner, The Complete Plays, ed. Michael Patterson (London: Methuen, 1987), p. 249; quoted in P. Schneider's Lenz, p. 5.

page of Schneider's novel creates a kind of identification between the two. Both Marx and Büchner's Lenz are thus connected, and this identification obviously extends to Schneider's main character, who is named after Büchner's protagonist. The image of Marx can therefore be seen both as a figure with which Lenz identifies and as a figure he rejects; the ambivalence here could be compared with that of a father–son relationship.[21]

Ultimately, however, Lenz's questions are addressed more to the image of Marx he and his contemporaries have created rather than to the historical figure of Marx. He criticizes himself and his contemporaries primarily for the inability to bring an abstract Marxism into any kind of connection with their lives and for the idealistic, bourgeois tendency to separate experience from theory. Lenz sees this most clearly, of course, in his own situation: "Until now he has gained little practical knowledge of society; as an obedient son of his class, he has confronted life primarily through theory, even at the point when he found the political concepts to reject the bourgeois way of life, which views the struggles of the social base *from the secure distance either of property or theory*" (p. 44—my emphasis).

This formulation of Lenz's experience is itself a somewhat idealized one, part of a dualistic conceptualization he has developed to explain his failed sexual relationship with the woman L.; it is nonetheless interesting for its equation of theory with property as instruments used by the bourgeoisie to create distance between itself and the realm of material struggle where wealth is actually created. At another point in the novel, Lenz talks of "people who waited for the new Volkswagen model with the same impatience as he and his friends did for the latest political developments" (pp. 31–32). This equation of his own activism with the status of merely a privileged bourgeois diversion causes him an attack of alienation reminiscent of Büchner: "He went on, he became uneasy, he felt excluded. . . . Buildings towered before him like mountains. A strange anxiety overcame him" (pp. 32–33).[22]

Lenz does not ultimately fall victim to a class reductionism that would characterize all political activism on the part of intellectuals as inescapably bourgeois. The alienation he suffers, however, is to some extent the alienation the intellectual experiences when con-

[21] See Sahlberg, "Peter Schneider's Lenz-Figur," p. 141.

[22] For a thorough comparison of Schneider's *Lenz* to Büchner's *Lenz*, and a discussion of the extent to which Schneider imitates Büchner's style, see Dietmar Goltschnigg's chapter on Schneider in his book *Rezeptions- und Wirkungsgeschichte Georg Büchners* (Kronberg/Ts.: Scriptor, 1975), pp. 273–79.

fronted with realities that do not conform to the theoretical structure
he or she has constructed. The sectarian groups of the student Left,
like the one that controlled the *Betriebsgruppe*, the factory study
group to which Lenz belonged, tended to view the whole realm of
personal experience and emotions as a malleable mass to be re-
shaped in spite of itself, as it were, in accordance with theoretical
positions.[23] "The group had taken upon itself the task of taking a trip
together, so that private relationships would keep in step with political ones" (p. 51).

Lenz's resistance to this rather totalitarian attitude toward real
contradictions between personal feelings (fears, doubts, anxiety, depression) and political theory explains most of his behavior. And
indeed he does not take his vacation with the group; he decides to
drop everything and go to Italy, where he is able to find what he is
seeking, at least for awhile: in Trento he finds an environment in
which political activity does not mean guilty repression of one's
feelings (p. 82). Lenz demands that he be allowed to admit his
doubts and insecurities and that happiness and even dreams be
taken into account. That side of human experience discounted by
Western intellectual tradition as "irrational" cannot be repressed
without doing damage to the whole human being, including his or
her capacity to function politically. One is reminded again of what
has been called Ernst Bloch's "polemic against the irrationalism of
the rational, precisely because it fails to grasp what is 'rational
within the irrational.' " Bloch considered the historical tendency of
the German Left to discount the "irrational" as a nearly fatal flaw.[24]

The rationalistic dismissal of personal anxieties and fantasies as
irrelevant is based on fear: fear of those realms of human experience
that resist the control—and calculation—of reason, resulting in an
odd asceticism with regard to sensuality and pleasure. Lenz tells his
friend B. that he (like all his intellectual friends) is incapable of
dealing with sensual experience. He asserts that B. would not be
able to react to something as intimate as his wife's odor without recourse to dogma: "Can you tell her that you can't stand the way she
smells anymore without blaming capitalism for it? All of you can
only talk in general, conceptually, about what you hate or love;
you're afraid that something will please you and then you won't be
able to continue the struggle anymore" (p. 50).

Joy is suspect, especially when actually experienced instead of re-

[23] For a discussion of *Betriebsgruppen*, see Chapter 1 above; see also Hartung, "Versuch," pp. 33–41.

[24] Rabinbach, "Unclaimed Heritage," p. 19.

maining an abstract category. Lenz feels that no real struggle for emancipation can exist under such conditions. Peter Schneider's brother, Michael Schneider, a critic somewhat ambivalent toward *Lenz*, nonetheless agreed with this argument:

> Those who once dreamed of swimming like a fish in the waters of a new, leftist popular culture, now lay exhausted and dried up on the sandy banks of leftist dogmatism, cut off from the wild sea of the imagination.
>
> How could it have been otherwise?! Just as Athena had sprung forth from Zeus's head (and not like Dionysus from the thigh), so too was this movement of intellectuals *purely a birth from the head*. It had hardly come into sensual contact with the world when the latter became an academic concept for it.[25]

The overdominance of the rational, the "head," comes at the cost of alienation from the "body," the concrete, immediate, sensual experience of the material world. This generalized alienation, obviously related to the development of a rationalized, technological civilization, is intensified by a loss of faith in the abstract rhetoric of dogmatic Marxist-Leninism, leading to a rejection of reason in general. This backlash is, again, the "substitution of sense with sensuality" that Rutschky sees as so typical of West Germany in the 1970s. There is in turn one specific kind of sensuality that provides a fairly sure method of dissipating alienation from the body, the "sensuality of terror and pain."[26] How much relief this type of sensuality provides for feelings of meaninglessness is debatable, of course. Lenz, however, longs so strongly for contact with the "body" that pain is indeed preferable to the numbness he ordinarily experiences, at one point stating: "It has to hurt before you can feel your body" (p. 41).

To feel, to sense one's body, to experience the world through one's skin is what Lenz wants, for he is weary of the search for deeper meanings. Rejecting Hegel and embracing the Beats, as it were, he demands sensual experience of the surface of the world, he demands validation of a "superficial" perception of the world. The abstract essence of objects and experiences is not enough; one has a right to joy in the immediate perception of one's surroundings, of each object in its concrete specificity, its external texture and variety. Lenz formulates this during the auto trip from Rome to Trento:

[25] M. Schneider, "Von der alten Radikalität," p. 180. (An interesting—and problematic—reversal is achieved here with the classical allusion: intellectualism conceived negatively is gendered female, whereas healthy sensuality becomes male.)

[26] Rutschky, *Erfahrungshunger*, p. 150.

"He didn't want to disperse what he was seeing so quickly into con-
ceptualizations, not immediately reach the point where one saw
only the essence of things, but no longer their outsides" (p. 74). He
rejects the type of fleeting, hasty perception he sees as typical of the
bourgeois intellectual, who never takes time to do more than gener-
alize from details (barely) perceived. In Italy, this has begun to
change for Lenz (p. 76).

The fear of the specific, the concrete, the immediate, is one motivation behind the intellectual's drive to abstraction and generalization, according to Lenz. (Another, I would add, is the desire for control.) The consequences of this drive, at any rate, involve a
numbness to the world, an alienation from the physical, an impoverishment of sensual experience. These are conditions by no means
suffered by intellectuals alone, a fact that Lenz in his self-obsessed
misery seems to miss. His unhappiness with this alienation from the
physical, combined with his resignation about the search for meaning, cause him to make a fetish of sensuality, to cling somewhat ir-
rationally to the surface of the object world: "it became repulsive to
him that in the twilight objects lost their contours" (p. 79). His plea
for attention to the surface of the world is echoed in much of the
prose and poetry in West Germany over the next few years after the
appearance of Lenz.[27]

Abstract schematizations block the joy in the "superficial," the
sensual experience of life, but they can also hinder a differentiated
assessment of political realities. They are often based on idealistic
dichotomies that oversimplify complex situations—and Lenz finds
himself handicapped by them in both politics and love. In the same
way that middle-class students had a predetermined concept of the
proletariat that blinded them to the actual reality of the West German working class, so Lenz in his relationship with L. developed an
idealized scheme: "A young intellectual falls for a pretty girl from
the people" (p. 44).[28] L. thus provided a connection to the proletar-

---

[27] This literature, called at the time "New Subjectivity" (Neue Subjektivität), but
also derogatorily labeled "New Inwardness" (Neue Innerlichkeit) by some critics,
was not just "inward" and "subjective." It must also be seen in its neorealistic and
empiricist aspects, as Sensibilism before it. In his article "Language and Image," Russell Berman speaks of "depoliticized empiricism" in the prose of Peter Schneider and
Peter Handke (p. 214). In "The Recipient as Spectator: West German Film and Poetry
of the Seventies," German Quarterly 55 (1982), Berman labels the poetry of the 1970s
"new realist poetry" and finds it somewhat positivistic (p. 502). Harald Hartung
speaks of an "aesthetic of the surface" in the poetry of the 1970s in his article "Lyrik
zwischen Paul Celan und Nicolas Born. Skizze einer Poetik des Gedichts in den 70er
Jahren," Praxis Deutsch (1981-Sonderheft), p. 4.

[28] This formulation bears the trace of romantic, nineteenth-century clichés. Beller

iat, whose vitality and sensuality are supposed to embody the "praxis" from which bourgeois intellectuals are cut off, condemned as it were to theoretical sterility.

How much L. actually has to do with the proletariat is questionable; there is little in the meager description given of L. to indicate that she has a working-class background.[29] That is precisely the problem: the "reality" of this woman is irrelevant to the role Lenz has assigned her in the political allegory he has created, as he himself is increasingly aware: "Is that really all I've done, he asked himself—to attempt privately, through a love story, the impossible feat of overcoming the contradiction between the way two classes perceive and live privately?" (p. 46). L. herself is certainly aware that she has little to do with Lenz's formulation of their relationship: "You're only talking about yourself. I don't exist at all in what you're saying" (p. 43).

A private resolution of class contradictions, through a love story: one might conclude that Lenz's mistake has been to impose abstract, political categories onto his personal life, to mistake the private or intimate sphere as the correct place for the achievement of political goals (the resolution of class contradictions, no less!). Although there is some validity to such an interpretation, the situation is actually more complex. The abstract, idealized dichotomies that Lenz constructs may be clothed in political terminology, but in substance, as the above remark by L. indicates, they are projections based on inadequacies Lenz perceives in his own personality: he is not really talking about L. or the working class. He is talking about himself.

Wolfgang, the young worker in his study group, accuses him of more or less the same thing: "Actually, you think of me only as somebody you would very much like to be" (p. 34). The ideal woman, the working class, and the oppressed are, for Lenz, largely narcissistic projections of an existence in which his alienation, numbness, and inability to be sensual supposedly would not exist. Early in the book Lenz meets an unemployed Turkish immigrant in the employment office of the factory where he has just been hired: "Most of all he watched the Turk's eyes and the powerful, fighter-like movements of his arms. He had a strong desire to see the world through his eyes" (p. 11). Since Lenz gets a job, and the Turk does

---

writes that Schneider is ironizing Lenz by crediting him with this formulation "in the style of Biedermeier." "Lenz in Arkadien," p. 92. But there is also a more modern, leftist romanticism at work here.

[29] Sahlberg, "Peter Schneiders Lenz-Figur," p. 143.

not, one might suppose that seeing "the world through his eyes" would not be quite so romantic.[30]

Those whom he holds up as models of a vitality and wholeness that he lacks have their own anxieties and doubts. Wolfgang, for instance, is plagued by an obsession that the people around him—especially Lenz and his friends—are vampires, a rather apt image for some middle-class students of the sectarian Left. Idealizing the working class as the "subject" of history, as the source of vitality with which all injustice could finally be righted, they tried to harness this source of energy by ministering theory to workers, who in turn often felt misunderstood and used by the sects.[31] "Somehow I have the feeling," Wolfgang tells Lenz, ". . . you're all sucking the blood from my marrow" (p. 36).

It would seem that Peter Schneider wanted his main character at least on one level to serve as an allegorical figure representing the West German student movement in its unrequited love affair with the proletariat.[32] The affective power behind the abstract, schematized notions that characterized the student movement in its dogmatic phase can also be construed to be less the result of political analysis than of romantic idealization and narcissistic projections of the sort to which Lenz is subject. This is a further argument for the position that this supposedly "politicized" phase is characterized by "private" motivations that underlay its very politics. Just as feelings of powerlessness and resignation can be shown to underlie the very adoption of a dogmatic stance, so too can the adoption of an idealized concept of the "Other," in this case the proletariat, reveal the crisis of the subject, the "identity" crisis in the wake of the disappointments of the student movement.

Narcissistic projections are symptoms of disturbances at a fundamental level of one's psychic identity, where attitudes toward the "Other" result from the same process that defines a sense of "Self."

[30] Todd Gitlin, discussing how the Beat movement influenced the American student movement, cites a passage from Jack Kerouac's *On the Road* that is an equally insensitive romanticization of the "Other": "At lilac evening I walked . . . in the Denver colored section, wishing I were a Negro, feeling that the best the white world had offered was not enough ecstasy for me, not enough life, joy, kicks, darkness, music, not enough night." *The Sixties*, p. 47.

[31] See Hartung, "Versuch," pp. 40–41; also Mosler, *Was wir wollten*, pp. 68–69.

[32] Rejecting claims that Lenz is purely autobiographical, Schneider called him "a collective figure"—see "Antwort an einen anonymen Kritiker," in Peter Schneider, *Atempause: Versuch, meine Gedanken über Literatur und Kunst zu ordnen* (Reinbek: Rowohlt, 1977), p. 202. He also referred to Lenz as "part of a mass phenomenon" in "Gepräch mit Peter Schneider," interview by Jos Hoogeveen, Gerd Labroisse, and Dick van Stekelenburg, *Deutsche Bücher* 8 (1978), p. 254.

Narcissism is generally defined as a deflection of libidinal energy from objects in the world back toward a traumatized, "weak" ego. This results in an inability to deal with the world other than by means of the weak ego's constant search for the reflection of a more perfect self in the external world.[33] The social implications of such a psychological condition and its relation to the more generalized psychological alienation Lenz experiences—numbness, impoverishment of experience—are fairly clear, and much has been written about the prevalence of behavior traits in (post)modern society that bear similarity to classical narcissism, Christopher Lasch's *The Culture of Narcissism* being perhaps the most famous example.[34]

But before taking this analysis too far, in simply pathologizing Lenz and his contemporaries, let us examine the concept of "classical narcissism" historically. When applied as a conceptual aid in the analysis of postindustrial society as a whole (and not merely to pathologize activists of a certain generation), narcissism can elucidate somewhat the "identity crisis" of the late twentieth century. Fredric Jameson, discussing the concept of postmodernism, calls this crisis the "death of the subject"; writing of the collapse of the modernistic credo of originality, of unique personal style, he states: "[T]hose of us who work in the area of culture and cultural and formal change, are all exploring the notion that that kind of individualism and personal identity is a thing of the past; that the old individual or individualist subject is 'dead'; and that one might even describe the concept of the unique individual and the theoretical basis of individualism as ideological."[35]

Freud's system of analyzing the subject—with its various categories, narcissism versus a "strong ego" among them—is itself obviously a historical model, and the type of individual considered healthy bears an important relation to a historical ideology—that of late nineteenth-century bourgeois society. While helping to undermine the concept of the autonomous subject via the category of the unconscious, psychoanalysis nonetheless tends to validate the "ideal" bourgeois individual (as constituted in that ideology) as the norm of psychological health. The "narcissism" of Lenz is thus less

---

[33] Sigmund Freud's "Zur Einführung des Narzißmus" (1914), in his *Gesammelte Schriften* (Leipzig: Internationaler Psychoanalytischer Verlag, 1925), 6: 178. In English, the essay appears as "On Narcissism: An Introduction," in John Rickman, ed., *A General Selection from the Works of Sigmund Freud* (London: Hogarth Press, 1937).

[34] Christopher Lasch, *The Culture of Narcissism: American Life in an Age of Diminishing Expectations* (New York: W. W. Norton and Co., 1978).

[35] Jameson, "Postmodernism and Consumer Society," pp. 114–15.

"pathological" than it is symptomatic of crises affecting behavior among all individuals in postindustrial society; these are crises not just of leftist German students in the late 1960s (as Lenz himself might seem to think) but—to one extent or another—of individuals at most levels of Western society in the latter half of the twentieth century.

Personal Identity and the Past

It is interesting that only as such "narcissistic" characters like Lenz return to West German literature is there any hint of an attempt to deal with the German past, at least on the part of the generation that experienced the student movement. During the dogmatic phase the legacy of German fascism seemed to be as easily cast aside as the bourgeois identities of most of the activists: dedication to the proletariat and to the antiimperialist struggle were seen as sufficient for the absolution of such unpleasant memories. It would not be until the later 1970s that significant attempts to confront Germany's history would be undertaken by members of this generation. But even in Lenz, one of the first texts of the "New Subjectivity," the necessity of this confrontation is at least broached.

The need to confront one's past is an important motif in Lenz's identity crisis, and it is a motif that transcends the boundaries of Lenz's personal psychology, since the past inscribed in his psyche is not merely "his" but is also shaped by his parents and larger social and historical determinants. To the extent the text focuses on this extrapersonal aspect of Lenz's quest, one can refute some standard criticisms of the book, according to which the book is "apolitical" and "psychologistic," accusations evident in one critic's verdict, for example: "But only after his flight, in Italy, does he come near to an experience of praxis, a mystical experience that is in any case only significant for him. Only for this individual, this monad floating freely, this bourgeois on the loose, only for Lenz alone does it all have a meaning, a certain therapeutic meaning, and that only for a time."[36]

Upon examination, this mystical (or at any rate utopian) experience is not caused by Lenz's isolation from any social context but

---

[36] Götz Großklaus, "West-östliches Unbehagen. Literarische Gesellschaftskritik in Ulrich Plenzdorfs Die neuen Leiden des jungen W. und Peter Schneiders Lenz," Basis 5 (1975), p. 99. Similar critiques can be found in articles that consider Lenz an example of Innerlichkeit, or "inwardness"; see, for example, Hosfeld and Peitsch, " 'Weil uns diese Aktionen . . . ,' " pp. 108, 113, and Buselmeier, "Nach der Revolte," p. 166.

rather by the atmosphere of solidarity he experiences while living in a community of workers and students in the northern Italian city of Trento. There Lenz finds a "public sphere" in which personal needs as well as political goals and collective tasks are openly discussed. This atmosphere ends Lenz's isolation, and one can assume that it is not merely beneficial for him alone. If its therapeutic benefits for Lenz last only for a while, this is because its "mystical" nature is tempered by realism on Lenz's part. Even before the idyll is interrupted by the police, Lenz starts to realize that his place, and his struggle, are not in Trento. Suddenly aware of all the borrowed clothes he is wearing, he asks himself: "Just what are you doing in all these strange clothes?" (p. 89). His equanimity in the face of his deportation from Italy and his subsequent resolve to remain in Berlin must be read in light of this realization on his part.

Lenz's attempt to come to terms with his own past is a process that necessarily has a significance beyond that for him alone. There are obvious allusions in the text to social and political complexes relevant to the German experience since the defeat of fascism. During the train ride from Rome to Ostia with Pierra, Lenz remembers an incident on a train as a small boy; the articulation of his memories of this incident to Pierra is one of the first instances in which Lenz begins to recognize patterns in his behavior that originated in childhood:

> Then it occurred to him that he had traveled in trains through the whole war and never stayed in one place longer than half a year. He told Pierra about it, she wanted to know more, but he didn't want to go into it anymore. He said, "Maybe it actually has something to do with those early trips, that constant state of being on the move, that later I always felt more at home while traveling than when I was staying someplace and trying to settle down." (p. 66)

The memories of the train have an Oedipal component: they involve his mother, who took him on these train rides to escape enemy bombing missions and approaching enemy troops, and there is a connection between the constant traveling of this early period in his life and the restlessness he experienced after a certain point in his relationship with L. (cf. p. 45). The extrapersonal, historical factor in these memories of a formative phase in Lenz's development is equally significant: the Second World War, with enemy bombers and trains filled with citizens fleeing the ever-shrinking front lines, is imprinted in Lenz's earliest memories and in the memories of a whole generation. Rutschky, too, makes reference to such early memories in a personal anecdote about his sensitivity to certain loud noises: "I don't want to make too much of this sensitivity. But it does nonetheless indicate traces of the war in a generation that was for a long time assumed to be untroubled, unburdened, to have no need of feelings of anxiety or guilt."[37]

It is clear from the observations Lenz makes in Italy that his obsession with the past is not merely a personal affair. He is impressed by the apparent ease with which Italians live with their history, as he first observes in Rome: "Lenz was amazed that in this city, which was packed with monuments and ruins, people seemed livelier and more imaginative than in the cities he knew in Germany, cities without history" (p. 69). Here one senses above all a reproach against a contemporary Germany he sees as "without history," a condition due not merely to the destruction left by the war but to a certain attitude toward the past that dominated West Germany's reconstruction, a tendency indeed to ignore and repress questions dealing with guilt about and responsibility for the fascist period. It has been argued—the most famous formulation of this argument being Alexander and Margarethe Mitscherlich's The Inability to Mourn (1967)— that the results of this denial of history is the collective experience of a repressed condition similar to the numbing apathy experienced by a person unable to mourn the loss of a loved one.[38]

Lenz is fascinated by the much less repressed way of dealing with the past he encounters in Italy: "He said that for the first time he could conceive that this living alongside the past without anxiety made it easier for a person to live in the present" (pp. 69–70). The Italian accommodation with the past is of course not quite as unproblematic as Lenz thinks, but here again the conception of a way to live with the past that is "without anxiety" is significant for what it implies about Lenz and his view of Germany. During his discussion with Paolo and B. on the ride to Trento, he is impressed by Paolo's ability to combine Christian and Marxist doctrines, and he sees this as yet another example of a healthy attitude to the past: "Then it struck Lenz how in Rome new streets and houses were built around the ancient ruins, and in Paolo's discussions he noted

[37] Rutschky, Erfahrungshunger, p. 157. These remnants of the war are for Rutschky a significant factor in the behavior of his generation during the 1970s, contributing to the "substitution of sense with sensuality" just as the collapse of the protest movement did. See pp. 155–64.

[38] Alexander and Margarethe Mitscherlich, The Inability to Mourn: Principles of Collective Behavior, trans. Beverly R. Placzek (Ann Arbor: UMI Press, 1978). Orig.: Die Unfähigkeit zu trauern. Grundlagen kollektiven Verhaltens (Munich: Piper, 1967).

this same tendency to make use of the past rather than to eliminate it" (p. 77).

To make use of the past instead of trying to eliminate it, to learn from it instead of denying it: only then can the present be effectively dealt with, on an individual, "psychological" level as well as on a socio-cultural, "political" level. This idea can also be seen in relation to postmodernism: abandonment of the rhetoric of novelty, of rupture, the radical break with the past; an eclectic and pragmatic attitude toward tradition, and an irreverent attitude toward the sanctity, integrity, and supposed opposition of conceptual systems such as Christianity and Marxism. As has been said of postmodernist architecture, there is a new awareness of "the presence of the past" and "an ironic dialogue with the past of both art and society."[39]

At such moments in Lenz's development, it becomes more evident that his fetishization of immediacy and sensuality, his need to experience the moment and linger in the "superficial," is not merely a symptom of his own malady but rather in no small part a reflection of the malady he ascribes to the German nation: the rejection and repression of a disturbing past, which obstructs an effective dealing with the present. Repression of the past results in an alienation that affects experience of the present; the enjoyment of the present becomes a goal sought with an urgency that corresponds to the extent that alienation interferes with that enjoyment.

From this perspective, the attempt to immerse oneself in mindless sensuality (an endeavor at which Lenz is not very good, in any case) bears some relation to the immersion of West Germany in mindless economic consumption in the 1950s—both indeed can be seen in the context of "postmodern" consumer capitalism. Furthermore, the attempt to proclaim a "zero hour" or *Stunde Null* in 1945 to distance the recent German past is not entirely dissimilar to the dogmatic rejection of all "bourgeois" tradition in art and the attempt by students to deny their own primarily bourgeois identity.[40] Both were attempts to deny the past as well as any suspicions of historical continuity, and both have a relation (although not the same relation) to

[39] Hutcheon, *A Poetics of Postmodernism*, p. 4.

[40] The connection between the postwar tendency to repress the past and the desire of the student movement to abolish literature and literary tradition is made by Malcolm Pender in his article "Historical Awareness." In Schneider's novel Pender sees an attempt to restore the dimension of literary expression and to come to terms with the past. "The link with the past in Lenz has two aspects: firstly, the author finds support from the past in his attempt to depict the present [i.e., in citing Büchner]. . . . Secondly, within the framework of the 'Erzählung,' Schneider's hero achieves a liberating insight into his own past" (pp. 150–51).

repression of the guilt-ridden legacy of the Third Reich. *Lenz* is in part the story of a student's attempt to come to terms with his past, an attempt that has political significance not merely for his fellow activists but for West German society as a whole.

Language as Therapy

But how does Lenz come to terms with the past? He does so by being able to talk about his personal complexes to understanding comrades in Trento, and their understanding makes it quite easy for him to stop dwelling on these problems and become politically active within the group. This is a relatively painless escape from the conflicts between the personal and the political, let alone from the burden of German history (to which, it should be stressed, there are only brief and somewat indirect allusions). The view of language here is ultimately a perhaps overly optimistic one. Examining the role of language in the text can help elucidate Lenz's alienation and "recovery," and it is obviously relevant to the text's relation to its own mediation, as a literary text depicting Lenz's struggle to synthesize the personal with the political.

At the beginning of the text, Lenz appears to have a quite ambivalent attitude toward language. It seems to do little more than alienate the world of experience. For Lenz, language blocks authentic experience—but it is of course a certain type of language that has this effect. It is primarily the abstract rhetoric he hears again and again in his study group: "He heard the same words again and again: material knowledge, consciousness, proletariat, strategy. The solemn, unbroken melody of these sentences became fixed in his ears; it bothered him that there were no pauses, no new beginnings, no allusions to anything else" (p. 27).

The seamless language of this kind of "theory" flattens reality, washes away the contours of the surface of things, creating a separate, abstract, hermetically sealed world where nothing spontaneous can disturb the "correct" analysis of things. It is a language that repulses Lenz. In the discussion with his friend B., shortly before his decision to go to Italy, this repulsion once again becomes evident: "After a short time Lenz sensed again his hatred for the prepared sentences he and B. used. His answers became more and more impatient, more and more emphatic. He suggested that they break off the discussion, it was all only talk, it was too strange" (p. 48).

Earlier, when he first visits Marina, the same feeling overwhelms him while answering her pro forma question about his politics: "He interrupted himself, saying he was speaking bla-bla, nothing but predigested stuff. He desired her, and that was the real reason he had come. He went to her and took hold of her" (p. 9). Marina, however, demands more of a discussion before agreeing to any such spontaneous sensuality. Lenz then formulates his romantic notions of a return to preverbal (preoedipal?) bliss. His statement could stand as a program for a "new sensuality" in which work, imagination, and physical intimacy—but not rational discussion—are the basis for authentic communication: " 'You don't get to know someone through these questions and answers,' he replied. 'There are only a few ways to get to know someone, when you work together, when you get crazy together, when you touch each other' " (p. 9).

Schneider's novel is often associated with—and to a certain extent anticipates—the ascendance during the rest of the 1970s of trends that did indeed seem to demand this sort of "new sensuality" (to the point where a younger generation of West German protesters later in the 1970s did seem to reject all attempts at dialogue, and all but the crudest forms of articulation, in favor of "action").[41] But as I have indicated, regardless of these positions taken by Lenz early in the novel, the role of discussion is actually quite central to Lenz's recovery in Italy. Statements such as the ones made to Marina are made at a point when Lenz's relationship to language—as well as his state of mind—is at its most alienated or disturbed. These statements must be compared with other comments about language he makes in the course of the book, especially those made in Trento, where many of his problems are at least temporarily resolved.

Although the prefabricated sentences he hears himself and his friends using disgust him, Lenz has a deep need to use language to express himself "authentically"; he also despairs of not being able to communicate. When he writes a letter to L., it causes him great anxiety: "The thought that he wouldn't be able to make himself understood drove him out of the house" (p. 17). What he wants from language is nothing less than the "authentic" communication of feelings; language should serve as a nearly transparent medium through which the emotional state of a speaker is perceptible to the listener.

At a party of leftist intellectuals he attends in Berlin, Lenz annoys a critic (whose professional medium is of course language) by aping exaggerated agreement with everything he says. The critic asks him why he is behaving so oddly, and Lenz responds: "Because I don't

---

[41] See Hermann Glaser, *Im Packeis des Unbehagens: Eine persönliche Zwischenbilanz des Generationenkonflikts* (Berlin: J.H.W. Dietz, 1982), pp. 18, 24; on p. 30 he cites the protesters' slogan, "After action, satisfaction."

feel anything when you speak" (p. 39). His argument with B. shortly before his departure for Italy touches on the same demand: that people be able to feel what they express, and express what they feel, when they use language. "Can you tell your wife that she is beautiful when you feel that she's beautiful? Can you feel it when you say it?" (p. 49). He longs for a use of language that eliminates—rather than reinforces—the alienation that blocks him from other people, and from his own experiences and feelings.

Lenz notices this discrepancy between language and authentic communication once again in Rome, where, at a social gathering of the radical chic, the "body language" of the people whom Lenz observes appears totally at odds with the phrases they spout. "Whenever Lenz would listen to what was being said, he couldn't understand the gestures that accompanied the conversations; if he paid attention to the gestures, then he wouldn't understand what was being said" (p. 68). The inauthenticity of their utterances is reflected even more clearly in their clothes, of course: "Film directors in stylized navy jackets greeted authors who waved back wearing the uniform of the Red Army, or expensive blue jeans" (p. 68). Lenz notes a similar contradiction between verbalizations and body carriage in the behavior of his good friend B., who is depicted as much more earnest than the Italian radical chic. During their long conversation in the car between Rome and Trento, Lenz tells B., "When you speak, you seem the complete optimist. When I watch you sitting there, you seem somehow resigned. Why shouldn't I take the second appearance as seriously as I take the first?" (pp. 77–78).

His relationship with B. up to this point has been characterized by a use of language in which such physical observations had no place (p. 77). A discourse in which physical, emotional, and sensual perceptions can be articulated without withering away under the glare of the intellect, a language that confronts rather than reinforces the repression of emotions in modern civilization's overly instrumentalized beings—this is Lenz's rather utopian desire. Language should have a healing, therapeutic function, as opposed to being mainly a tool of abstraction. It should be used to bring repressed fears, needs, memories, and dreams to the surface—exactly those most personal elements that have so long been considered irrelevant to rational discourse. In the course of Lenz's development in the novel, language does seem to be able to fulfill this function, and in spite of the individual nature of this psychological therapy for the main character, there is a significant social aspect to this model.

In the beginning of the novel, Lenz's relationship to language reflects the isolation and alienation from which he suffers in general;

in Trento, as he begins to resolve some of his problems, his new relationship to language not only reflects, it *effects* his social reintegration. This is brought about by the somewhat idealized "public sphere" he encounters in the community of workers and students there; in this community, one is welcome to articulate all one's needs. "It became a given for him that people were just as interested in his doubts and insecurities as they were in his positions on the issues. Since he could speak about L., about a dream, about anxieties without giving it a second thought, it didn't seem as important any more to talk about them" (p. 82). Such a liberating atmosphere for verbalization of personal feelings is in turn directly related to an openness to sensual experience and affection: "He became accustomed to the idea that everybody touched everybody whenever they felt like it, without there being any hidden insinuation to it" (p. 82).

Language thus seems to embody the very process by which unresolved experiences are worked out. Articulating these experiences for Lenz is practically synonymous with resolving them, as he learns when he attempts to explain them to his new friends. "Whatever he told them didn't seem strange or out of the ordinary to them, but by talking about it, it all became more distant again. He realized that by describing an experience he began to leave it behind" (pp. 85–86). The process of telling one's story, of describing one's past, is an important method of coming to terms with that past, with one's identity, which in turn is necessary to dissipate the alienation, the numbness that blocks experience of the present moment.

But of course in *Lenz*, all this happens within a few pages; the mere articulation of the protagonist's problems seems to be enough to dispel them. Language here has the potential—at least in utopian Trento—of overcoming the alienation from sensual and emotional experience, the alienation from the body that seems to be the cost of advanced industrial society. Far from the linguistic pessimism with which Lenz is associated at the beginning of the novel, language is seen quite optimistically by the end. This optimistic view of the communicative powers of language—of ordinary speech!—is interesting to compare with Adorno's formulation of the potential of lyric poetry for communication. In this type of poetry, according to Adorno, language can at times escape reification and become the medium for authentic communication between poem and reader, individual and society, subjectivity and objectivity, in a somewhat mystical process whereby these dichotomies are transcended:

> The highest lyric creations are therefore those in which the subject,
> without any remnant of mere content, resounds in language, until lan-

guage itself becomes audible. The self-forgetfulness of the subject that submits itself to language, an objective entity, and the immediacy and involuntary nature of its expression are one and the same: thus does language mediate lyric poetry and society at the innermost level.[42]

Similarities between Adorno's expectations of the best lyric poetry—created by the most exacting struggle with reified language—and Lenz's hopes for ordinary, everyday speech are interesting in connection with Rutschky's speculations on the reception of Adorno among students and former students in the 1970s. He writes, for instance, that Adorno's critique of modern society was primarily theoretical, at a distance from everyday life that made possible a reflection about that life; what one notes in the 1970s are attempts "Kritik zu leben," to live critical theory, as it were. These attempts are manifestations of the attitude that critical theory "should no longer be a mode of thinking, speaking, writing from outside everyday reality; it should be realized directly within that reality."[43]

This hope that the utopian content of critical theory could simply be "lived," experienced without any mediation through theoretical efforts or confrontation with hermetic lyric texts, has its roots in the populist, anti-intellectual strains of the 1960s and 1970s. Expressed this way it is a rather naive hope. On the other hand, it bears similarity to an influential postmodern concept, what Thomas Elsaesser calls "the imaginary as political category."[44] This is the idea that there is no "outside" from which to theorize safely, there is no "subject position" outside the Imaginary where Science would guarantee the objectivity of critique. Only "inside," within "life," determined (and "compromised") by subjectivity, politics, ideology, history—only inside can critique (or any other intervention or activity) be undertaken. There is no escape from the realm of emotions (and laughter, as Peter Sloterdijk stresses in the Critique of Cynical Reason).[45]

But the novel's relation to questions of mediation and form is an-

<hr>

[42] Theodor W. Adorno, "Rede über Lyrik und Gesellschaft," in Adorno, Noten zur Literatur, vol. 1 (Frankfurt: Suhrkamp, 1963), p. 85.

[43] Rutschky, Erfahrungshunger, p. 76; see also pp. 58–81.

[44] Thomas Elsaesser, "American Grafitti und Neuer Deutscher Film: Filmemacher zwischen Avantgarde und Postmoderne," in Andreas Huyssen and Klaus R. Scherpe, eds., Postmoderne. Zeichen eines kulturellen Wandels (Reinbek: Rowohlt, 1986), pp. 305–10.

[45] "Modern ideology critique—this is my thesis—has dangerously cut itself off from the powerful traditions of laughter within satirical knowledge, which have their philosophical roots in ancient kynicism." Sloterdijk, "Cynicism," p. 202.

other issue. Questions about the novel's form have raised many objections: for all its thematization of the longing for the personal, the specific, the sensual, how does the novel formally relate to such categories? Adelson writes: "Thematically, Lenz is about the negation of individual experience by the primacy of the abstract concept. And yet, aesthetically, Peter Schneider reduces Lenz's experiences to their generalizable, conceptual typicality. . . . The character becomes the concept."[46]

To the extent the novel's form can be described as this kind of reductive, "naive" realism, it certainly contradicts Lenz's longing for the specific and the sensual. Another critic has ridiculed the "sensuality" that the text proclaims by pointing out how schematic, how lacking in sensuousness, its language is; for example, morning is described: "It was still early, the birds were squawking" (p. 6).[47] In fact, the text's style is almost a minimalist rather than a naive realism and would bear some comparison with American minimalism of the 1980s. The spareness of the style can perhaps be explained by the narrowness of the narrative perspective: there is almost no distance between the third-person narrator and Lenz's perspective, so the bleak world is thus mostly a reflection of Lenz's subjective alienation, which is only briefly transcended.

The text's "generality" probably had something to do with its tremendous popularity. Evelyne Keitel sees *Lenz* as the beginning of a literary trend in the 1970s (extending into the 1980s) that produced many texts she calls *Verständigungstexte*, texts that were primarily concerned with direct social communication rather than aesthetic experience. They appeared to assist readers in coming to an understanding of shared experiences (shared in this case by the West German counterculture, or subgroups within it). She asserts that these texts bore some functional relation to "trivial literature," except that they were directed toward a specific (and more educated) audience—precisely the leftist counterculture that grew out of the student protest movement in West Germany. These texts depend on reader identification, but they provide not escape but a stimulus to those with similar experiences to join in group discussions through

---

[46] Adelson, "Subjectivity Reconsidered," pp. 27–28; see the similar passage in her book, *Crisis of Subjectivity*, pp. 34–35. See also Klaus Hartung's polemical attack on what he sees as the abstract, two-dimensional quality of the character of Lenz, in his article "Die Repression wird zum Milieu. Die Beredsamkeit linker Literatur," *Literaturmagazin*, no. 11 (1979), pp. 52–79; see esp. pp. 55–58. Hartung sees Lenz as a construct mouthing Schneider's opinions on the course of the student movement (p. 58).

[47] Zeller, *Aufbrüche: Abschiede*, p. 9.

which these experiences can be better understood. As a stimulus to a type of group therapy, they do reduce experiences to what is typical for their readers.[48] In a more positive light, however, this therapeutic function is somewhat similar to the model for discussion Habermas calls "communicative action";[49] the texts therefore play a role that is older than the trivial novel, the role literature played for the bourgeoisie in the eighteenth century: a medium of *Verständigung*, a means of spreading social understanding and enlightenment.[50]

The problems of literary mediation—and of the crisis of subjectivity—are not necessarily resolved by a return to older, simpler models. Seen as a *Verständigungstext*, however, Schneider's *Lenz* does reflect upon its own textual strategy in an indirect way. It hearkens back—via Büchner—to the eighteenth-century writer Jakob Michael Reinhold Lenz in the era of the birth of bourgeois subjectivity in German literature.[51] Another important group of *Verständigungstexte* in the 1970s can perhaps be seen in connection with a different early bourgeois literary tradition: the diary- and letter-writing of eighteenth-century women. The first of this other group of texts in the 1970s was Karin Struck's *Class Love*.

THE OTHER BEGINS TO SPEAK: KARIN STRUCK'S *CLASS LOVE*

Men are regressing everywhere, in all areas. At present, women possess a much greater aptitude for intelligence. The criterion on which men judge intelligence is still the capacity to theorize and in all the move-

---

[48] Keitel, "Verständigungstexte," pp. 431–55. In developing this concept, she discusses the following: *Lenz*, Verena Stefan's *Shedding* (*Häutungen*), Svende Merian's *Der Tod des Märchenprinzen*, naming others as well (Judith Offenbach's *Sonja*, Bommi Baumann's *Wie alles anfing*, Christiane F.'s *Wir Kinder vom Bahnhof Zoo*). See also the discussion of *Verständigungstexte* in Beutin et al., *Deutsche Literaturgeschichte* (1984 ed.), pp. 561–62, 565–66.

[49] Jürgen Habermas, *Theorie des kommunikativen Handelns* (Frankfurt: Suhrkamp, 1981).

[50] See Keitel, "Verständigungstexte," pp. 452–53.

[51] Lenz was an acquaintance of Goethe; his mental breakdown in the late 1770s provided the basis for Büchner's *Lenz* (1835).

For a discussion focused on Peter Schneider's career, rather than on *Lenz* alone (which was by no means the beginning and end of that career), see Peter Labanyi, "When Wishing Still Helped: Peter Schneider's Left-Wing Melancholy," in Bullivant, *After the "Death" of Literature*, pp. 313–39. Labanyi is most concerned with the period of the 1970s, but he touches on Schneider's writings in the 1960s and in the 1980s.

ments . . . the theoretical sphere is losing influence. It has been under
attack for centuries. It ought to be crushed by now, it should lose itself
in a reawakening of the senses, blind itself and be still.[52]

In the radical formulation above, the French writer and filmmaker
Marguerite Duras expresses a feminist version of the sentiment
against the theoretical and for the sensual, linking the theoretical
mode she rejects with the male domination of modern society.[53] The
dissatisfaction with rationalism and the yearning for sensual experience and immediacy noted in Peter Schneider's *Lenz* were attitudes by no means limited to young men in West Germany during
the 1970s. The rise of the ecological movement in Western Europe
and the United States was an international manifestation of a loss of
faith in technology; the Duras quote illustrates a similar stance
within a feminist context, a context of increasing importance during
the 1970s, as a new, international women's movement emerged.

In 1973 the "first decisive breakthrough" for feminist literature
occurred in West Germany with the publication of Karin Struck's
Class Love (*Klassenliebe*, 1973). A runaway best-seller like *Lenz*, it
was actually published a few months before Schneider's novel.[54]
Like *Lenz*, Struck's text attacked the rationalistic abstractions of the
dogmatic Left while proclaiming the need for a type of political
commitment that was not antithetical to personal experience or repressive of the need for sensuality and immediacy. A comparison of
Karin Struck's *Class Love* with Schneider's novel brings many similarities—and many revealing contrasts—to light. The politics of
voicing subjectivity in the 1970s cannot be discussed without paying attention to the issue of gender.

[52] Marguerite Duras, "Smothered Creativity," trans. Virginia Hules, in Marks and
Courtivron, *New French Feminisms*, p. 111. Originally from an interview in Suzanne
Horer and Jacqueline Socquet, eds., *La création étouffée* (Horay, 1973).

[53] While this is one type of feminist critique of the "theoretical," it should be
stressed that Duras's equation of women with sensuality and her apparent willingness to cede all theoretical activity to men would be problematic for a great many
feminists; her praise of (the "antitheoretical") Reagan in the 1980s was even more
problematic.

[54] Karin Struck's *Class Love* appeared in early 1973, and by the Frankfurt Book Fair
that fall, it was in its seventh printing (38,000–45,000 copies). Möhrmann,
"Feministische Trends," p. 342.

"Class Love" is a very literal translation of *Klassenliebe*. In German *Klassenliebe*
implies "love between the classes" (among other things) more easily than the English
"class love" probably does, but one analogy I want to make in choosing this translation is to "class struggle," *Klassenkampf*. In German the title also evokes an association with a "class" in school (perhaps even more readily than with a socio-economic
class), but this meaning is just as strong in the English word "class."

On the thematic level, the connections in Struck's novel to the new style of politics of the 1970s are much more explicit than in *Lenz*. Struck's book in some ways anticipates the political program of the ecological movement and a number of the life-style issues of alternative groups for the next decade: the desire for a pollution-free environment; the distrust of technology; the interest in nutrition, organic farming, and "holistic" approaches to health; and the return to breast-feeding babies and natural childbirth.

This more explicit connection to the issues that were to dominate the new politics is no doubt related to the fact that female subjectivity (or at any rate *feminist* subjectivity) had more of an interest in undermining the facile, ideological division of life into public and private realms. This division had placed women's experience entirely in the private realm, regardless of the political nature of the oppression within that experience. Whereas Schneider's voicing of "male subjectivity," as it were, could be subsumed by critics into a conservative tradition of (male) literary "Inwardness" (*Innerlichkeit*), and then interpreted as a retreat from the political into the self, the situation for women was quite different, as Renate Möhrmann writes: "If in regard to the formal depiction of male subjectivity one spoke of a *regression*, a retreat, then the literary construction of female subjectivity can be called literally a *pro-gression*, an advance. For here there is no re-privatization at work, but rather—in contrast—the making public of centuries-old injuries, revoking a silencing that had for so long been habitual."[55]

Making public the personal suffering of a male character was certainly nothing new for German literature, in terms of a broad historical perspective—Goethe's *Werther* was published two centuries before Schneider's *Lenz*, after all, at a time when the historical Lenz was alive. The historical situation of women, however, is such that it has been a constant struggle (of varying intensity) for women to gain access to the public realm as writers. As the bourgeois ideology equating women with the private, intimate sphere consolidated (with the help of works like *Werther*), the concerns of women were even less frequently given public expression—by women themselves, at any rate. In the 1970s, on the crest of the "second wave" of feminism, a period of new gains for women began, and large numbers of women began again to attempt to overcome this habitual silencing by articulating their personal experiences and perceptions.[56]

[55] Möhrmann, "Feministische Trends," p. 341.

[56] The "first wave" of feminism is usually considered to have begun in the middle of the nineteenth century and lasted up until the 1920s, after the granting of women's suffrage; the "second wave" then began in the early 1960s, gaining strength in the

This could hardly be considered a *retreat* from the political; it was, as Möhrmann stresses, a move *into* the public realm. The silent "Other" was again beginning to speak, to leave the status of object, and in so doing become a plurality of active subjects. The resulting articulations of subjectivity were quite political, containing much previously unvoiced—and fundamental—dissatisfaction with the status quo.

The Sensual Is Political

"Why should everything be so anonymous, so that you can't touch anything anymore, perceive with the senses? Isn't a cancer in the breast perceptible with the senses?"[57] Already on the very first page of *Class Love*, one notes the same concern with sensual perception and specificity one finds in *Lenz*. The choice of image, however—breast cancer—is in one sense obviously female and is much more shocking in its biological physicality than, for example, the upside-down poster of Marx on the first page of *Lenz*. Also on the first page of *Class Love*, political work typical of the "dogmatic phase" of the student movement—students attempting to educate workers—is mentioned in a somewhat negative light: "A student read a report. Afterwards everyone sat there, stiff and dumb, and said nothing" (p. 7). Finally, the same longing is evident for some kind of utopian resolution of the contradictions between sense perception and personal experience on the one hand and political theory and abstraction on the other.

The novel's first-person narrator/protagonist—who, like the author, is named Karin—is a woman who longs not merely for the sensual, the immediate, the personal, the "body."[58] It is a synthesis of mind and body, theory and praxis, for which she longs, as does Lenz. But as he does, she often seems to reject the rational and to find the theoretical inaccessible. In the middle of her depression over Z., her lover, she wonders if she finds meaning only through her senses, if she finds "sense" only through sensual perception (p. 171). She realizes, however, that her hunger for the sensual is a symptom of deprivation—"The hungry senses of those who have

---

late 1960s, becoming influential in the 1970s, and suffering some setbacks in the 1980s.

[57] Karin Struck, *Klassenliebe. Roman* (Frankfurt: Suhrkamp, 1973), p. 7. All further references to *Klassenliebe* appear in the text.

[58] *Class Love*'s protagonist, Karin "Strauch" (given as her father's last name on p. 108), is obviously closely identified with Karin Struck, the author. In its German title, the book is identified as a novel (*Roman*).

been starved" (p. 258). Her problems with the theoretical are at least in part the result of deprivation that Lenz has not experienced, as Adelson stresses: "Karin's intense sensitivity for what is sensual and tangible reflects those domains which the capitalist division of labor reserves for women. It is difficult for her to perform the abstractions necessary for her studies."[59] Sensual experience alone is no solution; what Struck's protagonist really needs is, again, a synthesis of both body and mind: "Am I more a person of the senses or of the brain? Why is it mutually exclusive to be *both*? Is it mutually exclusive?" (p. 149).

Struck's novel demands that the concept of politics be expanded to include the personal, as does *Lenz*, but the revision of the concept in the former is more extensive. Dreams, fears, personal suffering, and sensual needs are included, but questions of sexuality and sexual roles, of health, nutrition, and the pollution of the environment, must also be addressed. Emphasis is placed on the "body" in a much more physical, biological sense, yet at the same time, through this biological emphasis, the personal level is transcended. The "body" ultimately takes on global significance in an ecological sense. Struck attacks the instrumentalized reason that unthinkingly plunders the physical environment and connects it to exploitation of human labor, reification of human relations, and mistreatment of the human body—more often than not the female body.

> I think that if the relationship of humanity to nature is one of plunder, then so is that of man to woman. Since the sixteenth century at the latest the relationship to nature has been totally exploitative, probably it was historically necessary, like the subjugation of the proletariat. Yes? And now? Hasn't the point been reached for some time now where both subjugations are anachronistic? "It isn't any more a question of controlling nature, but rather controlling the control of nature." (p. 23)

From this perspective, the orthodox Left is just as culpable as capitalists are: through its rationalistic faith in industrial technology; its support of depersonalized, factory-like medical care; and its implicit support of the pharmaceutical and pesticide industries. Questions of health and nutrition cannot be separated from psychological health, nor can they be considered apolitical, the narrator insists in her arguments with her more orthodox friends. These is-

---

[59] Leslie A. Adelson, "The Question of a Feminist Aesthetic and Karin Struck's *Klassenliebe*," in Susan L. Cocalis and Kay Goodman, eds., *Beyond the Eternal Feminine: Critical Essays on Women and German Literature* (Stuttgart: Hans-Dieter Heinz, 1982), p. 345.

sues are part of an inseparable whole—the physical, the personal, the political cannot be compartmentalized but rather demand a "holistic" approach that deals with the entire ecological system of their interactions on individual, social, and global levels.

> Is the plan to set up a group with doctors, psychiatrists, writers, farmers . . . who would research together the causes of diseases and treat patients as whole, not as beings with heads, with legs, with sex organs, beings with psyches, beings which eat . . . isn't this plan "political"? . . . Aren't we continually being halved, aren't we continually being treated like cabbages, I ask Dietger. Isn't that a political question, I ask Dietger. And isn't a doctor, a single doctor, who asks such a question already a political doctor, I ask Dietger. . . . Read your Marxist Bernal, I tell Dietger. Just read what he writes about the soil, read that radishes have something to do with politics. (pp. 124–25)

The idea that radishes have a political significance is certainly one for which Struck has been criticized—Möhrmann notes the negative response of many readers to what she calls Struck's *Reformhausideologie* ("ideology of the health-food store").[60] It is true that her protagonist in *Class Love* is identified with a somewhat eccentric macrobiotic approach—she writes that one friend calls her a "macro-idiot" ("Makroidiotin"; p. 57). Nonetheless, the novel certainly anticipated the emphasis on diet that was to become ever more influential in Germany's leftist counterculture, the *alternative Szene* ("alternative scene"). It is this same cultural milieu out of which the West German Greens developed. But these attitudes have by no means been restricted to West Germany's counterculture or to Western European and North American countercultures. The perception that problems in nutrition and in raising food are not minor issues easily solved by more technology, chemical fertilizers, and pesticides has become quite prevalent throughout the world. As the 1990s begin, with the concern over toxic waste, oil spills, and global warming constantly in the news, it is no longer so easy to deride the concept of organic farming and similar ideas that activists in the ecology movement advanced in the 1970s.

Class Love pleads for a new sensitivity to sensual experience and to biological and ecological realities and perspectives. The book's critique of the dogmatic Left is largely an attack on its rationalistic blindness with regard to these concerns. Such attitudes are of course also prevalent in the basic beliefs of the Greens in West Germany— and throughout the industrial countries where such movements

[60] Möhrmann, "Feministische Trends," p. 344.

have arisen. They reflect a shift in paradigm in the physical sciences in the second half of the twentieth century, a shift articulated to some extent by "Green" politics: the shift from a Cartesian model of the world, a mechanistic, atomistic model of the world as composed of interchangeable particles, to a holistic, ecocentric model of the world based on interconnectedness rather than interchangeability, emphasizing systems and processes of change rather than atomic particles of matter (which, as Einstein taught us, are actually systems of energy).

The book also explores the relationship of class origins to sensuality, and here again a comparison with Lenz is useful, since Schneider's novel criticizes the orthodox Left with regard to questions of the sensual while exploring—or at least portraying—Lenz's class-bound attitudes in this regard. Whereas Lenz has been involved with a Maoist group, Struck's protagonist has worked with groups associated with the German Communist Party, the DKP, which was (at that time) aligned with Moscow.[61] The critique of the dogmatic Left in Class Love nonetheless runs along lines similar to those in Lenz: sterility with regard to spontaneous, sensual experience, and enmity to the personal, individual nature of such experience prevent the dogmatic Left from being a truly liberating force.

But one notes a major shift in emphasis in Class Love, where leftist asceticism contributes to the oppression of a working class that Struck depicts as itself sensually deprived—indeed, more deprived than the bourgeois Left that romanticizes proletarian sensuality. It is this deprivation that elucidates the susceptibility of the working class to uncritical, even mindless, sensual pleasures. Struck's protagonist asserts that it also explains both her alienation from her proletarian husband H. and her attraction to the bourgeois Z.: "If only H. had nourished me more with sensitivity. Bastardized Marxist theory made H. sterile. I would never have fallen for Z.'s sensuality and vitality" (p. 226). H.'s politicization is thus seen to have reinforced his insensitivity and deficient sensuality, rather than to have enlightened and emancipated him in this regard. Sensuality in turn is seen not as the province of the proletariat (as Lenz sees it)

---

[61] In this, both protagonists conform to the past associations of their respective authors. In 1969 Karin Struck's first husband became the second president of the newly founded DKP. Manfred Jurgensen calls him "Heinz B."; he is the model for the book's "H." Jurgensen, Deutsche Frauenautoren der Gegenwart (Bern: Francke, 1983), p. 212. For more biographical information about Struck, see her "Mädchenjahre im Schatten des Krieges," in Jurgensen, Deutsche Frauenautoren, pp. 198–205; and Jürgen Serke, Frauen schreiben. Ein neues Kapitel deutschprachiger Literatur (Frankfurt: Fischer, 1982), pp. 249–63.

but rather as a bourgeois privilege Z. has had the luxury of cultivating.

This shift in emphasis from sensually repressed intellectuals to a sensually deprived working class is actually a shift in perspective: Struck's protagonist—like Struck herself—considers herself working-class in origin, and her dilemma is her position between the classes (p. 51), her feeling that she is caught between the working class and the bourgeois intellectuals with whom she has come to associate, through both her education and her political work. Her perspective is thus other than that of Lenz; both in terms of class origin and gender, she is identified with groups that have not been characterized by mastery of language. Rather, she is a member of groups who have had little access to language, who have been for the most part denied any public voice. Her position with regard to language is thus to some extent marginal: "What language can I speak?" (p. 82). Her diary and her aspiration to become a writer are attempts to change this.

"Otherness" and Multiple Voices

The concept of the "Other" coming to speech has a specific relevance to a comparison of *Lenz* and *Class Love*. Klaus Hartung, in a rather scathing discussion of Schneider's text, complains that L.'s story remains untold—and L., Lenz's girlfriend, is the only character he finds fascinating in the story. L. does remain mostly silent, and when she does speak, she takes on Lenz's part, repeating his standard formulation of their relationship, in which her role is that of a "girl from the people" (*Lenz*, p. 44).[62] As I have argued, she remains for him a projection, a proletarian mirror image that compensates harmoniously for the bourgeois flaws he perceives in himself.

Whereas L.'s story remains untold, in Karin Struck's *Class Love* one finds the story of a "girl from the people," and she herself tells the story. Struck's protagonist, like L., is "other" both in the sense of her working-class origins and in her being female. She suffers like L. in her relationship with a male bourgeois leftist who is unwilling to commit himself to a relationship (*Class Love*, p. 153; cf. *Lenz*, p. 45). She uses an image to describe the leftist bourgeois attitude vis-à-vis the working class that is almost identical with the fantasy of Wolfgang, the worker who befriends Lenz. Wolfgang fears that Lenz and his student friends are vampires (*Lenz*, pp. 34–35); in a section titled "Transfusions," Struck's protagonist writes: "Wolf N. wants

---

[62] Hartung, "Die Repression," p. 59.

to sleep with me: desire for a proletarian blood supply" (*Class Love*, p. 163).

The critique of the dogmatic phase of the student movement in Struck's novel has thus a quite different perspective from that in *Lenz*, for all the similarities. Whereas Lenz, through his contact with L., Wolfgang, and Roberto, begins to sense that the "Other" is much more complex and distinct from all his projections and assumptions, Struck's protagonist—like Struck herself—has a much clearer view of the bourgeois Left's distorted ideas about her own class— and gender. Even in her own hunger for the sensual, the perspective is different, since she cannot romanticize proletarian sensuality. Using images that are reminiscent of the drunken wedding feast in the film *Kuhle Wampe* (1932) she describes celebrations with her own relatives: "Confirmation: memories of nothing but empty beer bottles, on the table, on the tables, under the table, under the tables. Weddings: memories of gluttony and twenty-course meals and the stomach-pumping of children pumped full of beer and vomiting. That is the sensuality of the working class, dear Z. Which you so praise. On which you so place your hopes" (p. 99).

She is quick to attack the rosy vision of proletarian sexuality that she sees in the attitudes of Z. and in the writings of Gerhard Zwerenz. To explain the relation of the working class to sensuality, she cites Marx: "that the workers stuff themselves, get drunk, go whoring, because only what is immediate is available to them as pleasure, whatever takes little time—this is in *Das Kapital*" (p. 87). In the same manner, she explains her own obsession with sensuality (including the obsession with eating and food); it is a symptom of an alienated condition, not a solution.

A similar insight informs her critique of male sexuality in general. She finds myths of sexual conquest as alive within the Left as anywhere else, characterizing Zwerenz with the formula: "The world belongs to me as far as my cock will reach." She explains this attitude both for Zwerenz and for Z. as oedipal rebellion: "Fucking as the revolt against the overpowering father" (p. 83). Referring specifically to some of Brecht's poems, she calls him a "male imperialist" (p. 137). This was a relatively new interpretation of Brecht in 1973 (note also the use of the word "imperialist" as opposed to the one that became standard in both Germany and the United States, "chauvinist"). Wondering bitterly if there are really only women like those who appear in the works of Brecht and Zwerenz, women who just put up with men's arrogant behavior, she asks, "Why don't they fight?" (p. 138).

Class Love does not necessarily expound an explicitly feminist political line, and indeed in its discussion of abortion it opposes the position of the West German women's movement (p. 94); feminist critics in turn have not been entirely sympathetic to Karin Struck, either—not merely for her sentiments about abortion but also because of other substantive disagreements.[63] *Class Love*, as the title indicates, is more directly concerned with otherness in terms of class. It is structured, moreover, around the protagonist's relationship with a man: the narrative, to the extent there is one, centers on her love for, pregnancy, and rejection by Z. This narrative dependency on Z. would not seem to bespeak a fully awakened feminist self-awareness.

Nonetheless the protagonist is obviously interested in theoretical positions that envision new styles of politics based on reevaluations of the role of women: mentioning her interest in hearing about a conference in honor of Angela Davis, she cites Marcuse: "to bring the specifically feminine into politics" (p. 61). And on the personal side, from the very beginning of the novel there are traces of a new consciousness about her dependency and feelings of inferiority as a woman, as opposed to the long passages in which she details her insecurities about her class origins. On the second page of the text, some of the first insecurities are voiced, and they are not specifically tied either to class or to gender, but the passage as a whole evokes the emerging feminist critique:

> I went with you through the streets. . . . I felt like a shriveled being, shriveled up inside myself out of fear. Tied up: I don't have the confidence to go out without someone else taking me by the hand. . . . Lots of stairs, wooden stairs, brightly painted, and a blaring television, in a corridor with posters on the walls, one of them giant-sized, with a sterile-looking young woman in a brassiere displaying her breasts: that sure isn't me. I felt like an appendage: someone drags me through the streets of Frankfurt, up a gleaming staircase, past a large poster with a horrible brassiere-model on it. (p. 8)

---

[63] Relations between Struck and the women's movement have often been stormy. On Struck's negative attitude toward the first international women's film seminar in Berlin (1973)—she complained about the abortion films—see Möhrmann, *Die Frau mit der Kamera*, p. 28.

More substantive are the differences feminist critics like Möhrmann, Evelyn Torton Beck, and Biddy Martin have with Struck, and with what Möhrmann labels the "turn toward the natural" in subsequent women's literature of the 1970s (she cites Verena Stefan, Christa Reinig, Katrin Mosler, and Karin Petersen). Möhrmann sees a danger in this trend (anticipated by Struck) for its ahistorical tendency to essentialize the "eternal feminine" and "its likewise eternal sensuality" ("Feministische Trends," pp. 344, 348). See also Beck and Martin "Westdeutsche Frauenliteratur," pp. 141–42.

She addresses these lines to Z.; at this point in the novel, when her love for Z. seems secure, there are nonetheless moments when she feels like his appendage and is unable to venture out into the world without his guidance. In this state she is not capable of what Möhrmann calls the Vor-Zug, the "pro-gression" or advance into the public sphere, a sphere where in any case she finds nothing with which she can identify, only advertising images that objectify women, images that leave no place for her subjectivity or identity as a woman.[64]

And it is precisely the crisis with Z. that can be seen as the motivation for the protagonist's writing of her story. Her determination at the end of the book to have the baby on her own, without Z., is a sign of a new independence. This parallels her writing, which is often compared to the process of giving birth: "Desire to give birth to something. A child, a work, a love" (p. 93). At the end of the book she describes Kafka's writing as "writing before birth" (p. 275) in an obvious analogy to her own situation. Writing indeed becomes a way to end her dependency on Z. Although earlier in the novel much of what she wrote were letters to Z., or at least addressed to him, it is when she realizes that she cannot rely on him that her motivation for writing changes: "Now I'm writing just for myself" (p. 192).

The importance of writing for the "Other" 's coming to speech in Struck's novel is central, as is the potential function of literature; there is also a need to come to terms with male literary figures like Brecht and Kafka, and with literary tradition as a whole. This is another important area in which Lenz and Class Love show significant similarities and contrasts: the attitude in each text to language, writing, and literature. In Lenz the use of language for expression of personal traumas and exploration of the past in a supportive social environment (i.e., Trento) is therapeutic. In Class Love, not only is language used as therapy, but, in a manner obviously self-reflexive for the author, writing itself is depicted as therapeutic.

The protagonist is interested in actually working with patients in hospitals and psychiatric institutions for whom therapy consists in part of trying to write their stories. It is essential that those who have been silent learn to write, to tell their own stories—and this type of therapy is of course as "political" as is the question of which groups have been kept silent. "The history of the patients is unwritten, I read in a history of medicine," she writes, and then comments bitterly, "That is truly the least important part, isn't it? The history of

---

[64] Möhrmann, "Feministische Trends," p. 341.

the workers, the history of women, the history of the Blacks, the history of the children, the history of the people" (p. 139).

There is a tremendous faith in writing: "Man, what power there is in writing. Or could be" (p. 140). Writing is not only therapy, it is a means of liberation from the handicaps of class socialization; referring to her husband H., the protagonist writes: "he frees himself through writing" (p. 129), and of course writing does this for her too, "Writing as an affirmation of myself" (p. 209). It does not, however, remain a personal operation; the untold stories of those marginalized groups mentioned above can—and should—be written into history, according to the protagonist: "I demand that the greatest reality, the reality of the exploited, be written on the most sophisticated intellectual plane. That it be inscribed into history" (p. 206). Writing for her thus has a historical aspect that is political: "Everything is so buried. Hidden. To gather together the particles of past and present oppressions" (pp. 166–67). Writing is an attempt to delve into the rubble of history to bring forth such particles: "Writing as archaeology. . . . Writing rather as submerging" (p. 211).

Her faith in writing includes a great faith in literature. Here is another important area of the book's critique of aspects of the student movement: the idea that literature is dead is discarded as a privileged bourgeois delusion. For those who have been denied access to literature, it is quite alive and vital: "And we never were able to over-stuff ourselves with literature. For us literature is like our daily bread, like water. Does life come without bread? What do we care about the slogans of leftist little boys from the bourgoisie, that 'literature is shit'? Nothing at all. . . . Without imagination socialism is nothing" (p. 118).

Lenz is of course named after Georg Büchner's novella and begins with a direct quote from it; various passages in the book imitate Büchner's style.[65] The literary parallels to other trips to Italy, by Goethe and others, are also unavoidable. Schneider's text represents thus to some extent a rehabilitation of literary tradition as a valid source of models and material to rework in the attempt to give expression to personal conflicts. Literature itself is validated as a vehicle for this endeavor.

Struck alludes to the same passage by Büchner with which Schneider's *Lenz* opens (pp. 10–11).[66] But Struck's allusions to, and direct quotes from, this and other literary works make the attitude

---

[65] On Schneider's imitation of Büchner's style, see Goltschnigg, *Rezeptions- und Wirkungsgeschichte Georg Büchners*, pp. 273–79.

[66] There are also direct quotes from Büchner's *Lenz* (e.g., pp. 82, 106).

of her text to other literature much more explicit than Schneider's. The latter's attitude can be surmised from his work, but it is not explicitly stated in the narrative he constructs. Struck states plainly that literature can be used in the struggle to express—and survive— one's personal contradictions and traumas. She constantly cites Büchner, Kafka, Brecht, Martin Walser, Thomas Bernhard, Erika Runge, Zwerenz, and Christa Wolf, to mention only some of the most frequently mentioned. The citations are used to help express what *she* wants to say. Schneider's loose adaptation of Büchner is of course to be understood in the same way; he is not simply paying homage to a figure in the literary canon. Struck, however, "adapts" nothing; she appropriates many voices into her own, and the form that results is a unique, albeit chaotic, blend of the voices she quotes.

Struck's "protagonist" is the fictional construct who appropriates all these quotes, and her explanation to Z. can be viewed as a self-reflexive comment on this appropriation, for which of course the author herself is responsible: "You said, these quotes, I've assimilated them, they're hardly quotes at all any more. But I've also noticed your annoyance at my constant quoting. That I do it so often is an expression of my fear of memory loss, also the attempt to appropriate something for myself out of the monstrous mass of printed material around me, not as knowledge, but in relation to my own subjective experience" (p. 44).

Here again one notes the protagonist's inferiority complex—this time in regard not merely to her memory but even more so to the vast bourgeois canon of knowledge of which she feels she knows too little. Yet her open admission of the desire to use it piecemeal and to her own ends is what bothers the more classically educated Z. In regard to Struck's own appropriation of citations in the book, there is a definite similarity to the practice of many postmodernist artists in the 1970s, who were "working out of the ruins of the modernist edifice, raiding it for ideas, plundering its vocabulary and supplementing it with randomly chosen images and motifs from pre-modern and non-modern cultures as well as from contemporary mass culture."[67]

Schneider's *Lenz* is fairly traditional in terms of its form—certainly in its return to narrative realism, at any rate; Struck's *Class Love*, on the other hand, is not a novel at all in the traditional sense. The "fictional" protagonist who supposedly is the source of the diary entries and the gatherer of the quotes of others, the other

[67] Huyssen, "Mapping the Postmodern," p. 25.

"voices," is a transparent fiction; one cannot but identify her with the author. Schneider's *Lenz* is somewhat diaristic in form, alluding as it does to Büchner's novella, which in turn was based in part on Pastor Oberlin's diary accounts of the troubled Lenz. But Struck's novel seems to be an authentic diary.

This was the book's innovation: in 1975 one critic commented that what Struck presented as novels could never have been categorized as such five years earlier.[68] Both in form and in apparent "authenticity" the book proved to be exemplary, especially (but not only) for women's literature in West Germany during the rest of the 1970s.[69] One notes again the continuity with documentary literature of the mid- and late 1960s, the "autobiographical shift of the documentary";[70] one explanation for this phenomenon is that in such "authentic" works the "documentary gesture" had simply begun documenting the author's self-reflection.[71]

Class Love is organized like a diary: the only divisions in the text that are marked (other than by spacing alone) are introduced by dated entries, the first being 16 May 1972 (p. 7), the last being 25 August of the same year (p. 275). But the self-obsession one expects in a diary and that is obviously a part of *Class Love* is to some extent interrupted by the multitude of voices incorporated into it. The obsession of this insecure self is revealed to be a search for its own voice amidst this multitude of voices that it finds to be more "authoritative"—but manages somehow to appropriate.

In *Lenz* a third-person narrator hovers quite closely to the internal perspective of the protagonist, such that the reader experiences Lenz's inability to escape himself but cannot achieve much distance on it—indeed, no more distance than Lenz himself is able to develop in the course of the novel, since the narrator allows no other perspective. In *Class Love* the ego that is exposed is weak not through its isolation but rather through its dispersion and permeability. Rather than feeling trapped in one claustrophobic perspective, the reader, like the main character, seems to be floating in a sea of voices, grasping at each for orientation.

For the text is often like a sea of different voices. There are voices cited in indirect quotation; there are voices quoted directly with

---

[68] Heinrich Vormweg, rev. of *Die Mutter* by Karin Struck, *Merkur* 29 (1975), p. 474.

[69] To name just a few—quite varied—examples of what can be considered diaristic writing: Verena Stefan's *Shedding* (*Häutungen*), Peter Handke's *The Weight of the World* (*Das Gewicht der Welt*, 1977), and Botho Strauss's *Devotion* (*Die Widmung*, 1977).

[70] Schlichting, "Das Ungenügen," p. 35.

[71] Beicken, " 'Neue Subjektivität,' " p. 167.

quotation marks: " 'I saw you, you were visible,' H. said to me" (p. 14), and without them: "Why are you washing your hair after midnight, Z. asks, mistrustingly" (pp. 7–8). Quotes are printed sometimes in italics: " '*Can one touch capitalism?*' " (p. 7); sometimes they are ascribed to characters or famous authors: "Do you get the very strong feeling that Walser is a child when he writes the sentence: 'If an author doesn't need the labor of writing in order to change himself, then he won't be able to change anyone else either' " (p. 13). At other times they are not ascribed to anyone: " '*Sudden sympathy from a sudden reminiscence. Her face glistened in the mist*' " (p. 8).

The variety of ways in which quotes are presented makes it at times difficult to identify them and often impossible to identify their sources. The resulting confusion of voices reflects the protagonist's search for her own voice. "Subjectivity" in Struck's book is much less a retreat into interiority than a blurring of boundaries between "exterior" and "interior," and this probably has something to do with a kind of ego development that is less rigid than that which is clasically "male" and "bourgeois." This kind of development is not necessarily an advantage (in certain practical ways it is obviously a disadvantage), but it does mean that subjective writing will be something other than a withdrawal into a seemingly autonomous self: "*I never had an 'I.' When I tried to say 'I,' it was, 'Pull yourself together.' Don't take yourself so seriously. . . . I am nothing. . . . Nightmares: I run around my whole life long with books in my hand, quotes underlined, and I keep reading these quotes again and again, because I myself am a nothing, don't belong with these books*" (pp. 180, 182).[72]

The difficulty of saying "I" has of course been a special problem for women, relegated for the most part to public objectification and silence for so long.[73] Perhaps this also explains why the exposure of subjectivity, of an ego, in a novel like *Class Love* goes so much farther in deconstructing the fiction of a unified self, a realm of personal concerns divorced from the social milieu around it: the ego here is nothing but a multiplicity of determining and conflicting dis-

[72] Cf. Theodor Adorno's remarks in *Minima Moralia. Reflexionen aus dem beschädigten Leben* (1951; Frankfurt: Suhrkamp, 1985): "With many people it is already an insolence to say 'I' " (my translation, p. 57).

[73] One is compelled to think of Christa Wolf in this connection, especially since Struck alludes to her so often in the course of the book. See Christa Wolf, *Nachdenken über Christa T.* (1968; Neuwied [W. Ger.]: Luchterhand, 1971), p. 214. (In English: *The Quest for Christa T.*) Christa Wolf is mentioned in *Class Love* on pp. 18–19, 24, 55, 117, 142–44, 256, and passim.

courses—social, political, sensual, sexual, biological. The struggle to take control of these discourses, to write one's own story, can never be an operation of "withdrawal" into an interior with fixed boundaries; rather it must be a matter of bringing out the fluid interaction of "internal" and "external" voices, of personal and social influences, that occurs within each individual: not *Rückzug* but a *Vor-Zug*, not a retreat into alienated selves but an advance into a world in which individuals strive actively to define and effect the discourses that shape their social and personal realities.

Problematizing the supposed boundaries between the personal and the social, between the private and the public, is a feminist project. The undermining of such dichotomies is related to the undermining of that fundamental split between what is traditionally considered "male" and "female."[74] This dichotomy is in turn related to the psychological split between the "Self" and the "Other" so formative in the development of human self-consciousness. For women, the self/other dichotomy has traditionally been gendered in such a way that their sex has been placed on the side of the "Other," of object to the male subject, which has of course determined public discourse. When, however, what has been designated as the "Other" begins to enter the public discourse as an active, speaking subject— subjects—the neat dichotomy collapses; there is no longer any simple division of the world into such neat, complementary halves.

In Struck's text this can be seen in at least two major ways: first, as I have discussed above, in the multiplicity of voices that speak in her text (rather than a unified "Other" corresponding to/reflecting a unified, autonomous "Self"), and second in Struck's emphasis on her character's dilemma in existing *between* fixed identities. She is not at home in the working class or among the bourgeoisie; she is also between two men, the bourgeois Z. and her husband H. (H. is, like her, of working-class origins and now, like her, enrolled at the university, where he studies medicine.) She is interested in her identity as a woman and as a mother, but she rejects the traditional conception of that identity with regard to sexuality and family.

Her national identity is similarly "between" states, reflecting some of the most typical displacements (geographical and ideological) of postwar Germans: her parents fled Pomerania (now part of Poland) into what became East Germany at the end of the war, and

---

[74] See, for example, the investigation of dichotomies (which ultimately exclude women) in Hélène Cixous's and Catherine Clément's *The Newly Born Woman*, trans. Betsy Wing (Minneapolis: University of Minnesota Press, 1986), p. 63. Cf. Craig Owens's connection of the feminist and the postmodernist critiques of "binarism" in "The Discourse of Others," p. 62.

it was there that the protagonist was born (as was Karin Struck).[75] In 1953 the family fled to West Berlin, and from there into West Germany. The protagonist has thus lived in both German states and now, after a period of sympathy for the East German one, rejects both politically while remaining in the West (see, for example, pages 19–20 and 108–13). She sees herself without roots and without fixed identity: "Without a language, without a country, without a class" (p. 245).

Yet this very rootlessness has its positive side in its blurring of fixed categories, identities, and dichotomies, and in an affinity for a discourse that takes nothing for granted, a discourse that realizes the varieties of voices and determinants out of which it must be fashioned, and the limitations of each. The protagonist is between states, between classes, between men—and thus she must in the end determine her own identity as a woman: not as the complementary opposite of the other side of any dichotomy, but through a process of making her own choices within a complex multiplicity of relations.

She does not deny the myriad influences that determine her; she is open about her confusion in dealing with them. She also realizes the need to sort them out and expose those elements in her socialization that need exorcising. Socially conditioned inferiority complexes make the necessary task of exposing her vulnerability and mistakes a difficult one, as is evident in the following passage that is critical of the dogmatic Left. Although here the topic is a class-based inferiority complex, the passage points the way toward the project of subsequent feminist writing (anticipating most directly Verena Stefan): "Do you think, I ask Herbert Friedmann, that we'll ever get rid of those feelings of inferiority inside of us we've been prompted to learn? We have to write them and speak them out and shout them out and fight them out. . . . Dear H., shed your skin, let us shed ourselves of that false language, the sterile, bureaucratic, Communist language of defensiveness and fear" (p. 268).[76]

Writing as Sensuality?

Struck's faith that writing will help her work through and leave behind her conditioning is typical of an optimism about writing that is similar to the faith in language evident in *Lenz*. The power of writing, however, is not restricted to therapy on the personal level: in *Class Love*, a line by Christa Wolf is cited that defines writing as

[75] See Struck, "Mädchenjahre," pp. 198–205.
[76] The anticipation of at least the title of Stefan's *Shedding* (*Häutungen*) is obvious.

"the means to fuse with time," in the instant when both writer and time "experience their closest, most conflicted, and painful proximity" (p. 18), and a formulation ascribed to Martin Walser is quoted: "Literature as re-creation of wholeness" (p. 130). This is an optimism beyond the individual level, indeed utopian in scope: producing literature is seen as a means by which modern social alienation can be overcome, indeed as a way to overcome the gap between personal experience and history.

In *Class Love*, the optimism of the populist strain of 1960s postmodernism appears to get mixed up with a quite Romantic—and modernist—belief in the power of art. All the hopes that Struck's generation once placed on revolution now become centered on literature, in a manner that seems related to Herbert Marcuse's ideas on both art and revolution, ideas that of course shaped the New Left internationally.

Marcuse saw in art and artistic activity the anticipation of non-alienated and nonexploitative behavior that would be typical of society after a truly emancipatory social revolution. The end of alienation is caused by the synthesis of individual and social experience. For Marcuse this synthesis is not only the anticipated achievement of the postrevolutionary society but also what on another level he attempted in his theoretical work. It has been asserted that Marcuse's innovation within critical theory was primarily the attempt to synthesize Marx and Freud; in this synthesis of the sociological with the psychoanalytical, the role of the aesthetic was central:

> Along this line of thought, questions about aesthetics and art gain significance for Marcuse, since in these realms, the positive potential of human psychological drives is already evident today, even though its full realization would be possible only in an emancipated society.
>
>   . . . . [I]n terms of both function and origin, the aesthetic for Marcuse can serve as the basic characteristic of a "new sensibility" in a nonrepressive culture . . . : it springs from Eros, and is the expression of an attitude to the world that is based neither on domination nor in instrumental reason.[77]

As Marcuse himself wrote, "The definite negation of the established reality would be an 'aesthetic' universe."[78] The students of 1968 had in their most radical stage attempted to make this "aesthetic" revolution happen outside the traditional arts, in the streets;

---

[77] Gmünder, *Kritische Theorie*, pp. 103, 109.

[78] Marcuse, "Art in the One-Dimensional Society" (1967), cited in Gmünder, *Kritische Theorie*, p. 110.

when this proved impossible, they retreated with their utopian dreams to cultural experimentation with alternative life-styles, but also to the realm of art and, in West Germany, to literature especially.[79] This burdened literature (at least for them) with the function of resolving major contradictions in modern society—between the sensual and the theoretical, the personal and the social, and what is called the poetic and the political by Wilhelm Meister, the would-be writer in the film *Wrong Move* by Peter Handke and Wim Wenders.

It is doubtful whether literature is capable of *resolving* (as opposed to rethinking) such contradictions. The "subjective" West German literature that proclaimed its ambition to synthesize such oppositions often appears to achieve only a rather facile equation of the opposing terms, effacing distinctions (and difference) rather than problematizing dichotomies. *Class Love*, for example, treats writing at times as though it were not supposed to be merely the synthesis of the sensual and the rational (already a rather romantic idea). Writing actually seems to embody sensuality itself: Karin glowingly describes writing naked at the typewriter (p. 100)—perhaps an overly literal illustration of that conception of art as something which "springs from Eros." Manfred Jurgensen writes of Struck: "She conceives of her own body as language, love means for her the 'language of the senses.' "[80] These depictions of writing in connection with the sensual and the biological include its metaphorical equation with giving birth: "To be pregnant: pregnant with Elias and pregnant with ideas and pregnant with rage and with literary works" (p. 163).

The equation of writing with biological reproduction is somewhat problematic, both from a feminist perspective and from a concern for a demystified understanding of writing. The book's penchant for biological metaphor is related to its equally problematic views on abortion, since the equation of literary creativity with the biological capacity of women to give birth is a rather traditional one, and one that seems uncomfortably close to the view that biological reproduction is the essential element of female creativity—and identity.[81]

---

[79] The rehabilitation of the poetic, and of art in general, by the veterans of the student movement paralleled a similar shift on Marcuse's part. As Peter Uwe Hohendahl writes, "Marcuse spoke out against the total transformation of art into social praxis already in 1972 with *Counterrevolution and Revolt*, and he returned to the concept of the art work." Hohendahl, "Politisierung der Kunsttheorie: Zur ästhetischen Diskussion seit 1965," in Lützeler and Schwarz, *Deutsche Literatur*, p. 293.

[80] Jurgensen, *Deutsche Frauenautoren*, p. 227. He is discussing her third novel, *Lieben* (1977).

[81] Here, too, the book anticipates—in an odd way—Stefan's *Shedding*, not in its basing of female identity on motherhood, but rather in basing it on biology—specifi-

Class Love and *Lenz* tend to be extremely optimistic about language: both about speech and its therapeutic potential for individual self-awareness, and about literary discourse. Language and literature—distinctions between the two levels of discourse somewhat effaced—provided a new refuge for revolutionary optimism, as one skeptical writer pointed out in rejecting this concept of literature: "All those who never wanted to conceive of literature as the 'letter-carrier for the revolution' will not now want to accompany literature as a letter-carrier on its way to the therapist."[82]

Some of what is blurred with regard to literary discourse in *Class Love* includes the distinctions between the protagonist/first-person narrator and the author, and between text and author, and between writing and the institution that is "literature." The blurring of such boundaries is in one sense postmodern, and such distinctions can be undermined productively—for instance, by problematizing the distinctions between "fictional" and "documentary" texts.[83] But this is more likely to happen when the project is exposed, or when at least some postmodernist irony is in evidence. Irony seems lacking in both Schneider's and Struck's texts. Struck in addition appeared to want to present a text meant to be experienced (without irony) as unmediated subjectivity, as her "authentic" diary, a text with which she was not averse to being identified by the public in a most literal sense. Indeed, some of her behavior in the aftermath of the book's success (a book she nonetheless called a novel) seems to indicate she wanted to encourage this simple identity between her person and her book.[84]

The "authenticity" of literature is of course thematized in *Class Love* itself. The protagonist responds to Zwerenz's book *Kopf und Bauch* (*Head and Belly*) by writing to the author personally: "A book is a letter, a call, a call for help, it's always a calling for help.

<hr>

cally the female body—and nature. See Marlis Gerhardt, "Wohin geht Nora? Auf der Suche nach der verlorenen Frau," *Kursbuch*, no. 47 (1977), pp. 82–86; also Möhrmann, "Feministische Trends," pp. 344–48.

[82] Ursula Krechel, "Leben in Anführungszeichen. Das Authentische in der gegenwärtigen Literatur," *Literaturmagazin*, no. 11 (1979), p. 101; she is citing Reinhard Lettau in *Literaturmagazin*, no. 4 (1975), p. 19 ("Briefträger der Revolution"). On the question of "authenticity," see also Elisabeth Schmid, "Frauenleben und -liebe. Zu den Romanen von Karin Struck," in Zeller, *Aufbrüche, Abschiede*, pp. 83–91.

[83] See below, Chapter 4, especially the discussion of Helke Sander and Alexander Kluge.

[84] See Mechthild Curtius's "Der 'Fall' Karin Struck—ein Stück Literaturmarkt am krassen Beispiel," *Literatur und Kritik*, no. 85 (1974), pp. 296–306, esp. pp. 304–6 on the *Jasmin* affair. Kramer explains the latter event as follows: "The divulging of the personal, of the intimate in her works was complemented by the publication in *Jasmin* of naked photos of the author." Kramer, "/New Subjectivity/," p. 155.

But the fellow doesn't mean it seriously. The fellow's only writing 'literature' " (p. 81). Her disappointment in Zwerenz is followed later by her own pledge: "A book is always a cry for help. . . . And I mean the cry seriously, the cry should not be a dead letter" (p. 84). Karin the narrator thus commits herself to being identified with her writing, pledging that her writing will be the honest expression of herself. In turn Struck the author seems to be saying that she can be identified fully with the fictional voice of "Karin Strauch."

This equation of what Struck presents as a novel with other forms of expression like letters and verbal cries obviously oversimplifies the varying levels of mediation and codification that are involved in these different types of utterances. It does not seem to be a playful, ironic, or "double-coded" use of the codes of "realist" authenticity in such a way that they are invoked and relativized at the same time. In addition, if the book is simply a cry for help, part of a personal need for communication and therapy, why is Karin so fascinated with attaining the exalted status of "writer"? For, although at times she seems to believe everyone is (potentially) a "genius" (p. 260), at other times she finds such a democratic notion disappointing: "Z. says, I can 'bury' my desire to become a writer, I already am one, 'you already are one.' But should I be happy about that? He says everyone is a writer" (p. 121).

The elite status of being one of the few to have "succeeded" at writing (i.e., professionally) definitely attracts her, in spite of her feeling that everyone—including the oppressed, the mentally ill, and other marginalized groups (or rather especially all these groups)—should be able to actualize themselves through writing. Writers who base their writing on authenticity, on lived experience, seem to want to reject the older, more elitist concept of being a master at the craft of writing. Writing in Class Love seems to be valorized as a *social* process for overcoming marginalization, on behalf of groups without a voice. But the protagonist—and the author— also seems to be caught in the contradiction of nonetheless having the individualistic ambition to achieve the elite status associated with the (old-fashioned concept of the) "artist."[85]

On the other hand, in Class Love, the attraction to this status is quite openly admitted: "The word 'publication,' almost as magic as the word 'adulteress' " (p. 242). Access to the public sphere is a laudable goal; what is problematic in this ambition has to do with the way such access is controlled by the publishing industry, and how this institutionalized control keeps such access limited to the

---

[85] Krechel, "Leben," pp. 97–98.

success of "exceptional" individuals, never social groups (marginal ones at any rate). But of course this type of contradiction is faced by all writers; perhaps the honest admission of this contradictory (but quite common) ambition is more self-reflexive than is at first apparent.[86]

"Honest testimony" is indeed how one critic has described the way Struck exposes her own contradictions.[87] And what is exposed is no "autonomous subject." Rather, the reader is confronted with a variety of voices within and outside her, determining discourses, various conflicting "identities": a German from the East living in the West, someone with a certain class background (and yet "between" classes), a student politicized in the late 1960s, a woman searching among traditional and newer gender roles. To the extent that the book is an open admission of contradictions, a process of searching with no happy resolution at the end, or secure claims to truth, it *is* postmodernist.[88]

But part of what *Class Love* exposes is a hope in the revolutionary and therapeutic possibilities of literature. This hope was not fulfilled, based as it was on some overly optimistic thinking about the nature of language and literary production and reception in an advanced capitalist society like West Germany. Indeed, voices more skeptical of language, literature, and writing were also being heard.

---

[86] Struck's subsequent career after *Klassenliebe*, and her relation to the institution of publishing (and the critics), has been the subject of much controversy. Her subsequent novels, certainly beginning with *Lieben* if not with *Die Mutter*, have been more or less rejected by critics (e.g., see Möhrmann, "Feministische Trends," p. 348). In 1983, Christian Schulz-Gerstein wrote about Struck's rise and fall in an article that ostensibly blames the press's inconsistency for this phenomenon, maintaining that it was not Struck's works that changed but the interests and criteria of the critics. Nonetheless, the barely concealed *Schadenfreude* with which he describes the decline in her fortunes makes it difficult to take his criticism of the press as the main thrust of his article (" 'Sie sind eine wirkliche Schriftstellerin,' " *Der Spiegel*, 23 May 1983, pp. 159–61). Kramer's account of Struck's career (and Schultz-Gerstein's article) is more balanced and more perceptive with regard to the relation of a single author to institutionalized reception in the West German literary market of the 1970s (Kramer, "/New Subjectivity/," pp. 155–59). See also *Karin Struck*, ed. Hans Adler and Hans Joachim Schrimpf (Frankfurt: Suhrkamp, 1984), and the following books by Jurgensen: *Deutsche Frauenautoren*, pp. 198–205, the chapter on Struck in his *Frauenliteratur. Autorinnen—Perspektiven—Konzepte* (Bern: Peter Lang, 1983), and *Karin Struck: Eine Einführung* (Bern: Peter Lang, 1985). How Struck saw her own dilemma in the 1980s is clear from the title of a lecture she gave, appearing abridged in *Monatshefte* 75 (1983): "Ist nur eine tote erotische Autorin eine gute erotische Autorin?" ["Is only a dead erotic female author a good one?"] (pp. 353–57).

[87] Adelson, "The Question," p. 349.

[88] One definitive aspect of postmodernist art according to Hutcheon is the "deliberate refusal to resolve contradictions." *A Poetics of Postmodernism*, p. x.

CHAPTER THREE

Writing and
the "Erotic Gaze"

THE WORD is a virus from outer space.[1]

THE CRISIS OF LANGUAGE

The optimism about the therapeutic potential of language and writing for the expression of subjectivity implied the hope that literature could be a medium for collective *Verständigung*, a communal understanding of personal experiences shared by many. Such sentiments are evident in texts like Schneider's *Lenz* and Struck's *Class Love*, and they are related ultimately to the attitude formulated in the title of a 1975 issue of the journal *Literaturmagazin* (no. 3): "Literature as Utopia." With the failure of politics to bring on the millennium, various activists turned to literature, placing their hopes in it. This recourse to literature can be seen as yet another dialectical twist in the (con)fusion of politics and art begun in the 1960s, in which first literati had abandoned literature for cultural revolution, and now disillusioned political activists sought healing in literature.

The turn toward "inwardness" in literature had a more radical side, in which such optimism about language and writing were tempered by much greater skepticism. This more pessimistic trend involved a much more complex view of the relation of writing, language, and subjectivity. Peter Handke's remarks on the function of literature upon receiving the 1973 Büchner Prize, in which he spoke of "the power of poetic thinking to dissolve abstractions and thus exert a powerful influence upon the future,"[2] gave encouragement to the concept of literature as utopia. But for Handke, literature's utopian function in loosening the hold of conceptual systems and logic was the result of a demanding struggle with the medium of language, not a simple outpouring of "authentic" experience without any concern for the mediation of language. Language was corrupt, an integral part of social conditioning and abstraction. Thus for Handke language was inimical to authentic perception, a goal that seemed to require transcending language and conditioning through a more or less mystical experience—in his novel *A Moment of True Feeling* (1975), it is an experience that is largely *visual* in nature.[3]

---

[1] Cited in Laurie Anderson's concert film, *Home of the Brave* (1986). Cf. William S. Burroughs, "Ten Years and a Billion Dollars," in his book *The Adding Machine: Selected Essays* (New York: Seaver, 1986): "My general theory since 1971 has been that the Word is literally a virus" (p. 48).

[2] Reprinted as "Die Geborgenheit unter der Schädeldecke" ["Refuge Beneath the Roof of the Skull"], *Theater Heute*, no. 12 (1973), p. 2.

[3] Handke's protagonist sees three objects in the sand, and this vision causes a mystical experience—in a manner somewhat comparable to the experience of the protag-

The valuation of the visual over language implied by this incident in Handke's text reflects a general tendency of the 1970s in West Germany that perhaps explains in part the increased role that film-making was to play during the course of the decade. Relevant in this context are Rutschky's discussion of the meaning of filmgoing in the 1970s and the "specular subject" that Eric Rentschler asserts is at the center of Handke's prose—and his 1977 film The Left-Handed Woman.[4] Also significant is the very fact that Handke's fascination with the cinema led him to try his hand at directing the latter text as a film, having already written a screenplay for Wim Wenders's Wrong Move (Falsche Bewegung, 1973).

The attraction to direct sensual experience (visual and otherwise) and the enmity toward social conditioning and language found its most extreme form in those social tendencies that seemed to reject logic and technology entirely, even to reject civilization itself. Such positions were actually espoused only by certain fringe sections of the ecology movement, certain anarchistic young urban "Spontis" who renounced all negotiation in favor of "action,"[5] and (to some extent) by factions within the women's movement that equated all civilization with patriarchy, identifying the feminine exclusively with the irrational and with nature.

One could perhaps discuss Verena Stefan's autobiographical essay Shedding (Häutungen, 1975) in this last context, although the resonance the work found—another instant best-seller, and this for an unknown author published by a small feminist collective—is proof that it spoke for more than "fringe" groups. Certainly Stefan's dissatisfaction with the inherent sexism of the German language was shared by many women, and her determination to fundamentally rethink it was a lucid acknowledgment of the power of language as a medium and its complicity in constructing a dominant order that has kept women oppressed for centuries. As Stefan wrote in a fore-word to her book: "each word must be twisted and turned before it can be used. . . . In writing I ran smack into language."[6] Some of the

---

onist in Hugo von Hofmannsthal's Letter of Lord Chandos (Ein Brief, 1902). Handke, A Moment of True Feeling, trans. Ralph Manheim (New York: Farrar, Straus, and Giroux, 1977), pp. 63–65. Orig. Die Stunde der wahren Empfindung (Frankfurt: Suhrkamp, 1975), pp. 81–83.

[4] Rutschky, "Allegorese des Kinos," in Erfahrungshunger, pp. 167–92. Rentschler, West German Film, pp. 166–73.

[5] Glaser, Im Packeis des Unbehagens, pp. 18, 24, 30.

[6] Verena Stefan, Häutungen (Munich: Frauenoffensive, 1975), p. 4. The English version, Shedding, trans. Johanna Moore and Beth Weckmueller (New York: Daughters Publishing, Co., 1978), does not include this opening statement by the author, dated August 1975 in Berlin.

choices she made in attempting to create a nonpatriarchal discourse are, however, more problematic; her use of nature metaphors for discussing the female body drew the most criticism from feminists unwilling to settle for the mere equation of femininity with nature.[7]

Charles Newman has asserted that a fundamental—and painful—aspect of human existence is the "split between sensation and thinking."[8] At the very least, this is true of modern "rational" existence. Related to that split between body and consciousness is the determining role played by language within human consciousness, increasing the alienation between individual bodies and social consciousness, for language is an essentially social—or in any case certainly not an individual—medium. The social nature of language is a major obstacle to the expression of individual experience, emotion, and sensation; another is literature itself, as a social institution embodied in a tradition of aesthetic practices. These obstacles to the direct articulation of subjective experience are then greatly magnified by the vast institutional media that have developed to manipulate language—of which the publishing industry is one of the smallest. Within the literary profession, as well as in other media of artistic expression, the struggle with these problems is by no means new; it has been the topic of aesthetic debates since at least the turn of the century. It seems that no single formal strategy, including the "rejection" of form, is adequate to resolving these obstacles.

For the generation in West Germany that experienced the student movement, there were other shifts in the early 1970s besides the political one (the *Tendenzwende*), especially in artistic trends. The filmmaker Rainer Werner Fassbinder shifted from his early period of experimentation, influenced by Brecht and Godard, to a new phase of his career, inspired by his discovery of the "critical" Hollywood melodrama of Douglas Sirk. In this new phase, initiated with *The Merchant of Four Seasons* (*Der Händler der vier Jahreszeiten*, 1971), Fassbinder began his attempt to fuse Brechtian distantiation with Sirkian melodrama.[9] Meanwhile, Wenders, initially a "Sensibilist" with little patience for Brecht and a fascination (albeit an ambivalent one) for Hollywood cinema, discovered while making his first full-length feature film after film school that he could not be

[7] See Kramer, "/New Subjectivity/," pp. 333–41, esp. the section of her discussion of Stefan titled "Woman as Pumpkin."

[8] Newman, *The Post-Modern Aura*, p. 82.

[9] In an interview with Norbert Sparrow, Fassbinder talked of his admiration for Sirk's melodramas—and his revision of Brecht: "With Brecht you see the emotions and you reflect on them as you witness them but you never feel them. I let the audience feel and think." *Cineaste* 8, no. 1 (1977), no. 1, p. 20.

an "American" director; subsequently he found in the Japanese film maker Ozu a style that gave him confidence in a non-American idiom, one of the "two opposing grammars" within his own work.[10]

Common to both these stylistic transitions is an attempt to fuse strategies associated with the avant-garde with the strategies of "mass culture" in order to transcend the dead ends to which both have led. The result is a development of postmodernist techniques for "installing and subverting familiar conventions of both kinds of art."[11] Fassbinder wanted to enable the audience to experience emotions through identification while employing enough distantiation to allow critical reflection on the social determinations of these mediated emotions, and Wenders wanted to use narrative without sacrificing profilmic reality to narrative (and cinematographic) manipulation.

Another shift that is arguably postmodernist was made by Peter Handke around 1970.[12] Handke's novel *The Goalie's Anxiety at the Penalty Kick* (*Die Angst des Tormanns beim Elfmeter*, 1970) marks the end of his earlier experimental drama and prose and the beginning of his attempt to recuperate the realist narrative, a move that in some ways anticipated the "New Subjectivity." Handke's shift was comparable to his friend Wenders's interest in somehow preserving the immediate reality in front of the camera from the distorting mediation of conventional film language.[13]

Handke's next two books, in any case, were very influential on writers like Karin Struck. In 1972, both the autobiographically based novel *Short Letter, Long Farewell* (*Der kurze Brief zum langen Abschied*) and the biographical novel/essay on his mother's life *A Sor-*

---

[10] Wim Wenders, interview in Dawson, *Wim Wenders*, pp. 8–9. The film was *The Goalie's Anxiety at the Penalty Kick* (*Die Angst des Tormanns beim Elfmeter*, 1971) and was based on Handke's 1970 novel of the same name. The lesson about his inability to function as an "American" director is one he would have to repeat during the painful process of making *Hammet* (1982) in the United States.

[11] Hutcheon, *A Poetics of Postmodernism*, p. 44.

[12] See Jerome Klinkowitz and James Knowlton, *Peter Handke and the Postmodern Transformation* (Columbia: University of Missouri Press, 1983). They also see him making a shift in the 1970s (p. 13).

[13] The two friends have of course collaborated frequently; first they worked on the short film Wenders made while still in film school, *3 American LPs* (1969). In 1971, Wenders filmed Handke's novel *Goalie's Anxiety*; Handke wrote the original version of the screenplay for *Wrong Move* in 1973. Wenders produced Handke's directorial debut, the film *The Left-Handed Woman* (1977); he wrote a script based on Handke's novel *Slow Homecoming* (*Langsame Heimkehr*, 1979) but was denied funding to make a film; and in 1982 he was able to direct a theater production of Handke's *Über die Dörfer* in Salzburg. And of course their latest collaboration is the film *Wings of Desire* (*Himmel über Berlin*, 1987).

row *Beyond Dreams* (*Wunschloses Unglück*) appeared. In these works narrative realism, autobiographically "authentic" experience, and Handke's own reflections about his project are blended.[14] Even in the 1960s, Handke had been fascinated with the immediacy of experience that traditional realism attempted to simulate; these conventional fabrications had been the target of attack for his experimental works. His movement after *The Goalie's Anxiety* toward realism was not a simple return to narrativity, in apparent rejection of his earlier experimental work. It reflected a consistent "longing for an unmediated world," which motivated his ambivalent shifting and combining of narrative and antinarrative strategies.[15]

Handke was not the only one to move toward realism during the early 1970s, and in the literary debate of those years his style of realism was often rejected as "apolitical" and "subjectivist."[16] In this debate, one very controversial topic was the relation of subjectivity to realism. The debate managed quickly to fall into the pattern of the old realism/formalism debate fought by the German Left in the 1930s, a debate revolving around Expressionism. A certain school of West German writers in the 1970s, led by Uwe Timm, followed the Lukács/socialist-realist line. Their novels, published by the Bertelsmann Company in a series known as the *AutorenEdition*, were attempts to clothe an objective political analysis of the status quo with the trappings of the traditional realistic novel, guiding the readers by means of identification with a protagonist through a plot that was to enlighten both the latter and the former (*without* any "formalist" distantiation).[17]

The other pole of the debate was the "subjectivism" of writers such as Handke, Nicolas Born, and Botho Strauss. The latter authors were accused of refusing to subordinate their writing to any political

---

[14] The connection to the realist tradition is underscored by the allusion in *Short Letter* to the nineteenth-century realist Gottfried Keller.

[15] Nägele, "Geschichten," pp. 245–46. Toward the late 1970s, the traces of mysticism noted in *A Moment of True Feeling* became more prominent in his work; with *Slow Homecoming* Handke seemed to make a definite break with his neorealist phase of the early 1970s, as he moved in the direction of a certain elevated, manneristic neo-Romanticism.

[16] This was the attack on Handke from the (orthodox) Left. See, for example, Roman Ritter, "Die 'Neue Innerlichkeit'—von innen und außen betrachtet. (Karin Struck, Peter Handke, Rolf Dieter Brinkmann)," *Kontext* 1 (1976), pp. 245–46. Mainstream critics, on the other hand, attacked Handke for the self-reflexivity that disturbed the "realistic" flow of the narrative—for example, see Marcel Reich-Ranicki, "Die Angst des Dichters beim Erzählen," in his collection of essays, *Entgegnung. Zur deutschen Literatur der siebziger Jahre* (Stuttgart: Deutsche Verlags-Anstalt, 1979), pp. 320–22.

[17] See Adelson's discussion of the "realism debate" in *Crisis of Subjectivity*, pp. 54–60.

analysis of reality—or any systemic analysis: as Handke defiantly said, "What biology maintains, what psychoanalysis maintains, how Marxism defines me, all of this leaves me cold."[18] Which approach was more "realistic" or appropriate to postindustrial reality? Which approach was more beholden to the bourgeois concept of the autonomous subject? Framing the questions this way turns the debate on its head: "But precisely in the 'subjective' texts there is radical deconstruction of that which subjectivity is supposed to establish: the self-conscious subject. On the other side, the 'realists' make sincere efforts to reconstruct the subject and the individual, and thus are probably being much more idealistic than they believe."[19]

What unites Botho Strauss's novel *Devotion* and the film *Wrong Move*, which resulted from the collaboration of Handke and Wenders, is this more radical subjectivity that works toward problematizing the more conventional forms of realism of the 1970s—not only the *AutorenEdition* novels but *Verständigunstexte* like *Lenz* as well. *Devotion* and *Wrong Move*, however, are by no means complete departures from realism; they employ both realism and modernist irony in a postmodern mixture of formal strategies and genres (and in the case of *Wrong Move*, media as well). Skepticism about language and form is combined with an ironic self-reflexivity about the efficacy of writing itself, in the case of *Devotion* almost a bitter parody of "New Subjectivity," and in *Wrong Move* beyond this to an undermining of the related ideology of direct visual immediacy.

POSTMODERN PESSIMISM? BOTHO STRAUSS'S *DEVOTION*

It's been a week and a half since he last went to work. He neither quit nor called in sick. Even though he could easily have applied for a medically attested sick leave. To have been ditched is, after all, a worse affliction than appendicitis.[20]

---

[18] Peter Handke, quoted in Rentschler, *West German Film*, p. 167; originally in "Die Tyrannei der Systeme," *Die Zeit*, 9 January 1976.

[19] Nägele, "Geschichten," pp. 242–43; he is talking here about Wolfgang Hildesheimer and Herbert Achternbusch, both more experimental than Handke, Strauss, or Born, who probably represent some sort of (contradictory) middle ground between the poles of the old debate between "formalism" and realism.

[20] Botho Strauss, *Devotion*, trans. Sophie Wilkins (New York: Farrar, Straus, and Giroux, 1979), p. 5. All further references to this work appear in the text. Orig. *Die Widmung. Eine Erzählung* (Munich: Hanser, 1977); the German version I occasionally cite is the 1980 edition published by Deutscher Taschenbuch Verlag (Munich).

Reading Botho Strauss's *Devotion* (*Die Widmung*, 1977), one very quickly notes an ironic tone all too obviously lacking in texts like *Lenz* and *Class Love*. The comparison of abandonment to appendicitis can certainly be seen as serious from the perspective of the protagonist, yet at the same time it is an obvious trivialization of his emotional distress to rank it among causes of employee absenteeism. The ambivalence and the hint of ironic distance here are all the more significant since this is the first reference in the text to the abandonment with which Richard Schroubek attempts to deal throughout the narrative. Thus the status of the "love story" is relativized from its very entrance into the narrative. In fact, Richard's romantic relationship with Hannah is something about which the reader learns very little. While Strauss's text is much more *innerlich*—more "inward"—than those by Schneider and Struck, certainly in terms of physical isolation (Richard hardly leaves his room) it has much less to do with a failed romance.[21]

The relationship of *Devotion* to the proclaimed "New Subjectivity" of the mid-1970s is a complex one, not least because of the fact that Botho Strauss's career can be seen as almost paradigmatic of the *Tendenzwende* on the part of leftist intellectuals. In 1967 (the year he became twenty-three) Strauss began writing for *Theater Heute*, where his reviews attacked the political complacency of the West German theater. His enthusiastic review of Peter Stein's revolutionary production of Goethe's *Tasso* in 1969 preceded his becoming, a year later, the *Dramaturg* for Stein's troupe in their new home at the theater called the Schaubühne am Halleschen Ufer in West Berlin.[22] At that time, the *Schaubühne* troupe was arguably one of the most politically radical in West Germany; over the course of the 1970s, it became more famous for its innovative stagings than for its politics, but it remained the most popular troupe among the leftist intellectuals of the Berlin "scene."[23] Strauss meanwhile began writing his own plays, the first of which, *Hypochondriacs*, Stein produced in

[21] As Adelson writes, Strauss's novel "is anything but a narrative account of a love relationship gone bad." *Crisis of Subjectivity*, p. 138.

[22] Peter von Becker, "Minima Moralia der achtziger Jahre. Notizen zu Botho Strauß' 'Paare Passanten' und 'Kalldewey, Farce,' " *Merkur* 36 (1982), pp. 152–53.

[23] West German actor Dieter Laser, who joined the *Schaubühne* troupe before the move to West Berlin, described to me the legal problems the troupe had in their determination to collect money for the Vietcong after their performances in the late 1960s. The troupe was formally run as a collective into the mid-1970s, but Laser said that although everyone from the custodians to Peter Stein had the right to speak, in actuality no one paid especially much attention until it was time for Stein—or a few of the other most influential members—to speak. (Private conversations, October 1984, W. Berlin.)

1972.[24] It is for his dramatic works, usually produced first at the Schaubühne, that Strauss is most famous in Germany, but his works of narrative fiction have also received considerable critical attention.[25] Together, his plays and fiction have caused certain critics to categorize the once radical theater critic as the exemplary representative of the literature of German *Innerlichkeit* ("Inwardness").[26]

Devotion, appearing first in 1977, bears on some levels a great deal of similarity to other novels of the mid-1970s, not least for its use of a motif that is typical of the era: an abandoned male partner and his fixation on the suffering caused by abandonment.[27] But, as indicated above, this motif is treated differently in *Devotion*. It serves to no small extent as a pretext for addressing other issues entirely: questions about language, communication, and especially writing. These issues are certainly to be found in other texts, as my discussion of *Lenz* and *Class Love* has indicated, but Strauss does not see language and writing as a means of salvation; for him, it has been said, language is not a means of healing but rather of exploration.[28]

Indeed, because of Strauss's questioning of writing, any similarity between his text and the former two could almost be said to exist only at the level of bitter parody. In *Lenz* there is a faith that language (in a collective atmosphere of open, therapeutic discussion)

[24] Strauss's works for the theater include *Hypochondriacs* (*Die Hypochonder*, 1971), *Familiar Faces, Mixed Feelings* (*Bekannte Gesichter, gemischte Gefühle*, 1974), *Three Acts of Recognition* (*Trilogie des Wiedersehens*, 1976), *Big and Little* (*Groß und klein*, 1978), *Kalldewey Farce* (1981), and *The Park* (*Der Park*, 1983).

[25] Strauss's prose works include *Schützenehre* (1975), *Marlene's Sister* (1975), *Devotion* (*Die Widmung*, 1977), *Rumor* (1980), *Paare Passanten* (1981), and *The Young Man* (*Der junge Mann*, 1984).

[26] Michael Schneider, "Botho Strauß, das bürgerliche Feuilleton und der Kultus des Verfalls. Zur Diagnose eines neuen Lebensgefühls," in *Den Kopf verkehrt aufgesetzt—oder die melancholische Linke. Aspekte des Kulturzerfalls in den siebziger Jahren*, (Darmstadt: Luchterhand, 1981), p. 235. Schneider is actually reporting Strauss's reputation, and he distances himself somewhat from this verdict. The trend has continued, with both Strauss and Handke continually attacked by German critics; in the 1980s, they were usually attacked as "neo-Romantics." Martin Lüdke has addressed this phenomenon in a discussion of their reception; examining the controversy, he persuasively places them in the category "postmodern." See Lüdke, "Der neudeutsche Literaturstreit. Beschreibung einer Misere," *Literaturmagazin*, no. 17 (1986), pp. 28–45. On Strauss in the 1980s, see also Adelson, *Crisis of Subjectivity*, pp. 68, 222–43; and Michael Radix, ed., *Strauß Lesen* (Munich: Hanser, 1987).

[27] Kreuzer, "Neue Subjektivität," p. 90. Volker Hage discusses *Devotion* from this perspective in "Das Ende der Beziehungen: Über den Zustand der Liebe in neueren Romanen und Erzählungen: Eine Bestandsaufnahme," in Zeller, *Aufbrüche: Abschiede*, pp. 14–25. Adelson cites a number of other articles that do so as well: see *Crisis of Subjectivity*, note 2, p. 175.

[28] See Beicken, " 'Neue Subjektivität,' " p. 175.

can effect a synthesis of the personal and political; in *Class Love* there is a similarly utopian faith that writing in particular is an individual process for overcoming social alienation and marginality. Such faith is ridiculed in *Devotion*: Richard's writings, representing all his hopes for reestablishing a dialogue with Hannah, are neglected by her, left unread on the seat of a taxi (p. 113).

The dialogue with this woman, his only social connection (p. 53), which Richard has struggled so hard to maintain through his writing, is thus made to seem hopeless in a darkly absurd manner. The consequences of this hopelessness extend (quite obviously in this most self-reflexive text) to the situation of the writer, which is depicted in a more pessimistic manner even than the situation of Wilhelm in the film *Wrong Move*. Richard, unlike Wilhelm, *does* manage to write, but his manuscript will never be read by the audience to whom he dedicates it.

The optimistic faith in authentic, direct communication in the texts by Struck and Schneider is postmodern in the sense of its rejection of the rationalistic abstraction typical of modernist art; the optimism of the texts is a legacy of the still-utopian postmodern attitudes dominant in the 1960s. In *Devotion* one encounters a postmodernism characterized by a profound pessimism with regard to the possibilities of writing.[29] Richard has little hope that writers will discover the meaning of "the innumerable leftovers" of Western civilization, remnants that it is their task (or curse?) nonetheless to recycle (pp. 66–67).[30] The text seems to ridicule the notion that literature can express subjective "immediacy."

Devotion depicts Richard's writing and the fate of his text and thus self-reflexively comments on its own status as a text, its own materiality as writing. Strauss's novel represents a much more complex attempt to deal with the relation of writing to subjectivity and society than we have yet encountered. Is that relation depicted in solely negative, pessimistic terms? The text attacks illusory harmonies and unities, and it exposes gaps—between the protagonist and his "story," between writing and communication, between self and

[29] According to Huyssen, disillusionment with "enlightenment" (exacerbated no doubt by the student movement's "idolatry of the concept") on the one hand, combined with a disillusionment in mass culture on the other, is what distinguishes the skeptical, pessimistic postmodernist tendency (which became dominant in the 1970s). "Mapping the Postmodern," pp. 24–25.

[30] See ibid., p. 25; see also John Barth on Jorge Luis Borges in "The Literature of Exhaustion": "The infinite library of one of his most popular stories is an image particularly relevant to the literature of exhaustion: 'The Library of Babel' houses every possible combination of alphabetical characters and spaces, and thus every possible book and statement" (p. 31).

self-representation, self and other, memory and the present. But is this merely another type of "totalizing" discourse, a total negation fetishizing fragmentation and meaninglessness rather than whole-ness and meaning? Is Richard's hope for dialogue depicted only to ridicule the very idea of communication? Or is a "dialogue" possi-ble across the gaps that are revealed—between self and other, indi-vidual and society, text and history? For the text does describe writ-ing as a "diachronic longing" (p. 64). Is this longing for a dialogue with history doomed?[31]

Broken Dialogues

Anyway, what good is noticing things in this random way, always mak-ing this quick grab for meaning, all this running busily in every direc-tion at once, what for? Whatever is truly worth seeing is sure to turn up only as a fragment of something deeply, powerfully archetypal, some-thing as hard for us to comprehend and retain as the pigeon on the gir-affe's head is for the retarded boy. (p. 9)

The above is an excerpt from a passage reported by the third-per-son narrator; in it Richard reflects on having observed a mentally disabled child with his mother at the zoo. The child he has observed had in turn been observing a giraffe, upon whose head a pigeon was sitting. The child had tried to articulate this experience and com-municate it to his mother, but all he could produce was the word "giraffe." Upon hearing this, his mother had not bothered to look up from her knitting but had simply replied, "Yes, Herbert, that is a giraffe. The giraffe is the tallest animal in the world" (p. 8).[32]

This somewhat bizarre yet compelling anecdote is typical of Strauss's novel, which has a fairly minimal plot but is strewn with many such anecdotal digressions, fragmentary narratives concern-

---

[31] See Adelson's insightful discussion of "diachronic longing" in *Crisis of Subjec-tivity*: for example, p. 68, as well as the entire chapter on *Die Widmung* (*Devotion*), pp. 138–80, esp. pp. 159–74.

[32] Gerhard vom Hofe and Peter Pfaff interpret the *Taube* (pigeon or dove) on the giraffe's head as a reference to the Biblical image of the Holy Ghost as a dove: *Das Elend des Polyphem: Zum Thema der Subjektivität bei Thomas Bernhard, Peter Handke, Wolfgang Koeppen und Botho Strauß* (Königstein/Ts.: Athenäum, 1980), p. 110. This reading can be elaborated further: the association between the child's strug-gle with language and a symbol of the Holy Ghost can also be connected to the men-tion later in the text of a "topsy-turvy Pentecost" (*Devotion*, p. 79), where an anti-Pentecostal "slime" has descended upon the tongue, instead of the Holy Ghost's gift of the universal language understood by all. This image comes in turn within a page of the discussion of Dante's "accidioso," who, after having torn out his tongue, gur-gles in "bloody slime" (p. 78).

ing people with whom Richard usually has little or no connection.[33] Like the others, this one is also humorous in the style of "black comedy," depicting human attempts to perceive and articulate the specificity of external reality as absurdly futile. This is indeed the interpretation Richard provides of the episode with the child and the giraffe; what is perceived visually as unique in its particularity is only part of an even greater ("archetypal") generality, one we have as little chance of understanding and articulating as the disabled child has with regard to the pigeon and the giraffe. Sensual perception, so desired by once-dogmatic leftists as an antidote to the tyranny of abstraction and generalization, captures nothing meaningful in and of itself. It grasps only fragments of underlying "archetypes" that, in turn, are beyond our comprehension anyway. Two contradictory longings are both depicted as futile here: the longing for the truly unique, the escape from the general, the typical, via openness to sensual experience; and the longing for some kind of understanding of the whole.

Richard's conclusion is that observation of external, empirical reality is useless. The trip to the zoo is virtually the last time he leaves his apartment until he speaks to Hannah on the telephone (p. 104). After the incident at the zoo, he remains in his room and begins writing the text he dedicates to her, more or less equivalent to the second section of *Devotion*, "For H." (pp. 13–99). In a chronological sense, this section represents the period of isolation for Richard that begins with the day at the zoo and ends with his brief telephone conversation with Hannah.

His disinterest in the outside world and his resignation about the possibility of finding any utopian wholeness, any meaning behind the countless fragments he perceives, can be read as symptomatic of postmodern despair. In the rubble heap of the relics of a civilization, all sense of history is lost, and the present loses its contours as surely as do past eras; in the vacuum of *post-histoire*, the era "after" history, all meaningful relationships between present and past, between fragments and wholes, have been erased. "Here it is today

---

[33] Similar digressions occur on pp. 3–4, 26–27, 50, 85–86, 93–94, and 119–20; all of them are based on events overheard, read in the newspaper, or viewed from a safe distance (whether on television or not). Thus, in addition to having the character of anecdotes that intrude upon the minimal plot of the "main narrative," they are also based on a voyeuristic interest on Richard's part for the world outside with which he no longer interacts. Even the episodes with the honey and the toilet (pp. 55–58) intrude as distractions from writing, and they are experienced voyeuristically not merely by the reader, but also by Richard himself, who refers to the toilet episode as a "silent film" (p. 58).

again. Which part of which whole?" (p. 24). Such passages undoubtedly give the book the atmosphere Michael Schneider characterized
as infected by the gentle "pestilence" of melancholy.[34] Another
critic called it "the toxic, lukewarm air of melancholy," wafting
from the "gutter of modernity."[35]

But even this atmosphere of despair is undermined by the pervasive irony of Strauss's text, irony that is at least as strong in the depiction of Richard as in the depiction of the disabled child. Richard's interpretation of the child's dilemma ought not to be taken at
face value. Why, after all, should the reader be any less condescend-
ing in evaluating Richard than Richard is observing the child who
sees the giraffe? This little parable on the limitations of the human
perspective vis-à-vis some larger reality (or "archetype") is itself
structured by perspectives within perspectives that can only reflect
upon the mediation of what is being reported. Attention is drawn
not only to the narrator's reporting of what Richard interprets to be
the child's experience but also to the construction of the narrative
structure as a whole by the author.

It is furthermore debatable whether the child's dilemma is his inability to "comprehend and retain" the pigeon on the giraffe's head;
rather the dilemma seems to be his inability to communicate to his
mother the wonder he sees. He seems to recognize well enough the
strange new element on the giraffe's head, but he lacks the vocabulary to articulate this—and a rhetorical strategy to get the attention
of his somewhat insensitive mother. It is an example of a failed dialogue, one that is echoed throughout the text: in the burlesque encounter between Fritz "the school porter" and Richard (pp. 35–48);
in Richard's account of his conversations with his cleaning woman,
Frau N. (pp. 51–52); in the imaginary "Interrogation" apparently
conducted by psychiatrists (pp. 72–75);[36] but most notably of course
in Richard's attempt to reestablish a dialogue with Hannah. Thus it
is all the more ironic that Richard misreads the child's dilemma, or
rather, that he appropriates it to make his point about the limitations
of human perception. His point is perhaps better illustrated by his
own limitations than the child's.

Richard, in any case, retreats to a realm where the sensory intrusions of the exterior world are kept to a minimum: "All day long
with the curtains closed so tight, not a ray of sunlight comes

[34] M. Schneider, *Den Kopf verkehrt aufgesetzt*, p. 239.

[35] Hubert Winkels, "Selbstheilung des Fragments. Zur Krise des Sinns bei Botho
Strauß und Peter Handke," *Sprache im technischen Zeitalter* 85 (1983), pp. 90–91.

[36] During the "Interrogation" someone—presumably Richard—is questioned about
an incident in his childhood; he can recall almost nothing.

through" (p. 18). His attempt to ignore what is "truly worth seeing," however, is an attempt not to cut himself off from the world but rather to reestablish his connection to Hannah—his only social connection—on a level deeper than the visual: through writing. For Richard, then, isolation is not solipsistic but is rather his last chance for integration. The dialogue possible in the world of Berlin outside his apartment—the "verbal free-for-all in which most of the things said reduce themselves to meaninglessness" (p. 4)—does not provide any real connection, an empty babble in which nothing is communicated except the fact of participation in a comforting social ritual.

Thus, speech, as "yakking," as "superabundance" (p. 5), is described in a manner similar to the text's description of television. From television Richard gets a sense of security, being "one of twenty million brainwashed viewers sitting in the same radiation cage, the same isolation, in passive attendance on the same events" (p. 83). This kind of social community, which is a kind of *collective* solipsism, a delirium that has in addition completely depoliticized him, is rejected in favor of writing, the fixed "tracing" of language; it is writing that can connect him "even from his most remote private outpost" in active participation in the collective, historical reality of the German language, and therefore leave him "with the sense of having gone out to share what he'd been writing in conversation with friends" (pp. 83–84). Through writing, then, the feeling of an authentic dialogue with others, even with history, can be reestablished.

Richard, therefore, even in the depths of his melancholy, is not totally resigned with regard to communication but actually retains some of the utopian faith in writing we have noted in Karin Struck. Here again, however, the structure of this ironic narrative, and its very ironic depiction of Richard, tend to ridicule this faith; Richard's writing may give him the *feeling* of creating a dialogue, but certainly the reality of his dialogue is disappointing for him: his writing is never read by the one to whom it is dedicated. How seriously, though, can the reader take Hannah as the goal of Richard's writing? Writing itself is thematized on so many levels in *Devotion* that it demands closer attention before determining the consequences—or even the exact targets—of the text's irony.

The Thematization of Writing

I'm ashamed to tell of it. I'm ashamed of my handwriting. It exposes me in all my spiritual nakedness. My handwriting shows me more naked than I am with all my clothes off. No leg, no breath, no clothes, no sound. . . . Instead, a man's whole being, shriveled and misshapen, like his scribble-scrabble. His lines are all that's left of him, as well as his self-propagation. The uneven tracings of his pencil on paper, so minimal that a blind man's fingertips would hardly detect them, become the final measure of the whole fellow. (pp. 15–16)

This description of writing is found on the first page of the middle section of *Devotion*, "For H.," which is by far the longest of the three subdivisions of the text. The conception of writing in this passage as both a physical, sensual activity (writing by hand) and a (barely) physical trace revealing the "naked" interior truth and wholeness of the writing subject bears some resemblance to that found in *Class Love*. It is this idea of writing, however, that the text elsewhere—and in general—seems to parody or reject. Indeed, the idea here that the essence of the "whole fellow" is "shriveled and misshapen" in the scrawl of his or her handwriting is a comical one; in addition, it defines writing as a complex (and distorting) process of mediation, as opposed to the idealistic notion of writing as the transparent essence of the subject.

The formulation of writing as a physical, almost biological trace of the living—or once living—subject has already been encountered in the text; in fact, it is mentioned a few pages earlier. The first word Richard ever wrote was his own name, the reader learns; his parents then placed it in the folder with his first tooth, fingernails, pieces of hair on his head: "They placed his script among the lifeless relics of his body that they collected for him" (p. 12). This relation of writing to the body—and to death—is what has always bound Richard to literature.[37]

The text contains other biological images that are associated with writing. Richard writes that Fritz is swollen not so much with fatty tissue "as the result of a pathological constipation of the expressive faculty" (p. 87). In the original German—*Ausdrucksverstopfung*, literally "expressive constipation"—the implication is even more clear that writing is considered to be a kind of defecation.[38] This in

---

[37] This motif of death and resurrection becomes anchored in the specific historical context of postwar Germany as well: "Years later there came the time of the stragglers returning home from Russian captivity, the religion of the Missing Men, the powerfully moving family reunions in West German railway stations, as he experienced them in the weekly newsreels of his first visits to the movies—Sauerbrot resurrections, but real" (p. 12). The Sauerbrot allusion is to the "Madame Sauerbrot" illustrations by Wilhelm Busch that his father showed him when he was a child (pp. 11–12).

[38] Writing is also connected with constipation on p. 20: "hence my writing (which I need in any case, so that at least something emerges into the open and I don't just

turn puts an interesting light on the *Ausdrucksnot*, the "need to express oneself," mentioned earlier in the text.[39] Writing is defined as a necessary, indeed hygienic, process of discarding "indigestible" emotional experience.

Less sarcastic and more complex is the connection of writing with skin: "Writing brings on more writing, that much he knew for sure. The skin keeps growing, but it feels to him as though the skin is being pulled over his ears" (pp. 45–46). Here the process of writing is compared to skin growing or getting thicker, presumably over a wound—the healing process—and at the same time to *being* skinned—getting more sensitive, feeling even more pain. The idea here is of skin as a membrane where the internal meets the external world, and Richard is not sure whether writing increases the insulation provided by this membrane or whether it removes it.[40]

The scars on this membrane are also significant in this regard. Later in the text, as Richard begins to write down sentences "whose source isn't recollection at all," he reports—in the third person—the story of a man whose skin is afflicted with all sorts of disfiguring eruptions. The man's lover is disgusted by his constant "onanistic" attention to his skin with creams and ointments (she thinks of him as "a monster" of self-fingering), but she also is concerned and puzzled about the meaning of his ailment, of all his sores: "How on earth am I to understand all those ugly signals?" (pp. 88–90). She cannot decipher these many ugly signals or signs—*Zeichen*—that have been the object of such self-obsessed concern by the man.[41]

These unintelligible signs are obviously an open allusion to Richard's writing; the part played by the woman in this episode represents Richard's fears that Hannah will not be able to make anything of what he has written for her—indeed, that his writing has no relation to anything except that which his wounds have to his own body. It is a dialogue with himself that no one else can understand, one that remains, as the woman puts it, in "animal-like silence" (p. 90), its communication to others impossible. His skin, and the paper on which he writes, bear scars that reflect internal wounds, an interior reality undecipherable to those outside it.

This is a nightmarish version of the naive view of writing as the transparent expression of subjectivity: writing here "expresses" in-

---

swallow myself up entirely) gets to be the eruptive core of everything that's otherwise constipated, partitioned, tied up in knots."

[39] Strauss, *Die Widmung*, pp. 7, 85.

[40] Martin Roda Becher discusses Strauss's "vital interest in the skin" in his article "Poesie der Unglücksfälle," *Merkur* 32 (1978), p. 625.

[41] Strauss, *Die Widmung*, p. 87.

ternal reality, but it is hardly transparent. It is opaque, communicating nothing but ugly and undecipherable signs, meaningless scars of internal processes. The connection of writing to biological processes and traces (scars, eruptions, excretions) in *Devotion* depicts it nihilistically as an activity leading only to solipsism. But is this the only way writing is depicted? Even within the "skin" symbolism, Richard is not sure whether writing will increase insulation from the world or strip it away—a painful and perhaps deadly process, "for skin conditions are seldom curable" (p. 89).

The depictions of writing as the physical "expression" of the internal subject must be compared to the motif of "copying" in *Devotion*. Copying seems related to the naive view of writing that Strauss seems to be parodying. It is based on a sort of *Widerspiegelung* (the "reflection" of objective reality proclaimed by famous theories of realism), but it is a reflection turned inward: "authentic" writing should faithfully mirror subjective reality. These faithful reflections are in a sense "copies" of the subject who produces them.

The first instance of the copying motif in *Devotion* deals explicitly with the copying of handwriting. Richard tells the story of the writer Z., who, after being abandoned by his wife of many years, stopped his own writing and began to copy his wife's letters, becoming ever more perfect in his imitation of her handwriting until the original letters were lost amidst innumerable perfect copies (p. 16). Such fetishization of his wife's letters is obviously based on the neurotic attempt to produce a substitute for her, but copying her letters only makes these last "authentic" traces vanish as she has done; the process only increases the gap between the written and the writer, making her absence more clear. Z.'s folly is thus closely related to the mistaken idea that writing can provide a copy of the writing subject.

The futility of copying is underscored shortly thereafter in the text, when Richard relates the anecdote about the prisoner who committed suicide after giving up his beloved hobby, painting. Before imprisonment, he had painted landscapes ("from nature"); in prison he turned to the painting of historical costumes and uniforms from models in books. In so doing he eventually reached "that deadly limit to imitation": "He'd never meant to be a copyist but at last understood, in despair, that, in giving his utmost, all he could achieve was an utmost likeness" (pp. 22–23). Representation is here once again depicted as the neurotic attempt to re-create what is absent, an attempt that produces only ever more frustrating demonstrations of absence.

This reading has obvious relevance, then, to the end of the novel, when Richard watches an elderly singer on television fail quite miserably at his attempt to "lip-synch" one of his once-popular songs (pp. 119–20). This passage has been read as a completely negative, resigned anecdote about the end of all art.[42] But it is also the third example of copying, once again portraying the absurdity of art that attempts to efface its own historical mediation in the attempt to re-create (or simulate) "reality" as though its object were present in the here and now. This anecdote is actually the most humorous of the three anecdotes dealing with copying. An unwanted gap between present and past is captured on television, of all media the one depicted in the text as the most complicit with conventional represen-tation and the effacement of history. It is not often that elements so "out of synch" are allowed to disturb the harmonious functioning of television's "reality": "The camera dared to move in for a close-up just once, but instantly beat a retreat. For while memory still sang in expansive tones, the old man's mouth suddenly shriveled and twitched, mumbling a curse at having forgotten the text" (p. 120).[43]

"Copying" is depicted here as the model for a simplistic type of representational art. The rejection of such art, and a preference for exposing the gaps between the artistic subject, the art produced, and external, historical "reality," is evident in *Devotion* on many levels. The text's self-reflexivity is not limited to the mere depiction of writing; it calls attention throughout to its own construction, to the gaps between its (rather noneventful) "story," its "protagonist," and its discursive activity. I have alluded to this self-reflexivity above, but it is useful at this point to examine aspects of it more systemat-ically.

Devotion, depicting as it does a man who writes a text "devoted" to a beloved reader, makes obvious reference to its own discursive nature, its own dependence on being read, its own nature as some-thing not self-sufficient or closed in upon itself. The fate of Rich-ard's text in the narrative invites speculation as to the fate of the encompassing text, and of writing in general. Beyond these impli-cations of the plot, however, there are two major factors that prob-lematize the relation of Richard's text to the narrative, as well as Richard's unity as the fictional "subject" of the narrative. The first is the framing of Richard's text, "For H.," between two sections of third-person narration explaining what happens before and after the writing of his text; the second factor is the interplay of first- and third-person narration within his "text" itself. These strategies un-dermine the self-sufficiency of Richard's text and expose and pene-

---

[42] vom Hofe and Pfaff, *Das Elend*, p. 128.

[43] As Adelson writes, "It is not by any means tragic that the singer cannot synchro-nize his own text. . . . What is crucial in the image of this 'Wunschkonzert' is pre-cisely the disjuncture between the present and the past." *Crisis of Subjectivity*, p. 154.

trate the boundaries between narrated and narrator, between fiction
and its construction.

"Now the writing begins" (p. 15): thus begins the central portion
of *Devotion*, and beyond the obvious self-reflexivity of such a sentence is its underscoring of the division in the text marked by the
previous page, containing only the words "For H." It draws attention to the artificiality of the division; it tells the reader that the writing has not begun until this point some eleven pages into the text,
and it calls into question the very effect it wants to achieve: the
identification of the *writing* that begins here with what *Richard*
writes. Indeed, the very formulation "Now the writing begins"
throws Richard's status both as author and as "autonomous subject"
into question. This is made even more explicit a few pages later,
when Richard writes, "after overthrowing the subject, life has taken
upon itself the task of finishing his story" (p. 18).

But more radical in calling into question Richard's status as "narrator" of his writing is the fact that "his" first-person narration is
constantly replaced by third-person narration throughout "his" text.
"For H." has eleven sections, and the first, second, sixth, eighth, and
ninth are narrated by Richard's "I," whereas the third, fourth, fifth,
seventh, and tenth are in third-person narration; the eleventh is primarily a return to first-person narration, with some use of third-person narration, constructed, seemingly, by the first-person narrator.
These transitions are not as neatly marked as this breakdown implies; as in the first section, where the first grammatical subject is
"the writing," and only thereafter does one see *I*, neither subject
pronoun necessarily appears at the beginning of each section; in the
sixth section, for example, the narrative *I* does not appear for over a
page, effacing itself in narration about Frau N (pp. 49–50). Adelson
calls the complex interplay of voices here "narrative schizophrenia"
(a very postmodern phenomenon).[44] The confusion is increased by
a passage that focuses on the issue of narration itself: "Now his face
buried in his outspread hands. . . . In whose hands? Who is suddenly holding his head like a melon cut open? Does it hurt or is it a
kind of shelter, to feel oneself being described by a stranger, a faithful biographer of the empty hours, by someone who retains his perspective until the last moment?" (p. 34).

This passage opens the third section, and its use of *his* marks the
first use of the third-person narrative perspective since the opening
frame of the novel; the paragraph that follows begins "Richard put

[44] Ibid., p. 159. Cf. Owens and Jameson: both mention schizophrenia in defining
postmodern art and culture; Jameson indeed calls it the "second basic feature of postmodernism" in his definition. Owens, "The Discourse of Others," p. 57, and Jameson,
"Postmodernism and Consumer Society," p. 118.

his notes of the preceding days in order." The shift of voice in the passage could be ascribed to Richard's own choice as the supposed narrator of "For H." The passage would thus reveal his rationale for switching narrative voice in order to experiment with the feeling of being described by someone who had a "perspective," a view (or better *overview*: *Überblick*).[45] It would also correspond to similar reflections in the previous section: "Exploration of the subjective personality has naturally always been a job for someone else" (p. 32). In order to establish distance, to pretend to assume the comforting position of omniscience with regard to his life, Richard, according to this interpretation, becomes an "other" to examine his own subjectivity.

Nonetheless, this explanation of the shift in voice, which would seemingly anchor the idiosyncratic use of narrative voices in the logic of the narrative, is not satisfactory. For one thing, one cannot help but hear the author behind the passage, reflecting on his own shifting of narrative voice, since it is he, and not the fictional Richard, who is responsible for it. And attributing it to Richard himself does not undo the disorientation that the constant shifting causes.

Furthermore, the sections narrated in third-person relate events that appear to be distractions for Richard, keeping him from writing. They are in fact intrusions of a more conventional narrativity into the text, intrusions that are alien to what Richard writes about, since his writing consists of rambling essayistic reflections and anecdotes based in part on observations of others. "Much digression in my writings" (p. 70), he writes. The first-person narration does not provide the kind of information about Richard that the reader gets, for example, in the episode with Fritz (pp. 35–48), or the episode in which his misadventures with the honey and the toilet are recounted (pp. 57–59). These incidents are presented to the reader by an omniscient narrator with the illusion of immediacy typical of conventional realist narrative, not the distanced exploration of subjectivity Richard wants to conduct.

The shifts in narrative voice draw attention to the complexity of the game of self-reflexivity Strauss has constructed, in which the substance of the fictional protagonist's "story" is the process of writing. The shifting helps to undermine all simple identification between "Richard's text" and Richard as a fictional character, between the section "For H." and what Richard writes, between the text of *Devotion* as a whole and the fiction it constructs, and between Strauss and *his* text. For the discourse here undermines the "integrity" of the elements on both sides of these supposed dichotomies.

[45] Strauss, *Die Widmung*, p. 35.

This is further amplified by the final section, "Berlin without End" (pp. 102–20), which completes the opening "frame" around "For H." The completed frame, of course, could be seen to function as a simple distantiation technique relativizing "Richard's perspective" by revealing what "happened" to his manuscript. But the very opposition between "Richard's perspective" and the "frame" is also undermined, since, as I have demonstrated, "For H." does not simply present the perspective of the protagonist. The doubt cast on narrative perspective in that section cannot fail to affect the return to consistent third-person narration in the final section, where it seems that an unhindered overview—*Überblick*—of Richard's situation is again provided. For this is precisely the kind of narration that has been described so ironically earlier, an omniscience for which Richard's subjectivity is an object known "like a melon cut open" (p. 34).[46]

Thus the final frame is itself relativized. And its third-person narration is also fragmented, if only briefly: "But she isn't waiting for me at all! For heaven's sake, I mustn't let her go! He ran after her" (p. 113). It also contains yet another attempt by Richard at writing (p. 119), which further breaks the identification of his writing with the previous section of the text. It is a very brief attempt: he writes "I haven't quite reached my goal yet," a somewhat humorous remark in light of having just found his unread and abandoned manuscript. Then he erases what he has written. This is followed by the anecdote about the elderly singer on television, which ends the novel.

This ironic ending is by no means a closure. The book does not end conclusively with Richard giving up writing, as the logic of the narrative might seem to demand; it ends instead with another anecdotal distraction, one that shows the laughable consequences of the identification of an artist with a text.

Solipsism versus History

"I must speak to you."
   He heard her voice and humbly nodded his head several
times, but forgot to reply.
   "Do you hear me?" (p. 104)

---

[46] Adelson makes the connection between this sort of narrative overview and the historical situation of West Germany in the 1970s: "The narrative *Überblick* is analogous to psychoanalytical and leftist political categories that deny the human subject any status as a living being whose experience extends beyond the realm of existing categories" (*Crisis of Subjectivity*, p. 160).

Richard has spent so much energy devoting himself to the text meant to fill the "dangerous interruption" in his dialogue with Hannah (p. 28) that, when she finally telephones him, and he once again hears Hannah's voice, he *forgets to reply*. This moment of failed communication encapsulates all those narrative events to come in the last section of the book that highlight the nonexistence of dialogue between Hannah and Richard.[47]

The relevance of the telephone to the concept of dialogue is echoed in earlier passages of the text: his chosen isolation from the world includes allowing his phone service to be shut off (p. 46). Hannah then undoes this by paying his bill in order to call him (p. 47), but her call is received by Richard's rival Fritz, since Richard, ironically enough, has locked himself in Hannah's room. He has done so in order to cut off the unwanted dialogue with Fritz, and as a result he misses Hannah's call. Still, Richard rejoices: "The connection has been restored . . . !" (p. 48). From then on he awaits another call from her. Later, as the heat wave in Berlin continues, apartment windows are left open, and Richard hears telephones "ringing at night from very far away" (p. 86); there is a hint of longing in this mention of open windows and hot nights as well as a kind of (auditory) sexual voyeurism, since the telephone has been equated with his "connection" to Hannah.

That Richard's concept of dialogue is intimately related to sexuality is clear: "I've never felt so free or so sure of myself as in the kind of dialogue prompted by physical desire" (p. 21). This may be a key to his dilemma, in that he transfers the concept of sexual dialogue to writing; writing *as* sexuality can be only a substitute for the object of desire, a fetish. Fetishes are strategies for avoiding the threat of vulnerability associated with interpersonal sexuality, and Richard devotes himself to his fetishistic text as though the trauma of separation could be resolved through this self-absorbed activity alone, without any interaction with anyone else. In denying the possibility of dialogue with the similarly abandoned Fritz (" 'are we going to have a conversation or not?' . . . . 'No!' Richard shouted" (p. 44)—he cuts off his chance to receive Hannah's call (p. 46).

Richard certainly seems to be aware of the intersubjective nature of the dialogue for which he longs: "We depend upon being heard" (p. 76); nor is only being heard enough, as he explains in his rejection of what a psychoanalyst could offer: "I listen in vain for an answer out of the depths of his ear" (p. 77). He also maintains that total

---

[47] These events include his meeting with her on the street in front of the bar, when he realizes she is not waiting for him, and when, actually face to face with her, he barely recognizes her (p. 113). Most significant, of course, is his realization that she left the manuscript in the very taxi they were taking when he gave it to her (p. 119).

withdrawal from communication with others makes the very idea of "privacy" meaningless. He makes this clear—in an obvious allusion to the debates in West Germany about "New Subjectivity"—when he discusses Dante's *accidioso*, who pulls out his tongue: "Well, they'll say that he has withdrawn into a 'private world,' when in fact he has denied himself precisely this sanctuary, has made uninhabitable the ultimate shelter of his most private self, his body" (p. 78).

But in spite of this insight into the social—and linguistic—nature of subjectivity, he continues to search for the answer to his failed dialogue with Hannah within himself: "I myself am the whole reason and I cannot comprehend it"; the "almost theological torment" provided by this introspection is ultimately solipsistic, granting Hannah no role in the breakup of the dialogue (pp. 92–93). His writing, which he identifies with this search, is thus meant to insulate him from the threat of her ability to affect him in ways beyond his control and calculation. It is no surprise, then, that when he is actually confronted by her voice, he "forgets" to respond; nor is it a surprise that his writing cannot speak to her.

The consequences of her rejection of his text must in turn be deadly as long as he identifies it not merely with his own subjectivity but as the intersubjective ground that makes his subjectivity possible. The text as fetish replaces the Other necessary for the dialogue in which subjectivity originates. The exposure of the text's impotent solipsism is deeply traumatic but also potentially liberating.

Richard has already had insights about the kind of truly intersubjective dialogue he seeks. One particular passage merits attention, because of its relation of sexuality to intersubjectivity: Richard's discussion of the erotic *Blick*. Wilkins translates this as "the erotic eye" (p. 54), but it can also be translated as an erotic *gaze*.[48] Richard compares the situation of his housecleaner, Frau N., a "working woman turned middle class" (p. 50), to his own sheltered existence (p. 52). By no means does he idealize her as a compensatory "Other" for his own inadequacies (as Schneider's Lenz had done with his beloved L.); instead he tries to determine how two such persons of diverse backgrounds and socialization could end up similarly crippled with regard to the natural capacity to exert any erotic attraction (p. 52). He concludes that she has lost this capacity through functionalization of her body in the struggle to maintain the economic status she has fought so hard to achieve; she is directed exclusively to this external goal. Her body has thus become external also, merely another tool for the achievement of her goal. How much more so then are

---

[48] Strauss, *Die Widmung*, p. 54.

other people "external" to her, having meaning only in terms of how they help or hinder her struggle? She has no energy left to be open to them in any less instrumental way: "complete loss of erotic capacity and any interest in strangers" (p. 54).

Richard, on the other hand, has not turned his body into a tool. He is barely aware of his body, "a worn costume, shabby, quite unused, unexercised." Rather than controlling his body, he is instead, in his ignorance of it, controlled by it: "dominance of physical sensitivity, together with its flow of delusions" (p. 53). Having achieved no awareness or knowledge of his body is as dangerous to the erotic capacity as having instrumentalized it: instead of making his body into its external puppet, his sense of self is too helpless in the face of physical sensations, too isolated within the body. His longing for the Other thus implodes inward into a vacuum that he claims has destroyed his capacity to exert erotic attraction outwardly. He defines this internal vacuum (very much like his self-imposed isolation in the apartment) as consisting of longing, loss of the visual connection to the external world ("empty eyes"), silence, "having nowhere to go," and writing (p. 54).[49]

The erotic gaze, on the other hand, is a concept that implies a kind of perception directed outward, not at objects upon whose surface an insecure self can be mirrored, nor at objects to be scrutinized for their instrumentality, but at "the interesting new person" (p. 54). The interest in this person is inspired neither by his or her "wholeness," nor by an ego's misrecognition while searching for its ideal image, nor by any one particular aspect that might be useful in terms of psychic, or any other, economy. It is rather the discovery of "a thousand subtle inconsistencies" that is the goal of the erotic gaze:

> One doesn't fall in love with a whole person. It is only when the other starts falling apart that one knows one's attentions have paid off, he is now ready to let himself be loved. Whatever it is that makes all the difference is something ephemeral, it isn't his face, not something to be idolized, not the beauty of some part of his body; it isn't something that can be relished, it can only be caught in passing. (p. 54)

Gratification has less to do with this type of love than does the subtlety of perception through which something as insignificant as a short turn of phrase or a hand gesture becomes recognized as something at once familiar and unknown: "Something familiar ap-

---

[49] Cf. the statement in Wenders's film *Alice in the Cities* (1973): "The ability to see and hear fade away when one has lost one's sense of self." Quoted in Peter Buchka, *Augen kann man nicht kaufen: Wim Wenders und seine Filme* (Munich: Hanser, 1983), p. 81.

pears suddenly, prematurely, in the stranger's looks." This is not narcissistic misrecognition in the Other, although there is certainly something mystical in this simultaneous recognition of similarity and difference.

The despair in Strauss's works has been interpreted as a bitter longing for "erotic transcendence," and thus Richard's inability to achieve such transcendence has been seen as a metaphor for the impossibility of art, most clearly illustrated in the final anecdote about the elderly singer on television.[50] But the failure of the singer is rather a parable about the type of fetishistic "copying" that has plagued Richard's writing, not necessarily a parable about all art. At the end of the novel, there is the hope at least that he will some day attempt interaction with more than a petrified version of himself.

Ultimately, of course, it is not important what happens to the fictional character Richard. The passage on the erotic gaze is indeed as much a discussion of "art" as it is of Richard's vision of love, but it does not glorify (or mourn the futility of) the self-contained text Richard produces. I would argue rather that it speaks of a discourse that is not centered on ego gratification, not fixated on an "object" to be worshiped (which ennobles the "subject"). It is centered on a *relationship* between Self and Other. It is a relationship that does not deny difference and is open to "a thousand subtle inconsistencies."

This is the dialogue for which the text longs, a dialogue with that beyond itself. This includes an awareness of the *impossibility* of any absolute totality within itself and a rejection of any hope for absolute synthesis with the Other outside. Instead there is the hope of dialogue between the two sides of various relations that cannot be equated with any system of absolute dichotomies: male/female, subjectivity/objectivity, literature/reality, present/past. Contradictions are explored not with their elimination through some manipulations of logic in mind, not with closure as a goal; rather there is an "erotic" openness to contradiction.

Thus there is the longing for a dialogue between the dehistoricized present and the past. The concept of a dialogue with history is opposed to history's effacement in the present via the illusion of narrative realism, the perfection of which is associated in the text with theater and film: "Appearance fleshed out, faces, bodies, voices, *actors*—who think that they, with their heads rinsed in television, their car-driving legs, can show us how Caesar walked!" (p.

[50] See vom Hofe and Pfaff, *Das Elend*, pp. 113, 124–29.

65).[51] *Devotion* criticizes the easy effacement of the differences between the present and the past as in the costume drama, in which a costume change makes possible the "depiction" of any historical era; the novel implies that open acknowledgment of difference is necessary.

Reading the literature of past eras is a method portrayed as suitable for such an exploration of historical difference, but the valorization of literature here should not be read merely as an example of art's melancholy obsession with its own past.[52] Literature is depicted as facilitating a kind of dialogue between the present and the past, and not one that remains merely within *literary* history, as the discussion of the historicity of the concepts "honor" and "shame" indicates (pp. 64–67). Literature is depicted here as a medium of interaction between two different cultures, the culture in which it originated and the culture in which it is read.

What does *Devotion* itself tell the reader about the culture in which it originated? There is more of a dialogue in the text with postwar German society than it would seem. The intrusions of the historical reality of West Germany, and Berlin especially, into Richard's life seem primarily annoyances that demonstrate his isolation and basic disinterest in such issues. On the level of the narrative, this is accurate; interest in the political is in Richard's view primarily a façade behind which other, more self-interested motives operate, as the reader is shown in the first few pages of the text. Richard is sure that the manicurist speaks so vehemently about the Israeli action at Entebbe in order to please her customer (pp. 3–4); she is merely participating in a kind of conversation that exists "wherever consumers congregate," a "verbal free-for-all" that resounds "as in a vast overarching dome, in German over Germany" (p. 4).

Other than this function as a topic for the functional conversations that lubricate the exchange of services within West German consumer society, political discourse has another dimension in ventilating psycho-sexual drives, as Richard learned when he reached "the age of enlightenment." Thereafter he saw through his father's behavior in political discussions and understood the adolescent rage that had accompanied his own politicization; now this analytical game of discovering "What's behind all this?" is the only thing that holds his interest when he listens to political discussions (p. 7).

---

[51] Strauss, of course, has written extensively for the theater. As to film, the view that it eliminates historical difference is justified only to the extent that it has been used as one of the primary media for the most depoliticized, ahistorical narrative realism.

[52] Cf. vom Hofe and Pfaff, *Das Elend*, p. 127.

Later in the text he writes that he has been "depoliticized . . . to the core" (p. 83).

Even here, this depoliticization is obviously something of which Richard is aware, and of which he to a certain extent complains. But there is of course more to the text than the awareness of the fictional protagonist. One finds that Richard and his situation are actually associated with the political reality of Germany and Berlin in quite an interesting fashion. His complaint about West Berlin in the second paragraph of the text, "Lacking everywhere is the normal, which it would do him good to see just now" (p. 3), is echoed by the title given to the third section of the text, "Berlin without End" (p. 100). The abnormality of his situation, first after Hannah's abandonment of him, and later after her abandonment of his manuscript, is thus identified with Berlin, and this situation is considered endless. The constancy of the "abnormal" is echoed in another passage:

> It is only in the course of the normal failure, so physical, so analytical, that one first experiences the nature of the normal and its overwhelming power. Everyone who suffers a separation or a breakup experiences it as something negative and personal, whereas staying together seems positive and universal. Actually, it's the other way around, of course: what is universal is precisely the negative, the shipwreck, the breakup, the misunderstandings, as attested by all the figures and the facts. (pp. 18–19)

That separation (Trennung) represents the normal state of affairs is a perception typical of Richard, and his longing for what is special parallels the text's hope for a dialogue crossing the boundaries of separation and dichotomy. The association of the "normal abnormality" of separation with Berlin could perhaps be seen as merely a snide political joke in the text, not having much more significance than the derogatory observations about Berlin that Richard makes at the hairdresser's (p. 5). The association, however, occurs again: "mornings down the Kaiserdamm, the Bismarckallee, June 17 Boulevard, all the way to the barrier; crossing the border at noon, afternoons walking back Unter den Linden, again as far as the approach to the barrier. Walking the whole length of the dividing line [Trennung], not without a certain schizophiliac satisfaction, as a collector of the partitioned" (p. 31).[53]

Separation, dividing lines, partition: the specific connection to

[53] Note that in the original German, Trennung is used in the passage on normalcy as well as in the one on the walk to the border. See Strauss, Die Widmung, pp. 21, 32. (Now, of course, after the opening of the Berlin Wall in 1989, the peculiarity of the "normalcy" of "separation" is more striking than during the frozen state of affairs maintained by the Cold War.)

Berlin's situation creates a kind of political allegory for Richard's plight. Similar political allusions would include the description of Richard's isolation as "the realm [*Reich*] of separation [*Trennung*]"[54] and the connection drawn between Richard and the Berlin Wall by a group of Bavarian tourists: they refer to him as one of the "Wall monsters of Berlin" (p. 107). In addition to the association of Richard with Berlin, there is a related association to West Germany as a whole:

> Thirty-one, he thinks, a physical fact, half a life and no biography. The times have been quiet, not the kind that shape destinies. An epoch in which he could not really come to maturity. From first consciousness to this day, his condition has been rigidly the same, permitting some growth, comfort, reform, but lacking all political energy, lacking in struggles, in incentive to make some kind of a break. Thirty years of a measured present tense in which he grew big and stayed little, surrounded by that ambience of public smugness so impervious to our existence. (p. 10)

He is thinking of his own life, but the parallels to the history of the Federal Republic of Germany are clear. Since Richard's ordeal is set in the drought-ridden summer of 1976, his thirty-one years began in 1945; this fragment of a life, "half a life," has been characterized by "growth, comfort, and reform," a summary of West Germany's economic and political history from the Adenauer years through Brandt and Schmidt. Being "without a sense of the past," *ohne Vergangenheitssinn*, is a condition that must be seen in relation to the whole problem of West Germany's (difficulties in) "coming to terms with" or "mastering" the past—*Vergangenheitsbewältigung*.[55]

Thus the "measured present tense" of which the text complains is not merely some vague sentiment of *post-histoire* but rather is determined to some extent by a particular kind of loss of history peculiar to West Germany. Strauss's next published work, the play *Big and Little* (*Groß und klein*, 1978), a title that alludes to the passage quoted above, can also be seen as a statement on the difficulty of human communication in a specifically West German setting.[56]

[54] See ibid., p. 80. Wilkins's translation (Strauss, *Devotion*, p. 82) leaves out any direct reference to *Trennung*.

[55] "ohne Vergangenheitssinn": Strauss, *Die Widmung*, p. 11. There are other passages in the text that allude to Germany's past and its imprint on Richard's generation: of particular interest are the passages connecting adult maleness in Richard's mind with fascism. *Devotion*, pp. 5, 50.

[56] "Big and Little"—"Groß und klein"—is, as von Becker has pointed out ("Minima Moralia," p. 157), the title Adorno gave to a section of *Minima Moralia*, pp. 161–64.

While *Devotion* is not one of Hutcheon's "historiographic meta-fictions," its "diachronic longing" can be related to her definition of a basic tendency in postmodern art: the opposition to "modernism's attempts to be *outside* history," which results in a constant confrontation of formalism with historical realities—without attempting to resolve the contradictions.[57] *Devotion*, as we have seen, makes some allusions to a specifically West German historical context. Its "diachronic longing" seems in some measure to relate to the specific need for opening up the repressed dialogue with German history since National Socialism and the war.

THE WRITER IN FILM: *WRONG MOVE* BY PETER HANDKE AND WIM WENDERS[58]

> Wilhelm and the old man. Wilhelm: "Do you believe that writing is possible if everything to do with politics has become alien to a person?"
> The old man: "Yes—if one could describe how this alienation has come about. It must not appear to be the natural state of affairs."
> Wilhelm: "Then I would have to tell the whole history of the West."
> The old man: "Indeed."[59]

The passage above occurs at a central point in both Peter Handke's screenplay *Wrong Move* (*Falsche Bewegung*, 1973) and Wim Wenders's film by the same name (1974). It demonstrates that, for both the script and the final film, the ongoing German debate on the relationship of politics and literature is quite relevant. As the passage also indicates, this debate is much older than its latest manifestations during and after the West German student protest movement of the late 1960s.

One of the most decisive periods in the long history of conflict in Western culture between literature and politics, between art and society, was the late eighteenth century. As the aristocracy's control

Von Becker cites Adorno's discussion in "Groß und klein" of the "hierarchy of important matters" that tends to intrude surreptitiously into theoretical discourse. Adelson discusses Adorno's relevance to the works of Botho Strauss (and West German literature of the 1970s in general) in *Crisis of Subjectivity*, pp. 45–54 and 60–65.

[57] Hutcheon, *A Poetics of Postmodernism*, pp. 100–101.

[58] A shorter, earlier version of this section, written with a somewhat different emphasis, appears as "*Wilhelm Meister* Revisited: *Falsche Bewegung* by Peter Handke and Wim Wenders" in Gertrud Bauer Pickar and Sabine Cramer, eds., *The Age of Goethe Today: Critical Reexamination and Literary Reflection* (Munich: Wilhelm Fink, 1990).

[59] Peter Handke, *Falsche Bewegung* (Frankfurt: Suhrkamp, 1975), p. 51. All further references to this work appear in the text.

over society was overthrown in France, a new age was dawning for artists as well, in which their activity began to be freed from the control of aristocratic patrons through its increasing orientation toward a marketplace consisting of a bourgeois audience. In Germany, where the bourgeoisie was too weak to emulate the French in the political realm, Kant was writing of a new art that was pleasing yet free of all bias or "interest"—and unbeholden to political interests.[60] Johann Wolfgang von Goethe, an artist still very much beholden to an aristocratic patron, polemicized against revolution.[61] In 1796, his novel *Wilhelm Meister's Apprenticeship* appeared, in which a young man departs from bourgeois life to join a traveling theater troupe, but through his experiences he is finally reconciled with bourgeois society, renouncing art for what Schiller called "tätiges Leben"—the "active life."[62]

Handke alludes directly to *Wilhelm Meister* in his screenplay for the film *Wrong Move*, naming his protagonist after the title figure in that novel, naming two female characters "Therese" and "Mignon" as well, and giving the latter an elderly companion ("the old man"), a musician haunted by a dark secret, much like the character to whom Goethe refers as the "harper."[63] The resulting text is a site of complex interaction between literature and history. On one level there is the allusion to Goethe's seminal *Bildungsroman*, with its reduction of artistic rebellion to a phase in the process of healthy integration into the status quo. The relevance of the allusion to Goethe must be seen in at least two historical contexts: Goethe's contribution to the negative German reaction to the French revolution, and his role as a dominant influence on attempts by subsequent German writers to define themselves vis-à-vis politics and society for at least the next century.

Of more direct historical relevance is the role played by Handke, the writer of the initial version of the film's script, setting this very loose adaptation of Goethe's text in contemporary West Germany. Handke had been the *enfant terrible* of German letters since the late

---

[60] Immanuel Kant, *Kritik der Urteilskraft*, in *Kant's Werke*, vol. 10 (Berlin: Königliche Preußische Akademie der Wissenschaften, 1908), p. 211.

[61] By the mid-1790s, both Goethe and Schiller vehemently condemned the French Revolution (as did most German writers, except those called "Jacobins" because of their sympathies). Goethe wrote in opposition to attempts "to stir up similar scenes in Germany artificially." Cited in Beutin, *Deutsche Literaturgeschichte* (1984), p. 150.

[62] Friedrich von Schiller, quoted in *Kindlers Literatur Lexikon*, vol. 7 (Zürich: Kindler, 1965), p. 1129.

[63] A detailed comparison of Handke's script with Goethe's novel is not my main focus here. A discussion of similarities between the two texts and Handke's script can be found in Geist, *The Cinema of Wim Wenders*, pp. 43–47.

1960s. In 1966, while still in his early twenties, Handke, an Austrian, had managed to get himself invited to the annual meeting of the older, established writers of postwar West Germany (Gruppe 47—"Group 47"); at the meeting he created a scandal with his polemical attack against the group.[64] Soon thereafter he also distanced himself from the activists who were his own contemporaries, defiantly proclaiming himself an "ivory-tower dweller."[65] Handke's screenplay for *Wrong Move*, therefore, with references to writing and politics like those cited above, resonates with the controversy surrounding not merely his own career but the whole issue of the role of the writer in West German society.

Furthermore, in that his text (like Strauss's *Devotion*) alludes to an "erotic gaze" (p. 58), the commentary in it on the state of writing in West Germany is made more complex by its own status as a *film* script, for here Handke's concern with the relation of specularity to writing is coupled with the practical experience of writing for the visual medium of film. It was not his first (or last) collaboration with Wenders, nor was it his first try at a film script, but it was the first full-length screenplay he had written that was filmed.[66] *Wrong Move*, as a cinematic reflection on writing and the writer in West Germany, is further complicated by Wenders's determining role in the film. His visualization—and revision—of Handke's script is of obvious significance, since the resulting film must also be seen in terms of the position of the *filmmaker* with regard to the artist's situation in West Germany and in terms of the specific historical context of filmmaking in that society.

Critics have written about incompatibility between Handke's language and Wenders's film.[67] Despite any such conflict within the film (or between Wenders's final draft and Handke's original script,

[64] Handke himself discussed the (in)famous 1966 meeting of the "Gruppe 47" (in Princeton, New Jersey) in an interview with Manfred Durzak ten years later. See Durzak, "Für mich ist Literatur auch eine Lebenshaltung. Gespräch mit Peter Handke," in Durzak, *Gespräche über den Roman* (Frankfurt: Suhrkamp, 1976), pp. 314–18.

[65] "Ich bin ein Bewohner des Elfenbeinturms" ("I am a Dweller in the Ivory Tower") is the title of a 1967 essay by Handke that appeared in a collection of his essays with the same title: *Ich bin ein Bewohner des Elfenbeinturms* (Frankfurt: Suhrkamp, 1972), pp. 19–28.

[66] In 1968–1969, as Rainer Nägele and Renate Voris report, Handke wrote a film script titled "Chronik der laufenden Ereignisse" ("Chronicle of the Flow of Events"); Nägele and Voris, *Peter Handke* (Munich: C. H. Beck, 1978), pp. 100–104.

[67] See, for instance, Friede Grafe, "Erhebungen überm Meerespiegel," rev. of *Falsche Bewegung*, dir. by Wim Wenders, *Süddeutsche Zeitung*, 11 April 1975; and Uwe Künzel, *Wim Wenders. Ein Filmbuch* (Freiburg: Dreisam-Verlag, 1981), p. 95. Geist reports that Wenders complained of the constraints of working with a "static script." *The Cinema of Wim Wenders*, p. 49.

which have significant differences), it should be noted that the artistic collaboration between the two friends has been for the most part smooth.[68] Eric Rentschler asserts that Wenders's early work, including his collaboration with Handke on the short film *3 American LPs* (1969), shows the influence of the "Sensibilism" prevalent in Munich in the late 1960s, a tendency evident in many of the student projects at the Academy for Television and Film where Wenders was enrolled. There is a clear connection between the preferred style (or antistyle) of the Sensibilists ("extended travelling shots and long takes," pointing "cameras out of apartment and car windows onto the streets")[69] and Wenders's style of filmmaking (e.g., his love of travelling shots, and his many "road movies," from *Summer in the City*, 1970, to *Paris, Texas*, 1984). The similarity between Sensibilism, in its search for immediacy and opposition to intellectualizing, and "New Subjectivity" has already been mentioned above.[70]

"New Subjectivity" as a literary trend was in turn much influenced by Handke, of course: his early stance against the subordination of literature to political activism would provide models for writers like Peter Schneider who subsequently switched from opposing Handke to supporting his position.[71] As mentioned above, the fusion of Handke's earlier experimental approach to the novel with a mode of narrative fiction—the detective genre, no less—in his novel *The Goalie's Anxiety* (1970) was a first indication of the coming return to narrative realism in the 1970s, and it marked the beginning of his transition from an experimental writer to one whose writing is based on experience.[72] This transition, and the emphasis on subjective and autobiographical experience in his works of the early 1970s, was very influential on young West German authors.[73]

The collaboration of Handke and Wenders on *Wrong Move* thus

[68] Rentschler, *West German Film*, note 63, p. 189; also note 56, p. 188.

[69] Ibid., p. 174. On "Sensibilism," see above, Chapter 1; see also Geist, "Wenders in the Cities," pp. 380–83, and Geist, *The Cinema of Wim Wenders*, pp. 14–17; Wolfram Schütte, "*Falsche Bewegung*: Wim Wenders neuer Film nach Peter Handkes Drehbuch," *Neue Zürcher Zeitung*, 18 April 1975; and Pflaum and Prinzler, *Cinema in the Federal Republic of Germany*, p. 31.

[70] See above, Chapter 1, "Dogmatization and Resignation."

[71] See P. Schneider, *Atempause*, especially his 1976 essay, "Über den Unterschied von Literatur und Politik," pp. 162–74.

[72] See Heinz Ludwig Arnold, "Gespräch mit Peter Handke," *Text & Kritik*, 24/24a (1976), p. 25. Handke continued to shift, moving from this neorealist phase of the early 1970s to what is often considered a manneristic "neo-Romanticism" by the 1980s.

[73] Karin Struck, for example, acknowledged this explicitly in *Class Love*. See *Class Love* (*Klassenliebe*), p. 117. (Handke discusses his devastating review of Struck's *Die Mutter* in Arnold, "Gespräch," p. 36.)

makes the resulting film a unique reflection upon the interaction in West Germany during the mid-1970s of writing, politics, specularity, "New Subjectivity," filmmaking, and history—political and literary history, both recent and more remote. The complexity of the interaction of these discourses in *Wrong Move* makes it in turn a "postmodernist" text: it is, after all, a curious mixture of "high art" and mass culture—and in some ways a "historiographical metafiction" as well. A work of German literary classicism—*Wilhelm Meister*, no less—is updated and adapted for the screen by Handke, is winner of the prestigious West German literary award, the Büchner Prize (that same year—1973), and then is filmed by Wenders, whose life had been "saved by rock and roll."[74] The first shot of this new Wilhelm Meister shows him playing an album by the Troggs and then putting his fist through the window. The tensions created in crossing boundaries of genre and media in this way are paralleled by those created in the obvious historical contrast between the Germany depicted by Goethe and that in the film: *Wrong Move* follows its Wilhelm Meister through a West German landscape increasingly dominated by massive high-rise apartment complexes and shopping centers.

In order to analyze the film in terms of these overlapping contexts, I first examine Handke's script in light of its depiction of writing and its relation to "New Subjectivity," and then look at how Wenders's film depicts the travels of Wilhelm Meister, Handke's would-be writer, in contemporary West Germany.[75]

Handke's Screenplay: Radical Innerlichkeit?

"I am convinced of the power of poetic thought to dissolve abstractions and thus exert a powerful influence on the future." Handke spoke these words in 1973, the same year he dates his script for *Wrong Move* (p. 81).[76] The faith in writing thus declared is quite similar to that expressed in Struck's *Class Love*. According to Handke's formulation, writing's utopian potential transcends any merely "private" qualities associated with writing. In a statement made a few years later, Handke rejects any "abstract utopia" as a conscious or preconceived goal or strategy for his writing, maintaining that the utopian perspective arises *of itself* from the process of

---

[74] In Dawson, *Wim Wenders*, p. 11.

[75] Rentschler calls Wenders's film a "Rerouting" of Handke's script. *West German Film*, p. 174.

[76] Handke, "Die Geborgenheit unter der Schädeldecke" ("Refuge under the Skull"), p. 2.

working with the realistic details he gathers from observation and experience. Such new perspectives open automatically from this process, providing solutions he had not planned: "The point of departure and the details must be realistic, completely realistic. When, however, new perspectives arise out of this, then I know that literature is simply superior to any other form of dealing with the world. And then I know—as dumb as it sounds—that it is needed. I have to have the feeling that other people need it, that it is useful literature, in the widest sense."[77]

The social character of literature is emphasized in this optimistic formulation of its potential; but its social and utopian character is guaranteed only by that which appears to be its radical privacy, for, as Handke said in the same interview in which he made the statement above, he believes "literature is only compelling when it penetrates the deepest levels of the self." Only through the most extreme subjectivity, he feels, is intersubjectivity possible.[78] Such sentiments are somewhat reminiscent of Adorno: for example, the idea that literature is "most deeply bound to the social when it does not speak as a mouthpiece for society," or that a poem is understood only when the reader "perceives in its loneliness the voice of humanity."[79] In *Wrong Move*, at a point later in the above-mentioned discussion on poetry and politics, the old man suggests to Wilhelm that he should "become politically active and stop writing," and Wilhelm responds:

> "But I had just realized—precisely *while* writing—that I couldn't formulate my needs in a political way. I found that up until then they had never been awakened by a politician, rather always exclusively by poets."
>
> The old man: "What does the world care about your most personal needs?"
>
> Wilhelm: "Everyone has his most personal needs, and those are the real ones. For me there are only most personal needs."
>
> The old man: "But they are impossible to fulfill, in contrast to the needs with which politics occupies itself. Those personal needs can be fulfilled only through the illusion of poetry."
>
> Wilhelm: "But that illusion implies the hope that they are capable of fulfillment—otherwise there wouldn't even be the illusion of it." (p. 52)

[77] Arnold, "Gespräch," p. 24.
[78] Ibid., p. 37.
[79] Adorno, "Rede über Lyrik und Gesellschaft," pp. 75, 85.

In this long passage, Wilhelm declares that it is the poet and not the politician who inspires authentic social interaction, who manages to communicate by working at the level of his most personal needs, since these are "the real ones." The politician uses language that is inauthentic, impersonal, and reified, a co-opted, conformist language that alienates the individual and thus increases social isolation. Poetry is thus the only means to intersubjective communication, and in its glimmer, where the old man sees only hallucinatory illusion, Wilhelm sees the hope for a utopian future where those intensely subjective needs can be fulfilled, where the longing for individuality and community are not mutually exclusive. For Wilhelm does see the need for that sort of "political" community that is a synthesis of the two:

> The old man: "Wilhelm, don't let yourself be led astray by your poetic feeling for the world."
> Wilhelm: "If only both, the poetic and the political, could be one."
> The old man: "That would be the end of longing—and the end of the world." (p. 52)

Once again, the old man underscores the utopian nature of Wilhelm's vision; from his perspective, however, this is a warning. It is at this point in the text where he discloses his secret to Wilhelm: that he had presided over the murder of Jews in Vilna during the war (p. 53). Later he will argue that an opposition to politics similar to that voiced by Wilhelm had, for the old man's generation, led ultimately to the "most terrible politics" (p. 73). But Wilhelm is not interested in his advice; he will instead attempt to drown the old man (p. 75).

The long discussion of poetry and politics must thus be seen in its textual context as somehow related to Germany's political past. One also cannot help but read it as almost a summary of arguments on the relation of literature and politics heard in West Germany between 1968 and the Tendenzwende, the tendential shift of 1973 and 1974. Some of the arguments of 1968, when literature was proclaimed dead, are echoed in the old man's suggestion to give up writing and become politically active.[80] Wilhelm of course voices arguments connected to the "New Subjectivity": at a time when political activism seemed futile, literature seemed once again viable, and, in its greater suitability for the communication of authentic subjective experience, it was argued that literary endeavors were in-

---

[80] See above, Chapter 1.

deed political.[81] It is surely significant that allusions to this debate are found in Handke's script immediately before crimes of the German past are exposed; the debate in the script is to some extent haunted by that past.

At the end of the screenplay, Wilhelm stands alone on the Zugspitze, a peak in southern Bavaria. The implication is that the isolation he achieves there will enable him to write; the only sounds called for in Handke's script as he stands there are those of a blizzard and the "noise of a typewriter . . . which gets stronger and stronger" (p. 81). Wilhelm's mother, at the beginning of the script, had sent him away from Heide in northern Germany so that he could fulfill his dream of becoming a writer (pp. 9–11). He then wanders the length of West Germany, meanwhile being followed by various people whom he encounters by chance in the course of his travels. Not until he has wandered all the way to southern Bavaria does he find the isolation and distance from others he needs to write. It is interesting to compare the development of Handke's protagonist with that of the protagonist in Goethe's novel: "In contrast to Goethe's Wilhelm Meister, Handke's Wilhelm doesn't search for himself in confrontation with society, but rather by increasing his distance from it. The journey into the world becomes here an escape from the world."[82]

The relation of Handke's script to Goethe's classic *Bildungsroman* is thus primarily one of negation; the allusions in the newer text to the older one demonstrate that the process of the development and education of the self can no longer be realized in the way it seemed possible in Goethe's Germany during the late eighteenth century.[83] In addition, both Handke's screenplay and Wenders's film can be seen as postmodern critiques of the ideology of the modern age, which was just beginning as Goethe wrote. Friedrich Kittler has written that *Bildung*—the perfecting of the individual through culture and education—replaced older (feudal) rites of passage for young men within the ascendant bourgeois culture of modernity. Now that the ideology of modernity is in crisis (or at least in major

---

[81] For example, Jürgen Theobaldy defended "New Subjective" poetry in the mid-1970s by asserting that "the turn toward one's own subjectivity" was a "step forward, through which social contradictions are experienced politically as well as personally." Theobaldy, "Literaturkritik, astrologisch. Zu Jörg Drews' Aufsatz über Selbsterfahrung und Neue Subjektivität in der Lyrik," *Akzente* 24 (1977), pp. 188–91.

[82] Nägele and Voris, *Peter Handke*, p. 105.

[83] Manfred Mixner makes this point in his book *Peter Handke* (Kronberg: Athenäum, 1977), p. 214.

transition), the ritualistic and mythological elements beneath the surface of its "enlightenment" have become more apparent.[84]

But even as a myth, the ideal of the harmonious integration of the developing young individual seems somewhat out of place in late twentieth-century technological society. Handke's critique of this myth, however, which Goethe can be said to have helped construct, is, for all its contemporary specificity, nonetheless remarkably similar to that of some very early detractors from Goethe, most notably Novalis. The latter's ultimate verdict is famous: "*Wilhelm Meister* is actually a *Candide* that is directed against poetry . . . , *Wilhelm Meister's Apprenticeship* is to a certain extent thoroughly prosaic and modern. All that is romantic gets lost in it, as does any sense of natural poetry, of the wondrous."[85]

Novalis's *Heinrich von Ofterdingen* has been called an "Anti-Meister."[86] Handke can perhaps be said to have begun a postmodern recycling of (neo-)Romantic attitudes during the course of the 1970s.[87] In any case, his screenplay for *Wrong Move* validates a view of art as both mystical and isolated from a corrupt and prosaic social reality. The social reality depicted there is specifically West German, a reality that has been criticized (and not merely by Handke) as one that presents all sorts of obstacles to an individual's search for an identity. Not the least of such obstacles is its political history.

In an authentic fashion, Handke seems to argue, the individual subject can develop only through "the illusion of poetry," to use the phrase the old man uses in his argument with Wilhelm. True self-realization comes through the process of writing, which is after all (according to Handke) "superior to any other form of dealing with the world."[88] For Wilhelm it is a manner of dealing with the world that requires being apart from it. Writing is a process of remembering in isolation. As he tells Therese: "When I am alone, I'll be able to remember, above all to remember you, and when I can remember again, I'll feel good and have the desire to write. As a process of

[84] Friedrich Kittler, "Über die Sozialisation Wilhelm Meisters," in Gerhard Kaiser and F. Kittler, eds., *Dichtung als Sozialisationsspiel. Studien zu Goethe und Gottfried Keller* (Göttingen: Vandenhoek and Ruprecht, 1978), p. 14.

[85] Novalis, *Fragmenten*, cited in the notes to Goethe's *Wilhelm Meisters Lehrjahre. Goethe: Berliner Ausgabe*, vol. 10 (East Berlin: Aufbau, 1971), p. 664.

[86] For instance, see Beutin et al., *Deutsche Literaturgeschichte* (1984 ed.), p. 163.

[87] Neo-Romanticism (in Germany, Rilke would be the best example) was a literary movement at the end of the nineteenth century. The original German romanticism came at the end of the eighteenth century—like Goethe and Schiller's classicism—at what can be considered the beginning of modernity, just after the Enlightenment.

[88] Arnold, "Gespräch," p. 24.

remembering, I think, writing will finally become automatic" (pp. 77–78).

Only later, apart from her, will he be able to love her: "I know that later I'll love you very much, Therese" (p. 78); living with her, he feels "als ob ich mich schwul zu mir selber verhalte"—that is, as if he felt homosexual desire for himself (p. 77). This sort of self-obsession is actually a sign of alienation from the self, which blocks him from experience of the world around him; to achieve contact with the people and things around him he must struggle alone with his memories of them in the process of writing. Communion with the world through radical privacy—via the process of writing: here again this somewhat mystical paradox emerges. The alienated individual is forced to remove himself or herself from the world in order to regain subjective access to it, a phenomenon that is depicted in more radical terms in Handke's *Left-Handed Woman*.[89] This need to withdraw is a striking indictment of what Handke sees as the numbing alienation of modern life; as Rentschler writes, it is a "critique of modernity" that has political significance insofar as it suggests the overwhelming power of "the forces that have imposed these limits on him [i.e., Handke] and other subjects who hunger for experience."[90]

This is a direct allusion to Rutschky's *Hunger for Experience*, the hunger considered symptomatic of the 1970s. It is in turn closely related to an emphasis on specularity, on what Rentschler calls "cinemorphic seeing."[91] There is a strong emphasis on visual perception in *Wrong Move*, given Wilhelm's concept of an "erotic gaze" (p. 58); furthermore, Wilhelm's rejection of inspiration (*einfallen*) as the impetus for writing, in favor of the more empirical concept of observation (*auffallen*), the position he takes in his discussion with Bernhard on poetry (pp. 55–56), can also be easily related to the concern with visual experience on the part of the "specular subject."

But Wilhelm's trajectory away from social contact into isolation (where he will be able to write) seems at odds with the hunger for unmediated experience, and with the passivity of purely visual experience. According to the screenplay, the film is supposed to end with a shot of Wilhelm dissolving into a shot of the Zugspitze in a blizzard (p. 81): the visual image of white snow and gray sky, an image in danger of losing all contour, is coupled with the sound of

[89] Handke's book *The Left-Handed Woman* (*Die linkshändige Frau*) appeared in 1976 (Frankfurt: Suhrkamp) and the film (which he directed) in 1978.

[90] Rentschler, *West German Film*, p. 173.

[91] Ibid., pp. 172–73. See also Russell Berman's discussion of Werner Herzog's "cult of primal seeing" in "The Recipient as Spectator," pp. 499–510.

a typewriter becoming ever louder. Visual experience is replaced by the whiteness of a blank page to be written upon; specularity is replaced by the solitary process of writing and remembering. For only in remembering does the visual truly open itself to experience; only through "after-images" is the experience clear, as stated explicitly in the following passage, which, significantly, is supposed to appear as "Writing over the image": "Sometimes I would stare in front of me, with the intention of not looking at anything in particular. Then I would close my eyes, and only with the after-image that then appeared would I realize what had been before me. When I'm writing, too, I'll close my eyes and see with total clarity something that I had refused to notice with my eyes open" (pp. 61–62).

Writing is thus in a sense opposed to direct visual experience, which in and of itself remains inadequate and incomplete, much as social interaction does: just as Wilhelm will be able to love Therese only later, so will he only later grasp what he has seen. It is writing alone that frees either interaction with his environment from alienation. When Therese criticizes him for overlooking a great deal in the world around him (pp. 32, 58), he admits she is right. Peter Buchka's thesis about Wenders's characters—that they cannot really hear or see—applies to Wilhelm in Handke's script as well.[92]

In spite of his inability to see with much sensitivity, Wilhelm maintains that the process of remembering is more important than registering whatever visual impressions offer themselves (p. 32). Later he formulates his concept of an "erotic gaze":

> Wilhelm: "I know that I don't have what is called a talent for observation, but I like to imagine that I have the capacity for a kind of erotic gaze. Suddenly something will catch my attention that I have always overlooked. Not only do I see it then, but simultaneously I get a feeling for it. That's what I mean by an erotic gaze. What I'm seeing is then no longer just an object being observed, but rather a very intimate part of myself as well. One used to call this seeing the essence of a phenomenon, I think. Something particular becomes a sign for the whole. I then write something that has not merely been observed, but something experienced. For this reason especially I want to be a writer." (p. 58)[93]

The erotic gaze is for Wilhelm something that overcomes him suddenly and changes what he observes—poorly—into something he

---

[92] Buchka, *Augen kann man nicht kaufen*, p. 81.

[93] The word I have translated here as "seeing the essence of a phenomenon" is *Wesenschau*, often translated as "phenomenology." Peter Pütz stresses the allusion here to Husserl. Pütz, " 'Schläft ein Lied in allen Dingen,' " in Raimund Fellinger, ed., *Peter Handke* (Frankfurt: Suhrkamp, 1985), p. 177.

experiences. Wilhelm's "erotic gaze" is roughly comparable to the erotic gaze discussed in Strauss's *Devotion*, although Wilhelm's formulation is less undifferentiated and more mystical. The mystical unity achieved between the perceived object and the perceiving subject in this experience is also closely related to writing; indeed, the experience sounds much like the descriptions of writing later in the text cited above—writing as a "process of remembering" that unites the subject with its alienated experience of itself and the world, ending the reified, objectified relation to both the self and others. The erotic gaze seems to effect the same unity and indeed to be part of the process of writing. It is a gaze, in fact, that is supposed to occur only "with eyes closed": the "after-images" he mentions in connection with his writing.

Thus for all the emphasis on specularity in Handke, there is, in *Wrong Move* at any rate, ambiguity as to which is more essential to the mystical experience: seeing or writing. Indeed, as I have argued, there is much evidence that seeing is definitely subordinated to writing; although this primacy is less clear in Handke's next work, the novel *A Moment of True Feeling*, in *Wrong Move* it seems that ultimately it is only writing that makes unmediated seeing possible; the erotic gaze is almost identical with the process of writing.[94] Immediacy of experience paradoxically depends on the mediation of writing, which in turn is a process that transcends all mediation—and alienation.

This is, once again, a utopian view of writing reminiscent of that in Karin Struck, although here there is more of an emphasis on writing as mediation, a process apart from sensual immediacy. But this mediation is conceived in a somewhat mystical, transcendent fashion, positing writing as a more idealistic, purer, more hermetic process than the openness to dialogue with extratextual realities implied in *Devotion*'s ironic foregrounding of its own inadequacies as a text. Rather than being open to extratextuality by reflecting on its own isolation and incompleteness like *Devotion*, *Wrong Move*, with its positive ending—the hero is finally able to write—implies a clo-

---

[94] Handke's *A Moment of True Feeling* (1975) is a text in which the mystical experience is posited apart from writing (see this chapter, note 3 above). Handke deemphasizes the mystical in his discussion of this novel with Arnold: "Gespräch," pp. 29–31. Nonetheless, the progression of his works has seemed to be in the direction of the mystical "erotic gaze." See, e.g., the discussion of Handke directing *The Left-Handed Woman* in Durzak, *Peter Handke und die deutsche Gegenwartsliteratur. Narziß auf Abwegen* (Stuttgart: Kohlhammer, 1982), p. 136. David Roberts writes, "Indeed Handke now once again seeks to endow the writer with magical powers of recreation of (an ideal) reality." "From the 1960s to the 1970s," p. xvii.

sure. In isolation the hero will transcend alienation, indeed history, since writing is the ground of transcendence, outside and beyond history. There is no "diachronic longing" here—history is a violent distraction, as the hero's irritation with the old man illustrates.[95]

Nonetheless there is tension between the text's emphasis on writing and *Innerlichkeit*, or "inwardness," and its stress on the visual, especially because of its status as a film script. Furthermore, the Handke's script was revised by Wenders in his filmic realization of *Wrong Move*, and the film treats writing—and Wilhelm the would-be writer—in a distinctly different fashion; writing (and art in general) loses much of its idealistic aura and its insulation from history.

Wenders's Re-Vision: The Writer in Film

Instead of the snowstorm on the Zugspitze Wilhelm had wanted to experience (p. 77), and which he finds at the end of Handke's script, there is, at the end of Wenders's film, a shot of Wilhelm with his back to the camera, gazing off into the mountains. The sky is clear, and on the sound track, the voice of the narrator speaks:

> I had told Therese I intended to stay in Germany because I knew too little to write about it. But it was only an excuse. I really wanted only to be alone, to be undisturbed in my torpor. I was waiting for some kind of experience, like a miracle, but the snowstorm never came. Why was I here instead of with the others? Why did I threaten the old man instead of letting him tell me more? I felt as if I had missed something, and I was still missing out—with every move I made.[96]

This is quite obviously a different ending. Wilhelm admits that his line about getting to know Germany (in the Handke script on p. 80) was merely an excuse to be alone; this isolation in turn is not any productive "process of remembering" but rather is described as "torpor." Wilhelm is filled with doubts about the choice he has made—not at all *fröhlich*, joyous, as in Handke's version (p. 78); and, most important, there is no snowstorm—and no sound of typ-

---

[95] Handke's text seems to plead for artistic autonomy and to demonstrate that passion for purity which Bürger finds typical of modernism. P. Bürger in C. and P. Bürger, *Postmoderne*, p. 10.

[96] Quoted in Buchka, *Augen kann man nicht Kaufen*, p. 51. Buchka also prints a still from this last shot across from a copy of Caspar David Friedrich's painting, "Wanderer above a Sea of Mist" ("Wanderer über dem Nebelmeer," ca. 1818), on pp. 52–53. The similarity between the two images was noted as early as 23 May 1975, in a review of the film by Frank Scurla in the *Saarbrücker Zeitung* ("Die Leiden des jungen Autors").

ing. The positive ending implied in Handke's script is totally inverted: Wilhelm does not succeed in becoming a writer, and his movement into isolation seems just as wrong as his other moves.[97]

"I want to become a writer. But how is that possible without any interest in people?" (p. 8). These lines at the beginning of the film, among the first to be heard as voice-over narration, indicate Wilhelm's social alienation; when one compares them with the lines in the voice-over at the end of the film (e.g., "Why was I here, instead of with the others?"), it is fairly clear that Wilhelm has changed little. By contrast, in Handke's version, his confident assertion to Therese—"I know that later I'll love you very much, Therese" (p. 78)—implies that, near the end of his travels, he at least knows how to overcome his numbness.[98] In the film he succeeds neither in acquiring desire for people nor in becoming a writer. Isolation will overcome neither his alienation from others nor his writing block.

The only thing positive about the film's ending, indeed, is its implication that Wilhelm is beginning to gain the ironic distance on himself that the film has had from the beginning, in a way less evident in Handke's script. The film distances the spectator from its protagonist by the use throughout the film of voice-over narration in the first person. It is often used to report what in Handke's script are notes Wilhelm makes in his diary, which are supposed to be shown (e.g., pp. 8–9) or even superimposed over the image (e.g., p. 61). Wenders accomplishes two things in having Wilhelm's words read over the sound track instead of showing them in written form: he deemphasizes Wilhelm's writing, increasing the impression the viewer has that Wilhelm never succeeds in writing much, that his internal monologue rarely is externalized in writing.[99] Furthermore, the distance between Wilhelm's internal perspective and the external, visual world is increased.

This gap between his perspective and the perspective of the camera mirrors his alienation, of course, and the gap is highlighted even when there is no voice-over. The camera distances the viewer from Wilhelm, but its perspective is not granted objectivity, either, as is

[97] On the comparison of Handke's screenplay to the film, Wenders himself said that he produced the final draft of the script: Dawson, *Wim Wenders*, p. 4. See also Rentschler, *West German Film*, p. 178, and Geist, *The Cinema of Wim Wenders*, p. 48. Geist provides information based on her own interview with Wenders that Handke did have a role in writing the final version of the script, but she nonetheless concludes that "Rentschler is probably right . . . that the changed view of Wilhelm's isolationism from positive to negative is Wenders' contribution."

[98] This line is in the film, too, but it is relativized by later narration, including the above voice-over.

[99] See Rentschler, *West German Film*, p. 175.

clear from the opening shot of the film. Handke's script calls for opening the film with an establishing shot of the town's central square before showing Wilhelm in his room (p. 7); instead, the film begins with a traveling aerial shot high above a town on a river, during which raindrops gather on the glass pane through which the camera films. Not only does this increase the contrast between the external world and the interior of Wilhelm's room, it increases the distance—literally—from which Wilhelm is filmed and foregrounds the camera's perspective in doing so. For this is obviously no "objective" establishing shot but rather an acknowledgment of the camera's position; the raindrops on the glass, indeed, come very close to a direct foregrounding of the camera's lens. The position of the camera in the first shot is further specified in the second shot, where, from inside Wilhelm's window, the viewer sees a helicopter above the town; bridging the two shots is the noise of the helicopter's engine, which replaces the opening music toward the end of the first shot.

The film's opening illustrates the distanced attitude that the film takes toward its protagonist, an attitude that is reflected in the filmmaker's admission of some personal dislike for the character.[100] This lack of sympathy is difficult to find in Handke's text; he seems to depict the protagonist's apparently negative traits as necessary to the existential position of the writer. It is the radical *Innerlichkeit* propagated in Handke's text that seems to be the object of criticism in Wenders's film. The split between Wilhelm and the world is not merely reproduced in the film but is depicted with irony.

The film has a somewhat surrealistic quality; its mood has been described as poetic and like a fairy tale.[101] This quality has doubtless to do with Handke's script and the fateful role chance plays in bringing a group together around Wilhelm and then dispersing it again.[102] Chance events—of varying degrees of improbability—abound in the script. For instance, at the very beginning Wilhelm encounters the old man and Mignon on the train to Hamburg (pp. 17–18); after Wilhelm changes trains in Hamburg, they appear once again on the new train. The conductor on this train immediately assumes that Wilhelm is paying for these two uninvited companions, and Wilhelm

---

[100] Cited in Geist, "Wenders in the Cities," p. 396.

[101] Mixner, *Peter Handke*, p. 215.

[102] Note the element of luck/fate in Joseph Freiherr von Eichendorff's *From the Life of a Ne'er-Do-Well* (*Aus dem Leben eines Taugenichts*, 1826), one of the two books Wilhelm brings along on his journey. In Eichendorff luck plays a role that is foregrounded more than in *Wilhelm Meister*, contributing to a fairy-tale atmosphere that Goethe's novel does not have.

good-naturedly acquiesces to this assumption (p. 22). Then it becomes apparent that the conductor and the old man know each
other from the war (p. 23; see also p. 53). Such events continue, such
as when, in the central episode of the script, Bernhard joins the
group by chance (p. 37), and he leads them, not to his uncle's house
in the country, but by mistake to the house of the suicidal industrialist. The latter in turn invites them in anyway: "I was just putting
the rifle into my mouth, and as I heard the car, I waited, hoping it
would stop" (p. 41).

The film's depiction of this chain of improbabilities is filled with
a humorous irony, a quality flaunting the "vraisemblable" of conventional narrative, the plausibility expected from a conventional
realist film.[103] The improbability of the chance encounters is especially accentuated around the character of Bernhard, usually in a
humorous way, as when Bernhard tells the others, "I think he isn't
my uncle at all. And it isn't the right house, either. We are altogether
in the wrong place, I'm afraid" (p. 41). In context, it is a somewhat
dark joke, and its evocation of the film's title makes it somehow emblematic.

Much of the humor can be explained in terms of the obvious dis-
comfort of a protagonist "without interest in people" who nonetheless finds ever more people following him. This humor is part of
Handke's story, for Wilhelm is a character who for most of the script
is a passive one, pushed out of the house by his mother and diverted
in his travels by the people who gather about him, including the
would-be poet, Bernhard, who does manage to write poetry—which
galls Wilhelm (p. 44), even though he considers it bad poetry (p. 56).

The group's dispersal takes place after the crucial walk in the hills
near the industrialist's house (pp. 50–61); after the industrialist's
suicide and Bernhard's unexplained departure from the group (pp.
61–62), however, chance plays a lesser role. It is Wilhelm who
drives off the old man and who decides to leave Therese. He begins
to take control by actively opting to be alone. But here again, though
Wenders follows the script so far, his changing of the ending mocks
this increased decisiveness on Wilhelm's part, for he does not find
the snowstorm, nor is he at all sure why he is there; no triumphal
sound of typing leaves the viewer with the idea that his aimless motion is over. The subject in the film has its autonomy undermined
throughout; isolation is no help.

[103] Timothy J. Corrigan uses Christian Metz's concept of the "vraisemblable" in his
essay, "The Realist Gesture in the Films of Wim Wenders: Hollywood and the New
German Cinema," *Quarterly Review of Film Studies* 5 (1980), pp. 210–11, and note
10, p. 215.

As I have noted, there is a tension in Handke's text between seeing and writing, indeed between seeing and spoken as well as written language. In terms of the attraction she exerts upon Wilhelm, the seductive and silent character Mignon is an incarnation of this tension.[104] Wilhelm has his own sullen struggle with articulation. In the same diary entry at the beginning of the script in which he announces his lack of interest in people, he writes: "For two days I haven't spoken a word. I feel as if my tongue has disappeared from my mouth. But in my sleep I talk all night long, my mother says" (p. 8).

Wilhelm, depicted as verbally uncommunicative and having difficulty writing, is thus peculiarly suited to being seduced by the silent Mignon, and in this he could stand for a whole generation disenchanted with verbal discourse and fixated on the immediacy of sensual experience—experience that often turned out to be a passive, hypnotic specularity, as opposed to anything much more active. The verbal communication so problematic for Wilhelm is in turn that which characterizes Therese, the actress, who also finds Wilhelm unsuited to be a writer, and who in anger eventually strikes him with the sheet of paper upon which he has been typing.[105] She is also, however, the woman who desires him—and the woman whose bed he is seeking when he mistakenly finds Mignon.

The scene in which this incident occurs illustrates Wilhelm's inability to determine what he wants, his indecisiveness and passivity in the face of the desires of others. For in spite of the attraction Mignon can be said to exert upon him, the fact that he accepts her embrace has more to do with another "wrong move" than any active longing on his part. He is expecting Therese, who has insisted that he find her: "But I don't want to be left unsatisfied today" (p. 44). Wilhelm embraces Mignon in the dark; discovering her identity, he slaps her, then caresses her, leaves the room, but, after leaning his head on the door, goes back to her (p. 47). The hero who speaks of his "erotic gaze" finds himself, confronted with the erotic desires of

---

[104] Mignon was played by Nastassia Kinski in her first film role; she was fourteen years old when she signed the contract to play the part. Dawson, *Wim Wenders*, p. 24.

[105] Therese of course has her own struggle with reified language as an actress condemned to speak the words of others—and as a woman condemned to speak words written (mostly) by men; see pp. 69–70. For a general discussion of the role of women in Wenders's films, see the following by Geist: "Wenders in the Cities"; *The Cinema of Wim Wenders*; and "Mothers and Children in the Films of Wim Wenders," in Sandra J. Frieden et al., eds., *Gender and German Cinema* (Oxford: Berg Publishers, forthcoming).

others, stumbling blindly in the dark.[106] He also finds it easier to succumb in silence to Mignon's advances than to deal with Therese, a grown woman who articulates her desires openly and directly.

In the midst of Handke's allusions to language, nonverbal experience, the visual, and the erotic in his treatment of the characters Therese (the actress), Wilhelm (the writer), and the silent Mignon, some simpler psycho-sexual patterns can be noted. Although Wilhelm's initial contact with Therese is established by his gaze through the train window, as soon as she takes the initiative—by sending him a message—and he has to speak to her, the problems begin. By the end of the script he feels he must leave her, but he gives the silent (and much younger) Mignon the option of joining him. Her silence is seductive—and nonthreatening.[107]

Mignon's attraction as a character is obviously much stronger in the film than in the script, since only visually is the full effect of the silence Handke planned for her appreciable. Her presence has been seen as all the more provocative around the other characters who voice the often long speeches of Handke's screenplay, which some critics consider somewhat stilted and wordy.[108] It is true that they are long, perhaps at times somewhat ponderous—certainly within the context of Wenders's work, with its generally laconic characters. But the tension between Wenders's camera and the scripted speeches is integral to the film: tension between the visual and the verbal was already built into Handke's script, as the character Mignon demonstrates.

For Mignon functions as a site of seductive, nonverbal immediacy, an object of the "erotic gaze" to the extent that it is not completely subsumed by writing and thus *competes* with writing as an

[106] Siegfried Schober called him "erotically blind" in his review, "Die Leiden des Wilhelm M.," *Der Spiegel*, 10 March 1975, p. 134.

[107] Here it is interesting to compare the "erotic gaze" of Wilhelm to Laura Mulvey's classic discussion of the "male gaze" in the ("classic") narrative cinema: "As the spectator identifies with the main male protagonist, he projects his look on to that of his like, his screen surrogate, so that the power of the male protagonist as he controls events coincides with the active power of the erotic look, both giving a satisfying sense of omnipotence . . . [reminiscent] of the more perfect, more complete, more powerful ideal ego conceived in the original moment of recognition in front of the mirror." Mulvey, "Visual Pleasure and Narrative Cinema" (1975), in Gerald Mast and Marshall Cohen, eds., *Film Theory and Criticism*, 3rd ed. (New York: Oxford University Press, 1985), p. 810. Wenders's film depicts Wilhelm's "look" as potent only for as long as it remains "cinemorphic" (passive), but when confronted with the actual woman on the other side of the train window, Wilhelm's impotence—narratively speaking and otherwise—is thematized.

[108] Among such critics are Künzel (*Wim Wenders*, p. 95) and Grafe ("Erhebungen"), as well as Sandford, *The New German Cinema*, p. 108.

avenue to some sort of mystical transcendence. The tension between the silent Mignon and the language of the other characters, between the visual and the verbal, must also be seen in relation to the text's existence as a film script. It carries over into Wenders's film as well, but it is articulated differently.

There is a mystical immediacy attached to visual experience both in Wilhelm's concept of the erotic gaze and in Handke's experimentation with the cinematic medium.[109] Handke's work is not lacking in self-reflexivity, of course, and his screenplay for *Wrong Move* is no exception. Wilhelm's concern with writing, and the desire to write (e.g., p. 46), is obviously central to the text, as are the intertextual allusions to Goethe and other writers: Wilhelm carries with him Eichendorff's *From the Life of A Ne'er-Do-Well* (*Aus dem Leben eines Taugenichts*, 1826) and Flaubert's *Sentimental Education* (*L'education sentimentale*, 1869) (p. 12). More striking—and cinematic—is his idea of superimposing writing over the image, an idea that Wenders rejects in this film but uses in the later work, *Nick's Film: Lightning over Water* (1980). The graphic representation of the materiality of writing that Handke proposes also would foreground the materiality of the film stock. But for Handke (logically enough) the emphasis here is clearly on writing.

What about Wenders's attitude to writing? As Buchka asserts, writing has played an important role in Wenders's work. His characters, experiencing difficulties with perception and verbal articulation, often attempt to overcome this alienation from the outer world—and inner self—by writing; thus there is an obvious parallel to the project of "New Subjectivity," and even more so to Handke's conception of writing in the early 1970s. But Buchka writes: "With *Wrong Move*, the dream of finding one's identity exclusively through writing is exhausted."[110] Wenders's generally negative depiction of Wilhelm supports this assertion.

Beyond the mere depiction of writing, there is the question of writing as filmmaking. As mentioned above, in the opening shot of the film, Wenders foregrounds his camera. As one critic asserts, Wenders is a filmmaker in whose films one notes "the clear presence of the camera within the images"; his films never remain exclusively bound to the narrative but expose their own cinematic means of expression. "They inscribe the trace of their own discourse upon

---

[109] See Nägele and Voris, *Peter Handke*, pp. 100–102, on the theoretical and experiential conflicts within Handke's attitude to film.

[110] Buchka, *Augen kann man nicht kaufen*, pp. 82, 88.

the stories."[111] He is thus a filmmaker for whom the notion of an "erotic gaze" might be somewhat problematic, in spite of his association with a cinema of "pure being as pure seeing."[112] A gaze that supposedly transcends mediation is rather close to the *illusion* of immediacy created in classic Hollywood cinema. Christian Metz (among others) defines that cinema in terms of the attempt to keep all evidence of cinematic discursivity (e.g., editing and camera work) as unnoticeable as possible, so that the "story" seems to be a reality unfolding immediately before the spectator.[113]

In opposition to that type of cinema, Wenders's filmmaking could perhaps be called (to borrow from Roland Barthes) "writerly," although this invocation of the readerly/writerly dichotomy might appear to make Wenders much more of a modernist than he is.[114] Taking into account his roots in Sensibilism, his love for the profilmic reality, and his consequent reticence about montage (at least in his earlier films), one would have to conclude that Wenders's style of *realism* (which, again, I would compare in certain ways to neorealism) is much too honest to efface the traces of its own construction. Precisely his respect for the profilmic reality seems to have compelled him to foreground his own intervention. It is this combination of self-reflexivity and narrative fiction, of neorealist and modernist influences, and his (ambivalent) interest in popular culture that reveals the postmodern origins of Wenders's films.

Wrong Move, besides alluding to the traces of its own cinematic enunciation, also alludes to the historical situation of the cinema in West Germany, as Rentschler has observed.[115] He interprets Wen-

---

[111] Norbert Grob, *Die Formen des filmischen Blicks. Wenders: Die frühen Filme* (Munich: Filmland Presse, 1984), pp. 99–100.

[112] In his book *New German Cinema*, Elsaesser writes that the desire for "an experience of 'pure being as pure seeing' " is probably "best met by the films of Wim Wenders and Werner Herzog" (p. 5).

[113] Christian Metz, "Story/Discourse: Notes on Two Kinds of Voyeurism," in Bill Nichols, ed., *Movies and Methods. Vol. 2: An Anthology* (Berkeley: University of California Press, 1985), pp. 543–49. Orig. "Histoire/Discours" in Julia Kristeva et al., eds., *Langue, Discours, Société* (Paris: Editions du Seuil, 1975).

[114] See Roland Barthes, *S/Z: An Essay* (1970), trans. Richard Miller (New York: Hill and Wang, 1974), pp. 3–4.

[115] In Glückstadt, his hometown in the film, Wilhelm rides on his bicycle past a cinema playing *Die Rückkehr der reitenden Leichen*; in Bonn he stands in front of a cinema playing Coppola's *The Conversation*; in Therese's apartment outside Frankfurt, Mignon and the old man watch Straub and Huillet's *Die Chronik der Anna Magdalena Bach* on television (in Handke's script they watch Dreyer's *Jeanne d'Arc*—p. 70); and, at a drive-in, Wilhelm, Therese, and Mignon watch Peter Lilienthal's *La Victoria*, about the situation in Chile. See Rentschler, *West German Film*, pp. 177–78.

ders's film as a critique of the radical *Innerlichkeit* bound up with the artist as depicted in Handke's script. After all, most independent filmmakers in West Germany were economically dependent on state subsidy during the uneasy political climate of the 1970s. This situation made impossible an art as autonomous as that to which Wilhelm seems to be drawn, although the attraction was understandable. Wenders's film reflects a skepticism with regard to Wilhelm's solution to the problem of the artist in West Germany. This skepticism is in turn caused by more than just the situation of the cinema there; Wilhelm's journey through Germany is changed in ways that make the historical and political background of the artist's dilemma there more evident than in the original screenplay.

The Writer in Germany

Wenders has said that it is impossible to make films in Germany without addressing the "hole" in German culture left by its misappropriation in the Third Reich.[116] In postwar West Germany, that cultural vacuum was not addressed, but an attempt was made to "fill" it by the *Wirtschaftswunder*, the "economic miracle" that created a new consumer culture. Consumerism meant goods and services, and it meant international (mostly American) mass culture as well: Hollywood movies, television, and—especially for Wenders's generation—rock and roll. *Wrong Move* is an attempt to explore this cultural (and political) legacy, and in fact the film's most "postmodernist" aspects are directly related to this historical investigation: it juxtaposes its allusions to Goethe and Eichendorff with the *Bundesbahn* and the *Autobahn* (modern trains and expressways); flickering television sets with the industrialist's long, brooding speeches about alienation in Germany; Beethoven's melody to the "Ode to Joy" ("An die Freude"—whistled by Mignon and Therese) with Laertes's disclosure of his war crimes in Vilna; and the scenic Rhine landscape of that sequence with the concrete monotony of Frankfurt-Hoechst, the location of Therese's suburban high-rise apartment.

Especially relevant to the film's critique of West German political and cultural history is a consideration of two of its elements: (1) the journey Wilhelm makes through that nation, and (2) the troublesome incarnation of the German past in the old man (called "Laertes" in the film credits) who accompanies Mignon and, uninvited,

---

[116] Dawson, *Wim Wenders*, p. 7.

follows Wilhelm around.[117] Both are elements central to Handke's screenplay, but the first, the journey that structures the narrative, is altered in a significant way by Wenders.

In the original script, the film opens in Heide (p. 7), where Wilhelm boards a train for Hamburg, carrying a ticket from his mother that she says will take him as far as Gießen, Bad Herzfeld, or Soest; he decides upon the latter destination: "Soest in Westphalia—immediately I smell fresh bread and hear the tolling of bells between the half-timbered buildings" (p. 15). It is in Soest where Therese and Bernhard join him, and it is near Soest where Bernhard leads the group to the industrialist's house. From there they drive (minus Bernhard) to Therese's apartment in Frankfurt-Höchst (p. 63).

The film, on the other hand, opens with a shot of Glückstadt on the Elbe that emphasizes the extreme width of the river at its mouth. The Elbe is of course not just any river but the one that symbolizes Germany's postwar division into two states.[118] The north-to-south journey through Germany in Handke's script is thus given a starting point that grazes, if ever so briefly and indirectly, the east-west rupture that has been so much more a determining factor of postwar German political realities than the much older north-south split in German culture. This starting point is displayed before the viewer sees Wilhelm; it precedes the narrative and alludes to the political and historical situation that determines Wilhelm's journey to Bonn instead of, say, Berlin.

For in the film he travels to Bonn, and this is the major alteration that Wenders makes in Wilhelm's itinerary. The picturesque half-timbered buildings (*Fachwerkhäuser*) of Soest are replaced by the more prosaic Bonn, the "provisional" capital of the Federal Republic of Germany, the sleepy, mid-sized town chosen in 1949 as a temporary substitute for the metropolis east of the Elbe. The small-town eccentricities Handke sets in Soest—for example, the man who screams "Do you know what pain is?" (p. 32)—have a political resonance entirely lacking in his version by being set in Bonn. As Rentschler writes, "The first signs of public insanity and collective

---

[117] Laertes was also the father of Odysseus, the wanderer. Wilhelm, the fatherless wanderer pushed out of the house by his mother, roams West Germany in search of an identity, finds Laertes, and sees in him a father figure he would like to kill: an appropriate reading for the intergenerational tensions in the film with regard to Germany's past.

[118] The Elbe was actually the border between East and West Germany for only a short stretch—which Wenders used in his next film, *Kings of the Road* (*Im Lauf der Zeit*, 1976)—yet it was perceived as the border in common speech ("East of the Elbe") and indeed was the meeting place of American, Russian, and British troops at the end of World War II. It actually provided a water link between the two states.

fear he encounters during a morning stroll do not transpire in an
obscure corner of North Rhine-Westphalia; they take place in the
capital of West Germany."[119]

It is also in Bonn that Wilhelm finally meets Therese and encounters Bernhard, two other persons with artistic aspirations. Therese
is an actress, and Bernhard, another would-be writer, serves as a sort
of parodistic alter-ego and rival for Wilhelm. This meeting of would-
be artists in the political capital of West Germany is also the prelude
to a more significant confrontation about art and politics: the above-
mentioned sequence in which, during the walk on the hills above
the Rhine, Laertes and Wilhelm discuss poetry and politics, and Laertes reveals the secret of his past.[120]

Laertes, "the old man" in Handke's script, is associated in both
versions with blood stains on the train seat that Wilhelm sees before
the old man with the bloody nose actually appears. The stains are
metonymic and metaphoric at the same time, with the latter function more pronounced in Handke's script, where the description
"The seat across from him with the large brown spot" (p. 17) evokes
by naming the color brown the Nazi past the old man symbolizes.
The blood on the white seat alludes most directly to the blood of
Laertes's victims.[121] It must also be seen in connection with the
blood Wilhelm draws by putting his fist through the window, which
he then sucks (p. 7).

In Wenders's film, the blood motif occurs one other time, at a
point not in the original script: while the industrialist speaks of
loneliness in Germany, he sticks a pen into his hand and draws
blood, seemingly unaware that he is doing so. Wilhelm then uses
this pen to write a diary entry, one of the few times in the film when
he manages to write. Once again, the film places him and his whole

[119] Rentschler, *West German Film*, p. 175.

[120] This is also one of the most cinematically impressive sequences of the film,
called a "marvel of figure groupings" by John L. Fell in his review, "The Wrong
Movement," *Film Quarterly* 32 (1978–1979), p. 50. James Franklin describes it this
way: "In a three-shot sequence . . . the main characters steadily but almost impercep-
tibly ascend a mountain." Franklin, *The New German Cinema*, p. 143. See Wenders's
description of it in Dawson, *Wim Wenders*, p. 24.

The construction of the sequence is foregrounded by its own virtuosity: that is,
minimal editing combined with the camera's role in the choreography. The camera
stays anchored to no single person's movement and does not disguise its own movement as independent from the characters.

[121] The blood on the white seat has also been compared to the blood on the snow
in *Parzival*. Shelley Frisch, "The Disenchanted Image: From Goethe's *Wilhelm Meister* to Wenders' *Wrong Movement*," *Literature/Film Quarterly* 7 (1979), p. 212. Wolfram Schütte also notes the Parzival allusion in the *Frankfurter Rundschau* version of
his review: "Träumerei oder Weg nach Innen," 25 April 1975.

approach to writing in a negative light. Laertes (admittedly a rather improbable war criminal) bleeds out of guilt for the suffering he has caused others; the shedding of his own blood for others, albeit a few decades too late, is in contrast to Wilhelm, who impatiently tells the old man "I have no feeling for the past" (p. 28), and who seems empowered to write by using the blood of another.[122]

The old man as a symbol of the crimes of the Nazi past "haunts" Wilhelm, just as those crimes continue to haunt Germany. The problem of postwar Germany has been the question of what to do about this legacy. One possible reading might be that Wilhelm's failure to kill Laertes symbolizes his inability to come to terms with politics, specifically Germany's political past, an inability seen as another sign of his general narcissistic withdrawal, his lack of resolve and passivity.[123] I would suggest that, on the contrary, it is his desire to kill the man that demonstrates his inability to deal with the past; this desire exposes a violence beneath his withdrawal from politics, a violence that illuminates the nature of that withdrawal.

Wilhelm finalizes his plans to murder the old man while writing—writing something he thinks will be political: "I'm writing a story about a man who is a good-natured person and at the same time incapable of a sort of pity. I want to prove that good-naturedness and the lack of pity belong together. I believe it will be a political story. By the way, I think I'd enjoy taking a boat-ride. Where is that possible around here?" (p. 72).

What one notices here is the obvious connection between the story he writes and his relation to the old man. There is, however, the odd problem of discerning whom he is writing about. Which one is basically good-natured but incapable of pity—the old man who committed war crimes at Vilna, or Wilhelm, who has decided to drown the old man? Besides the obvious insight that Wilhelm seems caught in repeating (on a very small scale) the old man's crimes, it also seems that Wilhelm is trying to eliminate the man in order to destroy the memory of those crimes.

The burden of politics in Germany is its association with such crimes, and it is a burden that has more than once in the history of West Germany vilified any type of politics beyond a supposedly value-free management of the economy.[124] Disturbing that repres-

---

[122] Compare this to the vampirism motif in *Lenz* and *Class Love* discussed above in Chapter 2. The *Erfahrungshunger*, the experiential hunger of this generation, is the common denominator, the need for a vicarious appropriation of the seeming vitality—or of the suffering—of others.

[123] See, for example, Frisch, "The Disenchanted Image," p. 213.

[124] Cf. Strauss's *Devotion* where Richard's father becomes angry at almost any type

sion of the political—and the repression of historical memory—has proved to be a dangerous activity inviting violence. Wilhelm's alienation from politics, when disturbed in confrontation with the old man, brings about a desire for violence that in its knee-jerk, reflex-like nature betrays more of a need to eliminate an obstacle to his narcissistic impassivity rather than any concern about justice for the old man's victims.

The old man has, after all, learned something from his experiences, and he is interested that Wilhelm should not repeat his mistakes. The latter finds the old man's advice and influence oppressive; in general Wilhelm would rather strike out in his impatience at the world he finds around him. The connection between his conflict with the old man and the problem of terrorism in West Germany after the demise of the student movement suggests itself rather clearly here. This is even clearer in another scene, during an exchange with Therese. During the walk in the hills, after the old man has disclosed his secret, Wilhelm explains to Therese his "erotic gaze" and his desire to become a writer. Therese expresses her irritation with the aimlessness of their situation in words that could easily apply to the quietism of which West Germany has so often been accused:

> Therese: "Something has to happen, Wilhelm. Everything is so automatic, so finished, so sewed-up tight. I'm not enjoying this walk anymore. It seems like a postponement to me. We have to do something."
> Wilhelm, *close-up*: "Have you ever wanted to kill someone?" (p. 58)

In the stultifying resignation of yet another failed German revolution, Wilhelm sees as the only action possible a despairing, individual act of violence. As I have stressed above, this type of political choice is more closely related to withdrawal into the "privacy" of art than is immediately apparent. The figure of Wilhelm embodies two "postrevolutionary" responses, both of which stem from resignation: terrorist violence as well as the withdrawal into aesthetics.

It is in this context, perhaps, that Wenders's film can be best distinguished from Handke's screenplay. For in the film, Wilhelm does not, after scaring off Laertes, go on into an isolation depicted as the solution to his writing block; instead he ends up on the Zugspitze with no blizzard, no sea of fog à la Caspar David Friedrich, only a merciless clarity that makes him doubt his move into isolation—and

---

of politics (p. 6). This attitude toward politics is older than the Third Reich and has its parallel throughout the West; in Germany, however, it has played an especially significant role—at least since the French Revolution.

his inability to learn from Laertes. Wenders's film suggests that, in a "postrevolutionary" era, it is important not to succumb to the conformism of the dominant social order, as Handke's adaptation of *Wilhelm Meister* stresses, but that it is also all the more important to learn from history rather than withdraw from it or attempt to eliminate it. Wenders has spoken clearly of the artist's necessity to confront the German past, that films cannot be made responsibly in Germany without addressing the "hole" in German culture left by fascism and the postwar repression of its memory. That is the vacuum into which Wilhelm apparently wants to escape.

CHAPTER FOUR

The Politics of Memory

THIS IS HOW one pictures the angel of history. His face is turned
toward the past. Where we perceive a chain of events, he sees
one single catastrophe which keeps piling wreckage upon
wreckage and hurls it in front of his feet. The angel
would like to stay, awaken the dead, and make
whole what has been smashed. But a storm
is blowing from Paradise; it has got caught
in his wings with such violence that the
angel can no longer close them. This
storm irresistibly propels him into
the future to which his back is
turned, while the pile of
debris before him
grows skyward.
This storm is
what we call
progress.[1]

1977: RETURN OF THE REPRESSED

Walter Benjamin made his remarks on the angel of history in reference to a painting by Klee. In the 1980s they were quoted in concert by Laurie Anderson, a contemporary composer of electronic music and a performance artist, a citation that illustrates a historical "constellation" that contains both Benjamin and the contemporary postmodern disposition toward "progress." (It is a pessimism that obviously does not—in Anderson's case certainly—renounce all technology.) Benjamin's attitude toward history is described by Habermas as "posthistoricist": "The modern, avant-garde spirit has sought to use the past in a different way; it disposes those pasts which have been made available by the objectifying scholarship of historicism, but it opposes at the same time a neutralized history which is locked up in the museum of historicism."[2]

A similar attitude to the past can be noted in the work of many West German artists of the generation that had been shaped by its experience of the late 1960s—especially in the late 1970s, once they began to turn their attention again toward history. For their concern with the self and its psychological development led ultimately toward examination of extrapersonal, historical factors as the 1970s progressed. As history once again became a topic of political and artistic discourse, the interest was not in neutral, "objectified" history but in a personally motivated investigation of the past.

These "posthistoricist" sentiments were not restricted to the realm of art and culture. Indeed, in the United States during the 1980s somewhat comparable attitudes toward history entered into academic debates, not merely within the field of history but in literary studies as well, in what has been somewhat ironically named "New Historicism."[3] Uniting these diverse academic and cultural activities is an awareness of the representation of history not as a neutral but as an active intervention on behalf of perspectives and experiences (both personal and political) repressed in standard interpretations.

[1] Walter Benjamin, "Theses on the Philosophy of History," in the collection of his essays *Illuminations*, trans. Harry Zohn, ed. Hannah Arendt (New York: Schocken, 1969), pp. 257–58. Quoted by Laurie Anderson on her "Natural History" tour (1986).

[2] Habermas, "Modernity," pp. 5–6.

[3] Hutcheon, *A Poetics of Postmodernism*, pp. 90–91. According to Stephen Greenblatt, who coined the term "New Historicism": "The term originated in a somewhat feeble witticism: a word play on the 'new criticsm' and also a tug of oppositions between 'new' and 'history.' " "A Conversation with Stephen Greenblatt," *California Monthly* (April 1988), p. 9.

In West Germany, there had been much repression of history. But by 1977, what had been repressed surfaced in ways that no one, on the right or the left, from the most "subjectivist" to the most orthodox, regardless of age, could afford to ignore. The year 1977 marked the ten-year anniversary of the murder of Benno Ohnesorg, one of the most dramatic mobilizing influences on the student movement. As ten-year anniversaries for various of the incidents that made up the history of the student movement approached, a series of articles and books appeared that attempted to make sense of this history.[4] All these writings may be seen as attempts to reclaim that history from the standard interpretations that had become dominant. Activists themselves attempted to write that history in accordance with their memories and with their analysis of those memories. Helke Sander, for instance, was motivated to begin the project that resulted in her film, *The Subjective Factor* (*Der subjektive Faktor*, 1980), by the various retrospectives put together by men who had been activists; she decided it was necessary to retell the story from a woman's point of view.

Another event that had its tenth anniversary was a 1967 speech given by Gudrun Ensslin at an SDS meeting in the period after Ohnesorg's death, a speech that could be used to mark the beginning of the process that would lead to the formation of the terrorist Red Army Faction, or RAF.[5] Around 1977, RAF entered a new phase of activity. Its founders had been in prison since 1972; Ulrike Meinhof had been found dead in her cell in May of 1976. The new phase was led by a new "generation" of terrorists whose motivation was hardly APO nostalgia.

The spectacular murders of 1977 represented a new escalation in terrorist violence in West Germany: a federal prosecutor, Siegfried Buback was murdered in April; Jürgen Ponto, the head of the Dresdner Bank, was shot in July; and leading industrialist Hanns Martin Schleyer was kidnapped in September and found dead in France in October, after the defeat of the Mogadishu skyjackers. The year also marked a major defeat for the terrorist strategy in West Germany, if not its complete elimination.[6]

[4] In 1977 alone, the following appeared: "Ten Years After," *Kursbuch*, no. 48 (June 1977); Mosler's *Was wir wollten, was wir wurden*; and Wolff and Windaus's *Studentenbewegung 1967–69*. For other titles, see Beutin et al., *Deutsche Literaturgeschichte* (1984 ed.), p. 562.

[5] See Lisa DiCaprio, "Marianne and Juliane/The German Sisters: Baader-Meinhof Fictionalized," *Jump Cut*, no. 29 (1984), p. 59.

[6] There has been some terrorist activity ascribed to RAF in the 1980s; this "revival" seemed to become serious after the West German *Bundestag* voted in November 1983

The kidnapping of Schleyer and the hijacking of a Lufthansa jet to Mogadishu, Somalia, were actions of the RAF meant to force the West German state to release Andreas Baader, Gudrun Ensslin, and Jan-Carl Raspe from their confinement in the maximum-security prison at Stammheim, near Stuttgart. Instead, a special unit of West German security forces stormed the Lufthansa jet in Mogadishu, freeing the passengers and killing the hijackers. In Stammheim the next morning, Baader, Ensslin, and Raspe were found dead in their cells, in what was somewhat suspiciously ruled a suicide (as had been the case with Meinhof in 1976).[7]

The hysteria with which West German society reacted to these events was great—as though this small band of terrorists could have brought down the West German state, almost as though the murders of Buback, Ponto, and Schleyer, inexcusable as they were, were the greatest crimes of the century. This atmosphere of national emergency created a situation in which almost anyone with leftist or oppositional views was considered a "sympathizer" whose influence had aided the terrorists. The presentation of events in the media did not deviate much from the dominant, rather one-dimensional perspective that defined public discourse in the autumn of 1977. Many leftists felt that civil liberties, especially freedom of expression, were in serious danger; some feared even that West German democracy was at an end.[8]

Why such tremendous fears—on both the right and the left— should have been prevalent is at first glance not clear to the foreigner. The answer has to do with the relation of the events in 1977 to what are undoubtedly the greatest (German) crimes of the century: the scuttling of German democracy by National Socialism, the resultant persecution of political dissidents and Jews; and the even-

---

to allow the United States to station its Pershing missiles in West Germany, in spite of widespread protests. In June 1990 it was revealed that some RAF members had been living in hiding in the GDR. Given the anarchistic inclinations of the group at its founding, it is ironic that some members ended up in the GDR. It also seems unlikely that the group was ever controlled by the GDR, in spite of any unholy collaboration that may have developed.

[7] The prisoners in Stammheim were found to have had guns in their cells; how this occurred in the highest-security prison in West Germany remains a mystery. The prisoners were also apparently in radio contact with the highjackers in Africa—another mystery. Such details and other inconsistencies in the official version of events have led to skepticism on the part of certain oppositional groups vis-à-vis that version. The Ensslin family, too—not just Gudrun's sister Christiane but also her father, a Lutheran minister—expressed doubts about the suicide thesis. Nonetheless the suicide version has not been disproved, at least officially. See Margit Mayer, "The German October of 1977," New German Critique, no. 13 (1977), p. 160.

[8] See Mayer, "The German October," pp. 155–63.

tual mass extermination of Jews, gypsies, homosexuals, and others. The fears of the Right go back at least to the revolutionary unrest after World War I in Germany; these fears contributed to the ultimate success of the Nazis. That success in turn explains the fears of the German Left.

The connection between 1977 and those events earlier in the century is a bit more concrete than my brief historical explanation above can convey. Schleyer, for instance, was not merely the head of Daimler-Benz (manufacturer of the Mercedes-Benz), as well as the leader of the organization of the largest employers in West Germany; he had also been in Hitler's S.S. In terms of symbolism, Schleyer was thus an especially appropriate target for terrorists who fancied that their self-appointed task was to purge the German past—or be purged by it. This rather dramatic self-image was already evident in the 1967 speech by Gudrun Ensslin to which I alluded above. In the aftermath of the Ohnesorg killing, she called the West German state not only "fascist" but determined to kill all the student protesters (at that time mostly nonviolent). She demanded meeting violence with violence, since negotiations were pointless with the "Auschwitz" generation.[9]

In 1977 another event, this one literary in nature, helped cause renewed interest in the past, the past of both the student movement and of German fascism. It was the posthumous publication in book form of *The Journey* (*Die Reise*), the never-completed autobiographical essay by Bernward Vesper, who had indeed once been Gudrun Ensslin's lover and was the son of the writer Will Vesper, a favorite of Hitler. Bernward had committed suicide in 1971, and it had taken six years for friends and editors to work out a publishing deal; but the book, a "ghostly journey into subjectivity and into the past," could not have met a more receptive audience than the one it found in 1977.[10] Readers were now interested not just in Vesper's illumination of aspects of the protest movement since forgotten (the drugs, the antiauthoritarian opposition to the dogmatic socialists, the sympathy with terrorism, the early example of radical "subjectivity" in Vesper's prose). There was also a special interest in Vesper's at-

---

[9] See DiCaprio, "Marianne and Juliane," p. 59. See also Rutschky's discussion of the relationship between the "German Autumn" of 1977 and the fascist legacy in *Erfahrungshunger*, pp. 145–64. Margarethe von Trotta's film *Marianne and Juliane* (*Die bleierne Zeit*, 1981) is a fictionalized account of events in Gudrun Ensslin's life from the point of view of her sister Christiane (to whom it is dedicated). Among other things, the film explores the connection between the terrorist sister Marianne's concern about the crimes of the German past and her move into terrorism.

[10] Beutin et al., *Deutsche Literaturgeschichte* (1984 ed.), p. 562.

tempts to deal both with the painful memories of his relationship to his authoritarian father and with his relationship to his father's political past.

Among other things, the success of Vesper's book contributed to a wave of Generationenliteratur, "generation literature," in the late 1970s. Written by people born in the 1930s and 1940s, these books dealt with the authors' relationships to their parents—usually their fathers—and the behavior of the parents during Nazism.[11] This was the personal side of the confrontation with the German past, with the parent in question personifying that past for the younger generation. These books were also part of the general autobiographical trend of the 1970s. Another influential book dealing with the fascist past was the autobiographical novel *Patterns of Childhood* (*Kindheitsmuster*, 1976) by East German writer Christa Wolf, which was based on personal, not parental, experience of fascism. (Wolf's works had influenced West German writers—especially women—since the 1969 publication of *The Quest for Christa T.* in West Germany.)[12]

The increasing interest in history was matched by an increase in the interest in literary history. To a certain extent, this interest had already been evident in *Lenz* (1972), *Wrong Move* (1975), and *The New Sorrows of Young W.* (*Die neuen Leiden des jungen W.*, 1973), by the East German writer Ulrich Plenzdorf (a big success in West Germany). But these works were followed by others devoted specifically to writers and artists from different historical eras, as opposed to the aforementioned modern adaptations. Peter Härtling's *Hölderlin*, Wolfgang Hildesheimer's *Mozart*, and Adolf Muschg's *Gottfried Keller* appeared in 1976 and 1977. This trend has been described as a search for "the way into history";[13] to it could be added Christa Wolf's *No Place on Earth* (*Kein Ort. Nirgends*, 1979), although that

---

[11] To name a few: Brigitte Schwaiger's *Lange Abwesenheit* (1980), Peter Härtling's *Nachgetragene Liebe* (1980), Heinrich Wiesner's *Der Riese am Tisch* (1979), Ruth Rehmann's *Der Mann auf der Kanzel* (1979), Siegfried Gauch's *Vaterspuren* (1979), Paul Kersten's *Der alltägliche Tod meines Vaters* (1980), Peter Henisch's *Die kleine Figur meines Vaters* (1980), and Christoph Meckel's *Suchbild. Über meinen Vater* (1980). Elisabeth Plessen's *Mitteilungen an den Adel* had appeared already in 1976. See Michael Schneider's essay "Fathers and Sons, Retrospectively: The Damaged Relations between Two Generations," trans. Jamie Owen Daniel, *New German Critique*, no. 31 (1984), pp. 3–51. Orig. "Väter und Söhne, posthum. Das beschädigte Verhältnis zweier Generationen," in his book *Den Kopf verkehrt aufgesetzt*, pp. 8–64.

[12] Christa Wolf had a great influence on West German "New Subjectivity"; cf. her passage on political slogans and personal identity, *Nachdenken über Christa T.*, pp. 71–72. Note also, for instance, how often Karin Struck cites her in *Class Love* (*Klassenliebe*); see above, Chapter 2, note 77.

[13] Kreuzer, "Neue Subjektivität," p. 92.

work must of course be read primarily as a response to East German reality.

The examination of history via literary tradition included an increasing validation of aesthetic complexity that ran counter to the trend of most "authentic," autobiographical writing. By the end of the 1970s and the early 1980s this new validation had resulted in announcements of a "resistance of aesthetics" and a repudiation of "authenticity."[14] Examples of the new formal rigor were produced by somewhat older writers, two of whom had been influential on the student movement: Hans Magnus Enzensberger and Peter Weiss. Enzensberger's *Sinking of the Titanic* (*Der Untergang der Titanic*, 1977), written in verse, is a parable on the defeat of the modern ideal of progress in the twentieth century, contrasting three historical perspectives (the 1912 Titanic disaster, his own utopian hopes of the late 1960s, and the pessimism of the mid-1970s); formally it alludes to as old a formal influence as Dante.[15] Peter Weiss's *The Aesthetics of Resistance* (*Die Ästhetik des Widerstands*) is a complex, multilayered novelistic attempt to come to terms with some painful history (personal and political). Uwe Johnson's *Anniversaries* (*Jahrestage*) represents a similar project and like Weiss's *Aesthetics of Resistance* is a work of monumental proportions: Weiss's novel appeared in three installments, 1975, 1978, and 1981, and Johnson's in four, 1970, 1971, 1973, and 1980.[16]

A similar concern with history and with the complexity of coming to terms with it both politically and via aesthetic means can be seen among members of the " '68 generation" who were involved with filmmaking—although here, too, the influence of the somewhat older Alexander Kluge was significant. In the "New German Cinema," there had been a shift toward "literary history" as well in the mid-1970s, but this shift had not meant any general increase in the level of *film* aesthetics, rather the contrary; aside from some films like Fassbinder's *Effi Briest* (1974), literary adaptation in West German cinema had resulted in the making of ever more uninspired films until one spoke of the *Literaturverfilmungskrise*, the crisis of (mediocre) filmed adaptations of literature.[17] This trend was in some sense related to the conservative *Tendenzwende*, but in film the rea-

[14] See Beutin et al., *Deutsche Literaturgeschichte* (1984 ed.), pp. 565–78, esp. p. 566 discussing the literary deficits of New Subjectivity; see also Krechel, "Leben in Anführungszeichen," pp. 80–107.

[15] See, for example, Hinrich Seeba, "Der Untergang der Utopie: Ein Schiffbruch in der Gegenwartsliteratur," *German Studies Review* 4 (1981), pp. 281–98.

[16] Beutin et al., *Deutsche Literaturgeschichte* (1984 ed.), pp. 540, 568–70.

[17] See Rentschler, *West German Film*, pp. 129–53; Pflaum and Prinzler, *Cinema in the Federal Republic of Germany*, pp. 25–30.

sons were much more transparent, having to do with the West German system of state subsidies for film projects, which required above all the approval of a script.[18] What better method to win approval for a project than to submit a script based on a "literary classic"?

Many filmmakers were quite dissatisfied with this situation, but it took two things to mobilize them into action. The first of these was a cinematic event: Joachim Fest's film *Hitler—A Career* (1977), a film that dealt with the troublesome German past in a fashion that disturbed the filmmakers. Wim Wenders especially lashed out at Fest's film, decrying the situation of West German film, explicating in turn its relation to the fascist past that Fest had ascribed to the aura of one man—an aura Fest's film reproduced uncritically.[19] The second mobilizing event was political: the hysteria that built up to the "German autumn" of 1977. Fassbinder, disgusted with the political and cinematic scene in West Germany, declared he would leave Germany. Actually, as it happened, it was Wenders who left, lured by Francis Coppola to direct *Hammet* in California.[20]

Fassbinder instead stayed to join in a collaborative effort with other filmmakers to put together some kind of alternative look at the events of Autumn 1977, from a perspective that differed from the government's polarizing rhetoric, the latter unchallenged by the official electronic media. The resulting film, *Germany in Autumn* (*Deutschland im Herbst*, 1978), was edited by Kluge and Beate Mainka-Jellinghaus. It was a collage of fictional, autobiographical, and documentary episodes; these episodes investigated historical and contemporary aspects of German reality considered relevant to the crisis of 1977 by the various collaborating directors and writers.[21]

---

[18] For background on the West German subsidy system, its history, and its relationship to the development of the New German Cinema, see Elsaesser, *New German Cinema*, pp. 8–35; Rentschler, *West German Film*, pp. 32–63; Pflaum and Prinzler, *Cinema in the Federal Republic of Germany*, pp. 5–80; Franklin, *The New German Cinema*, pp. 21–58; Sandford, *The New German Cinema*, pp. 9–16; and Phillips, *New German Filmmakers*, pp. ix–xxiii.

[19] See Wenders, "That's Entertainment: Hitler," in Rentschler, *West German Filmmakers on Film*, pp. 126–31. Orig. "That's Entertainment: Eine Polemik gegen Joachim C. Fests Film *Hitler—Eine Karriere*," *Die Zeit*, 5 August 1977, p. 34.

[20] Fassbinder declared at the 1977 Berlin International Film Festival that he wanted to emigrate; see Buchka, *Augen kann man nicht kaufen*, pp. 13–14. Pflaum and Prinzler write of "Fassbinder's polemical declaration that he would rather live as a roadsweeper in Mexico if politics developed in a way he felt possible." *Cinema in the Federal Republic of Germany*, p. 36.

[21] Among the collaborators were Kluge, Fassbinder, Volker Schlöndorff, Heinrich Böll, and Edgar Reitz. See Miriam Hansen's article "Cooperative Auteur Cinema," pp. 36–56; also Kaes, *Deutschlandbilder*, pp. 30–35. More or less the same group of film-

For Kluge, Fassbinder, and others, this began a period in which their work began to confront German history in ways that differed considerably from the adaptation of literary classics.[22] Fassbinder began his "BRD-Trilogie," a trilogy of films dealing with West Germany in the 1940s and 1950s: The Marriage of Maria Braun (Die Ehe der Maria Braun, 1979), Lola (1981), and The Longing of Veronika Voss (Die Sehnsucht der Veronika Voss, 1981).[23] These stylized melodramas explored the relationship between the conservative restoration in West Germany that dominated the 1950s and the emotional lives of individual Germans. Kluge's montage-style investigation of German history in Germany in Autumn would be further developed in his next film, The Patriot (Die Patriotin, 1979).[24]

Impulses comparable to those in Fassbinder's and Kluge's films can also be seen in films by women, who by the late 1970s began to exert an influence on West German cinema that could no longer be ignored. Confrontation with the past via "Brechtian" melodrama can be seen in the work of such filmmakers as Helma Sanders-Brahms and Jutta Brückner, and through juxtaposition of documentary footage with fictional sequences in the films of Brückner, Sanders-Brahms, and Helke Sander. Sander's The Subjective Factor (1981) was a mix of fictional and documentary footage; her 1977 film REDUPERS, one of the first films by West German women to achieve critical acclaim, used no "historical" documentary footage, but its

makers continued collaboration in subsequent attempts to influence political discourse in West Germany: in 1980, Der Kandidat appeared, a film about the archconservative Franz Josef Strauss made by Kluge, Schlöndorff, Alexander von Eschwege, and Stefan Aust. In 1982–1983 a similar collaboration by Kluge, Schlöndorff, Aust, and Axel Engstfeld resulted in Krieg und Frieden (War and Peace), a study of the nuclear arms race during the West German debate about accepting the deployment of U.S. Pershing missiles. See Pflaum and Prinzler, Cinema in the Federal Republic of Germany, pp. 73–74.

[22] The phenomenon of this "return to history" in West German film since the mid-1970s is the focus of Kaes's Deutschlandbilder, which has now appeared in English as From Heimat to Hitler. Kaes mentions the events of 1977 as one major motivation for the trend—certainly for Kluge and Fassbinder. Another important event at the end of the 1970s was the premiere of the American miniseries Holocaust on West German television in January 1979; the American series caused a popular reaction with regard to repressed German history that the more experimental Germany in Autumn was unable to create. See Kaes, Deutschlandbilder, pp. 35–42, and Elsaesser, New German Cinema, pp. 271–72.

[23] Fassbinder's Lili Marleen (1981) and Berlin Alexanderplatz (1980) treat politics, literature, and/or mass culture in other periods of German history: fascism, the Weimar Republic.

[24] Hans Jürgen Syberberg's Our Hitler (Hitler. Ein Film aus Deutschland, 1977) can also be seen in the context of these "history films." See especially Kaes's discussion of the film in Deutschlandbilder, pp. 135–70.

low-key narrative provided a format for documenting autobiographical, artistic, and political realities. As much as it is a fiction, it is a documentary on Berlin in 1977 and a self-reflexive examination of Sander's situation as a woman struggling to survive there as an artist.

The personal, autobiographical aspect of the confrontation with German history is much stronger in these films by women (or at least much more openly admitted). This can be partially explained in terms of the trend of "generational literature": the " '68 generation" wanted to confront personal history and German history by examining its relation to parents who had lived through fascism as adults. Fassbinder, too, reflects this tendency—it should be mentioned in this context that the original title idea for The Marriage of Maria Braun was "The Marriages of Our Parents."[25] But in the films by Brückner and Sanders-Brahms, a more explicitly feminist project must also be acknowledged: the need to explore their specific identity as women by looking at their parents, and especially their mothers.

The endeavors by Sander, Sanders-Brahms, and others to combine personal interests and feminist perspectives in the examination of larger historical issues—the fascist past, the student movement—make their films especially representative of a shift in the leftist counterculture in the late 1970s. During these years one noted a gradual move away from ghettoization and single-issue organizing toward an attempt at greater unity—and toward once again exerting influence on public policy in West Germany as a whole. This process resulted in the consolidation of a new peace movement and the formation of the Greens.

But these women did not confront such historical and political issues in their films by renouncing the feminist emphasis on personal politics. Instead it was through that very emphasis, politically and aesthetically, that they moved into a confrontation with the German past, much as feminist politics would lead many women into broad coalitions like the peace movement and the Greens. The films by Helma Sanders-Brahms and by Helke Sander examined here, for example, share a project similar to that of the Greens (and of Fassbinder's trilogy, for that matter): German history is reread in order to undermine conventional interpretations mired in Cold War thinking, as part of a broader critique of militarism—and patriarchy.

[25] See Kaes, "History, fiction, memory: Fassbinder's The Marriage of Maria Braun (1979)," in Eric Rentschler, ed., German Film and Literature: Adaptations and Transformations (New York: Methuen, 1986), p. 278.

WOMEN'S DISCOURSE AND THE GERMAN PAST: *GERMANY, PALE MOTHER* BY HELMA SANDERS-BRAHMS

"Germany, Pale Mother—the title is significant for that whole generation of those who are between thirty and forty, in whose childhood the 'fatherland' was a land of mothers."[26] That title also explains the relationship between Helma Sanders-Brahms's film and the historical position it articulates: the search for personal identity by members of her generation. Eventually this search involved the need to confront their parents' history, most specifically with regard to those questions, so long unspoken, that pertained to the years of fascism and the war. The role that fathers played had been at issue in much West German literature in the latter half of the 1970s.[27] The mother's role had been largely neglected, since it was less likely to be one of active compliance. Yet precisely because mothers were more likely to be at home during the war, their influence was all the more important in shaping the early years of a whole generation. The mother, after all, was often the only parent that both male and female children saw for long stretches of time during the war, and for some time afterwards.

In *A Sorrow Beyond Dreams* (1972), Peter Handke had dealt with the story of his mother's experiences during the war in Austria; in the late 1970s, however, it was primarily women who began to look at their mothers' lives, above all in connection with the feminist questioning of traditional sex roles.[28] In a series of films in the late 1970s and early 1980s, German women attempted to tell the stories of their mothers and of their relationship to their mothers. These films include Jutta Brückner's *Years of Hunger* (Hungerjahre, 1980), Recha Jungmann's *Etwas tut weh* (1980), *Germany, Pale Mother* (Deutschland, bleiche Mutter, 1979) by Helma Sanders-Brahms, and Jeanine Meerapfel's *Malou* (1983).[29]

[26] Christian Bauer, "Auf der Suche nach verlorenen Müttern," rev. of *Deutschland, bleiche Mutter*, dir. Helma Sanders-Brahms, *Süddeutsche Zeitung*, 3 January 1981.

[27] See above, note 11; see also Kaes, *Deutschlandbilder*, pp. 110–11.

[28] See, for example, Kaes, *Deutschlandbilder*, pp. 111–12.

[29] Wolfram Schütte discusses Jungman's, Brückner's, and Sanders-Brahms's films in "Mütter, Töchter, Krieg und Terror," *Frankfurter Rundschau*, 25 February 1980. For other discussions of the topic of daughters and mothers in film, see Jan Mouton's "The Absent Mother Makes an Appearance in the Films of West German Women Directors," *Women in German Yearbook* 4 (1988), pp. 69–81; and Eva Hiller's "mütter und töchter: zu 'deutschland, bleiche mutter,' (helma sanders-brahms), 'hungerjahre' (jutta brückner), 'daughter rite' (michelle citron)," *Frauen und Film*, no. 24 (1980), pp. 29–33.

Sanders-Brahms's film, in recounting the story of her mother, confronts the issue of fascism and the war in the most direct manner, for the filmmaker depicts her mother's experience of precisely those years. Her mother's attitude toward the National Socialists was hardly supportive but nonetheless problematic in its "apolitical" indifference to most of what they initiated. The relevance of Sanders-Brahms's project to feminism is evident in its presentation of an aspect of the history of the Second World War often neglected: a woman's experience.

Sanders-Brahms does not, however, recount this history by effacing her own interest and place in it for the sake of creating the illusion of "objective" history; she uses her mother's life as the focus of the narrative, and she foregrounds her own position of authority in reconstructing her mother's story. Sanders-Brahms's investigation of her relationship to her mother—the "dialogue" her narrative voice carries on with her mother's life—openly controls the trajectory of the film. This fusion of a historical and political investigation with an intensely subjective exploration of the mother–daughter relationship is exemplary of the feminist attempt to combine the personal and the political, to analyze the political nature of women's experience in the "private" or domestic sphere, and to bring women into history, the "public" realm traditionally defined by male experience.

Sanders-Brahms makes public her mother's "private" experience, confronting its intersection with fascism and the war, and at the same time edits her film so that her fictional reconstruction of her mother's story confronts the documentary record of the war. She provides documentary evidence of the horrors of the war that the National Socialists had been so eager to start; the impossibility of escaping the havoc they wreaked by withdrawing into a private realm of happiness (the dream of Sanders-Brahms's "apolitical" parents) is also amply demonstrated. Her film thus deals with the intersection of the personal and the political at many levels, reflecting the interests of feminism as well as the program announced by both male and female activists of her generation since the 1960s. It also alludes to the alliance of feminism and the peace movement that had developed by the beginning of the 1980s, in that it demonstrates the impossibility of trying to separate "women's issues" from other historical and political concerns—above all fascism and militarism. Those phenomena, in turn, cannot be discussed apart from questions of gendered socialization, as Klaus Theweleit's *Male Fantasies* so ably demonstrates.[30]

---

[30] Klaus Theweleit, *Male Fantasies*, trans. Stephan Conway et al., 2 vols. (Minne-

The "Public/Private" Dichotomy

As Judith Mayne has written, "Feminist theorists have always
stressed that the division of life between the realms of private and
public is a false dichotomy."[31] The place of women, according to
this dichotomy, is of course the private, domestic realm, a realm of
blissful warmth, free from the evils of politics, which are associated
with public life. Women are "privileged" by this association with
the warmth and intimacy of the home and its attendant "freedom"
from politics, and they are indeed responsible for its maintenance,
although *authority* for the home does not reside with them. This
"privilege" furthermore masks their exclusion from the realm of
power, bathing it in a positive light. Fully supportive of such an
ideology, the National Socialists enshrined the place of women in
the home.[32] Hitler awarded medals (the *Mutterkreuz*, or "mother's
cross") to women for having babies on the homefront, just as he
would award the "iron cross" to men for their valor on the battle-
fields; the dichotomy between women's domestic role and men's activity on the fields of history was thus sanctified by the highest authority.[33]

Sanders-Brahms's film does not depict Hans and Lene, the characters representing her parents, as Nazis; the question of their complicity with the regime has rather to do with their acceptance of the
public/private dichotomy in its traditional form. Sanders-Brahms
wrote that her intention was to address the situation of those oft-
neglected people in the Third Reich whose goals had little to do
with politics, who wanted "the simple life ... love, marriage, a

apolis: University of Minnesota Press, 1987). Orig. *Männerphantasien*, 2 vols. (Frankfurt: Roter Stern, 1977). This study analyzes attitudes toward women and sexuality
in the writings of German soldiers and members of protofascist paramilitary groups
during and after World War I. Also examined is the relationship between the misogyny of these men and the misogyny typical of male socialization in Western culture.

[31] Judith Mayne, "Female Narration, Women's Cinema," *New German Critique*,
nos. 24–25 (1981–1982), p. 160.

[32] For a comprehensive study of the situation of women during the Third Reich, see
Claudia Koonz's *Mothers in the Fatherland: Women, the Family and Nazi Politics*
(New York: St. Martin's Press, 1987). See also the following by Tim Mason: "Women
in Germany, 1925–1940: Family, Welfare, and Work," *History Workshop*, nos. 1 and
2 (1976); and *Zur Lage der Frauen in Deutschland. Wohlfahrt, Arbeit und Familie*
(Frankfurt: Suhrkamp, 1976).

[33] There is of course a contradiction here: Hitler/Public Power intrudes into the
private realm to reward women for "public service," thus increasing state control
over reproduction and the family.

child."[34] In other words, she wanted to focus on people who wanted little to do with the party, people who simply wanted private happiness. In the second sequence of the film, Hans reacts to an argument at the office between his friend and colleague Ulrich, a Nazi, and their socialist supervisor, by stating that such political controversies are of no concern to him: "I just want my peace and quiet. And the brunette. I only want to live my life, you know? The Führer can't have anything against that" (p. 30). Lene, for her part, does not want a man in the party, as she tells her sister Hanne, but not out of any interest in resisting it, as becomes clear soon thereafter in the same scene. In what seems to be a reference to *Kristallnacht* (9 November 1938), the "night of the broken glass," when Jewish homes, businesses, and synagogues in Germany were attacked by organized mobs, breaking glass is heard by the two sisters. They look out Lene's bedroom window to see Rahel Bernstein, a Jewish classmate of theirs, being carried away; it is Lene who closes the shutters to the disturbances outside and suggests they continue their talk about suitable mates.

The illusion that politics and the turbulence of historical forces can simply be shut out, and that Hans will be able to live in peace with his dark-haired sweetheart, is one that is soon shattered in the film. Hans's and Lene's domestic bliss is ultimately in the way of the plans of the "Führer": Hans is drafted and sent to the front. Lene now finds herself alone in the domestic sphere, a poor refuge from the world, since the "public" forces of history continue to intrude into it—such as when she gives birth during an air raid. Eventually her refuge is literally destroyed by those forces, and Lene finds herself in front of a pile of rubble. "This was our house," she tells the infant Anna, as they begin their life outside the home (p. 58). When, after the war, the traditional domestic sphere is reestablished, there is still no "peace"; Hans's and Lene's experiences have been too diverse, and the order restored in the new society after the war makes the home not a refuge but a site of strife. For Lene, at least, the home becomes almost as confining as a prison. Sanders-Brahms's voice, in

[34] Helma Sanders-Brahms, *Deutschland, bleiche Mutter. Film-Erzählung* (Reinbeck bei Hamburg: Rowohlt, 1980), p. 9. All subsequent references to this book are in the text. The book includes early statements about the project, an early version of the screenplay, the text of the Grimm Brothers' fairy tale ("The Robber Bridegroom") that Eva Mattes recites in the film, the text of the voice-overs that Sanders-Brahms reads, an epilogue written after the filming, and other materials. (Since there are differences between the version of the screenplay in the *Film-Erzählung* and the final film, I shall cite dialogue from the former only when I am sure that it agrees with the film.)

the role of the narrator, states: "Now the war began on the inside, just as outside there was peace" (p. 113).

Thus the illusion of private happiness separate from history and politics is demonstrated to be a deadly one, one that indeed facilitated through passive compliance the militaristic politics that proved so destructive to the private lives of so many. But the examination of the ideological dichotomy of the public and the private is carried on by Sanders-Brahms's film not only at the level of the main characters' values; it can be shown to structure the entire film.

The film's narrative can be divided into three parts: Lene's entry into the domestic sphere—her courtship, marriage, and the birth of her daughter; her wanderings with her child in search of food and shelter after her home has been destroyed; and her life after the return of Hans, when the domestic sphere is restored. This tripartite division of the plot is reflected in the film's mirror motif: at a significant point in each of the three sections of the narrative, a mirror appears, each time itself divided into three segments, forming thus a triptych.[35] The first mirror is seen when the newlyweds have just arrived in their new home, the side panels reflecting each partner separately, and the large central panel showing the two seated together, happily smiling. This stylized image presents their idealized hopes for their life together—and at the same time it fragments them. The next time a mirror appears, the togetherness promised by that first image has long been interrupted by Hans's absence, and now the physical locus representing that togetherness is in ruins. After identifying the pile of rubble for Anna as their former home, Lene, looking into an unbroken segment of mirror, says, "And that was me" (p. 58). Lene's identity from this point on is no longer determined by her position inside the house Hans owned.

Homeless, Lene carries Anna as she makes her way first to Berlin in search of her wealthy relatives and a chance to meet Hans on leave. Then she takes Anna out to the country, where they survive off the land, safe from the air raids in Berlin, if not from all soldiers, since they do encounter some—dead ones who provide both bits of clothing and sights Lene would rather Anna not see, and living ones who expose Anna to another horrific sight: they rape her mother. But Lene can survive the rape. She has gained a strength outside the domestic sphere she had not known when it was intact.

Once the war has ended, Lene is still active in the world outside

---

[35] For the "triptych" idea, I am indebted to Barbara Kosta, who used it in her paper "*Deutschland, bleiche Mutter*: An addendum to history" (unpublished essay, University of California, Berkeley, 1983), p. 9.

the home, negotiating in the black market and helping with other women to rebuild Germany out of the rubble; but when Hans returns from captivity this phase of her life ends. He gets a job, and soon there is a new house for the family, a house where Lene serves him coffee, and where he establishes his authority over Anna (insisting, for example, that the child write neatly). The strength and the skills Lene had developed caring for herself and her child are now irrelevant: "She had learned how far her energies could reach, and that she didn't need anything else but herself and her hope . . . and now that this hope had been fulfilled, but her energies were no longer needed, she lost her face" (p. 10).

It is the image of her face, deformed on one side by paralysis, that she confronts in the mirror in her new home after the war, and this mirror-image is the emblem of the last part of the film. In her face is reflected the crippling effects that the restoration of the old private sphere has brought with it, in a conservative West German state where certain lessons learned in the war and the immediate postwar era—the bankruptcy of militarism and the value of women's contribution to survival and reconstruction—are repressed. Authority is restored within the home, just as, outside, Germany is once again militarized.[36]

The division of the narrative into three parts centering on Lene's place inside and outside the domestic sphere corresponds more or less to the formal composition of the film as well: the beginning and end of the film consist entirely of fictional reenactments of scenes from the life of Sanders-Brahms's mother, but in the middle section of the film, documentary footage of the war and its immediate aftermath intrude into the fiction. It is the war that destroys the illusion of private happiness insulated from politics and history; it is the war that interrupts the private melodrama of Lene and Hans and forces Lene out into the public realm on her own. In that Sanders-Brahms's fiction reenacts her mother's personal experience in the war years, her juxtaposition of that personal story with the "public," documentary record of those years reflects both the intrusion of the historical reality into her mother's life and her entrance into the "public realm" of history.

One of the first sequences in the film where documentary and fictional footage are intercut is the birth sequence. Shots of Lene in labor, Lene in her most "private," most personal pain, are juxta-

---

[36] Cf. Fassbinder's *Marriage of Maria Braun* (1979), where a broadcast of Adenauer proudly proclaiming West German rearmament is heard just before Maria learns that she has been tricked by the men in her life.

posed with documentary footage of Allied planes bombing Germany. Lene's struggle to give birth is contextualized by the historical struggle being waged "over her head." This montage is not an arbitrary, "formalistic" trick but rather a way of depicting Lene's labor in the middle of an air raid. Later, when her husband remarks that she has had an easy time while he's been fighting, she tells him: "Do you know what it's like to give birth during an air raid?" (p. 67).

Not only does the documentary footage of the bombers put Anna's birth into historical context; that birth contextualizes the bombing as well: the experience of women and children was not "separate" from the history of the war. Indeed, in the Second World War, when bombing of civilian populations occurred on a scale unimaginable in previous wars, women and children were in effect conscious targets of military strategy. For those responsible for such strategy on both sides of the conflict, there was no refuge status granted the "private," domestic sphere of women and children. Sanders-Brahms's fictional sequences of the birth thus give us part of the historical reality of the war largely unrecorded by documentarists, but nonetheless an essential part, without which much of what is recorded does not make sense. Why would nonmilitary targets be bombed if there were no civilian population to terrorize in the midst of its daily life—working, eating, cooking, making love, sleeping, giving birth?

It would seem, in fact, that one of the most important points made by Sanders-Brahms's film is that the "public," historical record must be confronted by the experience of women, which it has tended to neglect, in order to make sense of both. The most radical of such "confrontations" in Sanders-Brahms's film occurs when the fictional Lene addresses the documentary image of a small boy being interviewed in Berlin at the end of the war. The intercutting of fictional and documentary footage is such that the two characters seem to be in dialogue; the actress Eva Mattes asks questions to which the boy's statements appear to be responses. With a confidence his age seems to belie, he explains—apparently to Lene, the newcomer— how to make one's way through the chaos of rubble that Berlin has by then become. Lene then asks where his family is; he says that he has been searching for them for months, as he walks away from the camera, looking even smaller under the weight of his backpack, disappearing into the ruined landscape that surrounds and overwhelms him.

The boy whose lonely search for his family was thus preserved for a few moments in some rare documentary footage has long since disappeared from history; the moments, however, are precious for their poignant illustration of the war's disruption of the family, its intrusion into the personal experience of those members of the civilian population normally most sheltered from "public life." The child has been forced to leave the domestic sphere and make his own way; he acquires skills in so doing, but his focus remains the search for his family. The boy's plight in turn has been recorded on documentary footage, and it has thus become part of the public record of the war. It is this (uniquely "personal") moment of official history into which Sanders-Brahms has chosen to suture her mother's story most tightly. Lene, too, has been forced out of her home, is acquiring skills never before required of her, and is searching for her relatives, hoping to meet Hans on leave, and of course all the while caring for her daughter, carrying her on her shoulders as the small boy does his possessions.

Beyond the parallels at the level of the narrative, however, this "dialogue" between the boy and Lene represents as well the project of Sanders-Brahms's film: just as her fictional character asks questions of the documentary record of the past, she too is holding a "dialogue" with her mother's past. In the role of the narrator, her voice-over addresses her mother from the beginning of the film: "My mother. . . . From you I learned to speak"; "But this is your love story, mother" (p. 112). In making the film, she is addressing not merely her mother's experience but that of many women as well, as her description of the film in her preface indicates: "A story constructed from personal experiences and the experiences of many women with whom I have spoken, from whom I have tape-recorded and written testimony" (p. 25). And of course she is not only addressing the past shared by German women, she is holding a dialogue with the collective German past as a whole, as is obvious in her use of Brecht's poem "Germany, Pale Mother" for the title and for the opening sequence of her film. This dialogue with the past is in turn reflected in her cinematic intervention in history, in her intercutting of the fictional with the documentary. This formal technique achieves a subversion of the dichotomy between personal memory and public record that is similar to the project of other filmmakers.[37] It is also related to one of feminism's main objectives: examining, rethinking, and undermining ideological dichotomies.

Melodrama and Distantiation

Sanders-Brahms's film has had a controversial reception; many critics—including feminist ones—have attacked it. In a long essay that is exemplary for the concerns it raises, Ellen Seiter criticizes the film

[37] To name a few: Alexander Kluge (e.g., *The Patriot*, 1979), Jutta Brückner (*Years of Hunger*, 1980), Helke Sander (*REDUPERS*, 1977; *The Subjective Factor*, 1980).

for its use of "realist and melodramatic codes." This use, she argues, has the tendency to depoliticize the film: "My concern . . . is with the way that the filmmaker's use of melodramatic codes obscures the ability to read the family narrative in political, rather than pathetic terms."[38] Seiter is certainly right that the film makes use of melodramatic codes; Lene's story is primarily one of suffering, indeed, one of excessive suffering. The question is whether this melodrama is the only content of the film. How is the melodrama used, and does its presence "obscure" a political reading of the film?

The problem of melodrama is a thorny one, and one that has much to do with the modernism-postmodernism debate. Obviously, Seiter's position is an antirealist one, and as such it is similar to a left-wing modernism that sees melodrama and realism as elements of a depoliticized mass culture. The emotionalism of mass culture is opposed to the rationalism of modernist distantiation techniques; a very "modern" dichotomy is clearly at work. One consequence of this either/or logic is the conflation of realism with melodrama, achieved as a result of the necessity of placing them both on the "mass culture" side of what Huyssen calls the "Great Divide."[39] One notes in Seiter's formulation above the same near-equation of realism and melodrama. This is problematic; after all, for many advocates of a politically committed realism, nothing could be less "realistic"—and apolitical—than melodrama. "Antirealists," meanwhile, considering realism inherently bourgeois and depoliticized, have championed melodrama as politically subversive precisely because its stylization and excess are not "realistic."[40]

The same dichotomy is evident in Christian Metz's short but influential essay "Story/Discourse," which in a sense combines a psychoanalytic approach with a valorization of the distantiation techniques

[38] Ellen Seiter, "Women's History, Women's Melodrama: *Deutschland, bleiche Mutter*," *German Quarterly* 59 (1986), p. 573. A somewhat similar position is taken by E. Ann Kaplan in her essay, "The Search for the Mother/Land in Sanders-Brahms's *Germany, Pale Mother* (1980)," in Rentschler, *German Film and Literature*, pp. 289–304. Kaplan finds the film "essentialist" and insufficiently "nonrealist," yet she comes to quite different conclusions from Seiter's, finding that the "historical address" conducted by the film gets in the way of the exploration of the mother–daughter relationship; Seiter, on the other hand, feels that the latter makes the film problematic precisely because its melodramatic depiction obscures the troubling German past in which the film is set.

[39] See Huyssen, *After the Great Divide*, e.g., pp. vii–15.

[40] See Christine Gledhill's "The Melodramatic Field: An Investigation," in Gledhill, ed., *Home Is Where the Heart Is: Studies in Melodrama and the Woman's Film* (London: BFI Publishing, 1987), pp. 5–39, esp. pp. 5–13, 28–38. See also Elsaesser's famous 1972 essay, "Tales of Sound and Fury: Observations on the Family Melodrama," in (e.g.) Gledhill's *Home Is Where the Heart Is*, pp. 43–69.

Brecht championed in his aesthetic theories. Discussing the "Hollywood film," Metz makes use of the distinction between story (*histoire*) and discourse (*discours*):

> In Emile Benveniste's terms, the traditional film is presented as story, and not as discourse. And yet it is discourse, if we refer it back to the film-maker's intentions, the influence he wields over the general public, etc.; but the basic characteristic of this kind of discourse, and the very principle of its effectiveness as discourse, is precisely that it obliterates all traces of the enunciation, and masquerades as story. The tense of story is of course always "past definite"; similarly, the narrative plenitude and transparency of this kind of film is based on a refusal to admit that anything is lacking, or that anything has to be sought for.[41]

The Hollywood film is thus a discourse, designed for a desired reception by a mass audience by various "enunciators" who collaborate in its production; it is then distributed by a vast and complicated institutional network. But it is a discourse that pretends not to be one, masquerading instead as a "story" that is completed—and invulnerable to intervention or mediation by contemporary human subjects. As much as possible, evidence of its designed construction is hidden; it must appear to "happen" as though it had no human author, drawing its authority instead from "fate" or "reality." At the same time, it appears to happen *now*, in the present, before the eyes of the spectators, having an aura of immediacy; as Metz writes, this type of fiction "presents the narrated without the narrator, rather like in dreams or phantasy."[42]

The value of this distinction, as well as its relevance to art in the twentieth century, is obvious—as is its proximity to the modernism/mass culture dichotomy, which blurs distinctions between various cinematic forms in its postulation of a monolithic "classical realism." The "New German Cinema" is often seen as opposing the Hollywood tradition; many of the filmmakers drew on Brecht's concept of distantiation in their resistance to its formal conventions. Women making films often felt an additional antipathy to Hollywood filmmaking, seeing its representation of woman as fundamentally patriarchal.[43] Helma Sanders-Brahms, by opening her film with a Brecht poem (read by his daughter, Hanna Hiob), would seem to be aligning her film with the Brechtian tradition, in which through the use of

[41] Metz, "Story/Discourse," p. 544. Metz sees the roots of the "Hollywood Film" in the novel of the nineteenth century, which it has replaced (pp. 546–47).

[42] Ibid.

[43] See, for example, Laura Mulvey's famous essay, "Visual Pleasure and Narrative Cinema."

distantiation techniques the audience's attention is drawn to the discursive nature of what it is watching—that is, that a play or a film is being narrated and has been constructed by an author within the institutional apparatus of the theater or the cinema.

But the New German Cinema ought not to be confused with the avant-garde; it was for the most part an attempt to create something that would not fit at either pole of the rigid dichotomy between the avant-garde and the commercial, something that would, in Fassbinder's words, let the audience "feel and think."[44] Fassbinder's contribution to the New German Cinema was specifically an attempt to fuse melodrama with Brechtian distantiation. Nor indeed was Brecht totally opposed to narrative realism; his goal was to interrupt, not eliminate, all illusion, in a move that as Hutcheon has noted is already "postmodern": that is, to work "*within* conventions in order to subvert them."[45] Furthermore, even "undiluted" melodrama has been considered a form that can distance the audience precisely through its antirealistic excess—a form that thus implies that realist representation is inadequate.[46]

In any event, the melodrama in Sanders-Brahms's film is by no means undiluted. There are many elements that distance the audience from unhindered identification with either its melodrama or its creation of an "illusion of the real." An examination of the film's formal structure makes clear how close the film's project is to that of Fassbinder and Brecht, and indeed how often the discursive nature of its "story" is foregrounded.

The most obvious device for distantiation that Sanders-Brahms uses is voice-over narration, a technique reminiscent of Brecht's own use of an onstage narrator.[47] It is a technique often used in the films of Jean-Luc Godard, known since the 1960s for his adaptation of Brecht's theories for the screen. Sanders-Brahms, like Godard, does the voice-over herself, but in a manner drawing much more attention to herself personally; it is no secret that the narrator addresses her parents, nor that Anna represents the filmmaker as a child. Indeed, if one pays attention to the credits at the end of the

[44] See Fassbinder, "I Let the Audience Feel and Think." Elsaesser makes a point of distinguishing the New German Cinema from both the cinematic avant-garde of the 1950s and 1960s and the broader historical avant-garde. See "American Grafitti," e.g., pp. 310–12, 315–16.

[45] Hutcheon, A Poetics of Postmodernism, pp. 5, 7.

[46] Patrice Petro, Joyless Streets: Women and Melodramatic Representation in Weimar Germany (Princeton, NJ: Princeton University Press, 1989), p. 30; see also her discussion of melodrama, pp. 25–36.

[47] One example would be The Caucasian Chalk-Circle (Der kaukasische Kreidekreis).

film, one learns that Anna is played at one point in the film by Anna Sanders-Brahms, Helma's daughter. The autobiographical nature of the film is thus doubly underscored, as Sanders-Brahms tells her mother's story while using her own daughter to represent her part in that story.

Sanders-Brahms's role as the "enunciator" of the film, as the one who constructs it, is therefore foregrounded in a way not evident in other, less openly autobiographical films; consistent with what has been defined as a feminist revision of modernism, the narration is connected to the perspective of a specific human subject rather than a more abstract, depersonalized instance of authority.[48] Beyond the autobiographical aspect of the film, however, Sanders-Brahms's voice-over also foregrounds its role in constructing the discourse, and by this I mean that it literally reveals choices made as to what is shown and what is not shown by the fiction. One of the best examples of such foregrounding occurs after the newly married Hans and Lene have arrived in their new home. Their tender scene of lovemaking, which begins with their gentle attempts to undress each other, is interrupted by the narrator: "I can't imagine your embrace. I can't imagine how you touched each other's skin. You are my parents. I am between you. I haven't gotten married. That I learned from your example" (p. 112).

Learning that the narrator decided not to marry because of her parents' marriage, the spectator is hindered in the enjoyment of, and identification with, the romance on the screen, because the narrator implies that this happy couple will not remain so. But not only does the voice-over undercut the mood of the scene; it tells the audience explicitly why only the beginning of the lovemaking is shown, why the filmmaker chooses to direct the scene as she does and cut it when she does.

Another example of the voice-over exposing the subjectivity behind the fiction has to do with the choice of Ernst Jacobi for the role of Hans, who represents the filmmaker's father. Jacobi appears much older than Eve Mattes, and this mismatch in age may distance the spectator further from the romance between Hans and Lene. What is more significant, Sanders-Brahms's voice-over directly addresses the age difference: "You were as young as she, my father. But in my memory your face is always as old as it was when you came back from the war" (p. 112). In this instance Sanders-Brahms exposes the rationale for her casting. The fiction is unmistakenly her construct, not a story presenting itself as unmediated reality. It is, as Seiter

<hr />

[48] Rich, "She Says, He Says," p. 44.

writes, the "daughter's version of the mother's story," but that fact
is never disguised.[49]

The film's use of voice-over thus draws attention to its own existence as a fictive discourse. At the same time, it distances the audience by providing a perspective on the events being narrated that is
separate from that of the main characters. The other major element
in the film with a similar function is the documentary footage,
which, as discussed above, breaks up the fiction at the same time it
contextualizes and is contextualized by it. The illusion of reality in
the Hollywood film (a "beautifully closed object," as Metz writes[50])
depends in part on its apparent self-sufficiency; in Sanders-
Brahms's film the fiction is called into question by the documentary
footage that intrudes upon it. Both perspectives, the fictional and the
documentary, relativize each other; the voice-over has a similar relationship to both these visual components of the film.

At some points the voice-over seems to conspire with the fictional
narrative, as when the homeless Lene and Anna are wandering. It
seems problematic that this period is presented as being so idyllic,
but here it is the documentary footage that provides the corrective.
"And so Lene and I loved each other in the bathtub and flew like
witches over the rooftops" (p. 113). The voice-over here intensifies
rather than undercuts the mood created by the shot of Lene and
Anna happily playing together in the bathtub (at the apartment of
Lene's rich relatives); here the objections of some critics that the reality of the war is effaced by a mythologized mother–daughter symbiosis seem warranted.[51] The voice-over here is providing the perspective of the daughter, the way she remembers those times. This
perspective is nonetheless immediately undercut by the sequence of
documentary footage that follows the voice-over: an aerial shot,
taken from a plane flying over Berlin in about 1945, displays for the
spectator a historical reality that contradicts the child's idealized
memories. "Flying over the roofs," as the child asserts she had done,
would in actuality have meant flying over miles of bombed buildings, many of which had no roofs, as the spectator can ascertain dur-

---

[49] Seiter, "Women's History," p. 571.

[50] Metz, "Story/Discourse," p. 546.

[51] This is Seiter's opinion ("Women's History," pp. 4–6) and Hiller's ("mütter und
töchter," pp. 30–31); for a similar reading, see also Angelika Bammer, "Through a
Daughter's Eyes: Helma Sanders-Brahms' Germany, Pale Mother," New German Critique, no. 36 (1985), pp. 103–106. Claudia Lenssen alludes to a similar interpretation
in her conversation with Helen Fehervary and Judith Mayne, "From Hitler to Hepburn: A Discussion of Women's Film Production and Reception," New German Critique, nos. 24–25 (1981–1982), p. 176.

ing this silent sequence of eerie footage showing Berlin in ruins (similar to a later sequence of greater length). The spectator is not allowed to participate in the joy shared by the mother and daughter—which is idyllic only in the memory of the child, in any case—without being confronted with visual evidence of how ghastly a world it was that she remembers so selectively.

Besides the use of voice-over and of documentary footage, there are many other ways in which Sanders-Brahms attempts to distance the audience from too uncritical an immersion in the melodrama of the narrative. Choice of actors has already been mentioned with regard to Ernst Jacobi; more disorienting for the audience is the use of Eva Mattes in the roles of a Polish peasant and a French partisan whom Hans and his fellow German soldiers execute. The first time Mattes appears playing someone other than Lene, it is especially confusing, since up to this point in the film her identification with the role of Lene has appeared complete, in accordance with the naturalistic acting one expects in conventional films. Precisely because of this, the audience is unsettled. Hans, breaking down and crying over his role in the shooting of the peasants, then explains to his comrades that one of the women looked just like his wife; this explanation only reinforces the rupture of naturalistic codes, for the audience is positive that this is *precisely* the same woman it knows as Lene.

Sanders-Brahms thus makes a statement about war: Hans's role as a soldier includes invading the "domestic sphere" of the enemy, driving out women and children—as his wife and child will be driven from their home—and killing them. Women "just like" his wife are the enemy; women are somehow on the "other side," opposing that for which he must fight—opposing him *actively* in the case of the French partisan woman. The harsh socialization he undergoes as a soldier (he soon loses the sensitivity he displays at his first murder of civilians) plays no small part in the growing distrust he feels for his wife, and later for both wife and child.

Another distantiation technique in the film involves the use of Jürgen Knieper's music on the sound track, which at times adds a somber, dissonant perspective to the narrative but includes other themes as well (for instance, a lyrical motif and a more tragic one). One of the most striking uses of the sound track comes early in the film, when, during the dance at the rowing club where Hans first speaks with Lene, there is no dance music at all; all one can hear are some ominous chords that are obviously nondiegetic. The eeriness of this sequence, in which happy couples dance to music that the spectator cannot hear, signifies the threat that political forces pose for all these "normal," private romances. This is made more explicit through editing and camera work. The scene opens with an extremely close shot of a huge swastika flag (so close that the gnats of the summer night are evident as they crawl all over it). Through editing, shots of two black-uniformed Nazis alternate with shots of the couples dancing, until finally the two are shown striding through the couples. Sinister political forces penetrate even the locus of romance, where indeed Hans has been asking Lene if joining or remaining outside the Party will help his chances with her.

In addition, there are two major sequences of the film that have distancing functions: the opening poem and the fairy tale narrated in its entirety to Anna by Lene in the middle of the film. The Brecht poem functions appropriately enough like the titles that precede the scenes in almost all Brecht's plays: the historical and political context of the story about to begin is emphasized. It is not only the story of Lene and Hans; it is the story of Germany. The poem can also be read (and its use here suggests such a reading) to imply the complex interrelationship between fascism, militarism, and gendered socialization that the film explores: Germany is a mother, despoiled by her sons. The use of the poem does not set up any simplistic allegory in which Lene is to be read simply as Germany—any attempt to interpret the story neatly as an allegory breaks down rather quickly, as Angelika Bammer has noted.[52] The use of a poem at the beginning of a narrative adds another perspective from which to view the fiction; it is meant to add complexity precisely through the impossibility of any seamless relation to the narrative, precisely because there is a "gap," a *Leerstelle*, in that relation.[53]

E. Ann Kaplan argues that the unproblematized use of the allegorical trope "Mother = Germany" in Brecht's poem is adopted by Sanders-Brahms and not undermined.[54] It is true that Lene's victimization by Nazi policies and by the results of those policies (war, bombardment, invasion) is depicted, but so is her complicity with National Socialist policies with regard to the Jews: she ignores Rahel

---

[52] Bammer, "Through a Daughter's Eyes," p. 96. Cf. Fassbinder's *Maria Braun*—which Bammer also cites—for a more convincing example of the allegorization of a female character. See also Elsaesser, *New German Cinema*, p. 270.

[53] Cf. Wolfgang Iser's famous essay, "Die Appellstruktur des Textes" (1970), in which he develops his concept of the "*Leerstelle*," acknowledging the influence of Roman Ingarden. See Iser, "Appellstruktur," in Rainer Warnung, ed., *Rezeptionsästhetik* (Munich: Wilhelm Fink, 1975), pp. 235ff. The essay appears in English translation as "Indeterminacy and the Reader's Response in Prose Fiction," in J. Hillis Miller, ed., *Aspects of Narrative* (New York: Columbia University Press, 1971), pp. 1–45.

[54] Kaplan, "The Search for the Mother/Land," p. 291.

and actively participates in looting Duckstein's shop. This places her in *both* roles in Brecht's poem: that of the shamed, victimized mother, and that of the sons who do the victimizing.

The fairy tale, "The Robber Bridegroom" ("Das Räuberbräutigam"), is described by Sanders-Brahms herself as a deliberate *Verfremdungseffekt*, or distantiation device.[55] It interrupts the fiction as would any story-within-a-story, but the interruption is more noticeable because of the way it is narrated. For one thing, it *is* narrated, not enacted; furthermore, the text of the tale (as recorded by the Brothers Grimm) is narrated in its entirety by Lene to Anna (pp. 92–96). The audience may not know this specifically, but it certainly knows that Lene is not speaking her own words, and that the sequence goes on at great length. While the audience hears Lene telling the story, it sees the visual settings of her wanderings with Anna—visually, in other words, the main fiction continues, while a different story is heard. This other story, the fairy tale, provides obvious commentary on the visual events, and thus on the main narrative of the film as well.

In the tale, a father unwittingly "gives the hand" of his daughter in marriage to a man who lives in the forest with a band of robbers—men who also capture, hack apart, and eat young virgin girls. While Lene narrates the tale, what is seen by the spectator? Lene and Anna wander through a forest, see a dead soldier in the bushes, and come to an abandoned factory with a tall smokestack and an oven inside, in front of which they rest; more documentary footage shot from an airplane of Berlin in ruins at the end of the Second World War is then shown; Lene and Anna wander through another abandoned factory hall and are accosted by two American soldiers, who rape Lene; finally, as Lene finishes telling the tale to Anna, they sit on the connector between two cars of a moving freight train. A corpse, a smokestack, an oven, a bombed city, a rape: certainly not an inappropriate visual accompaniment to this particular fairy tale, and one that makes clear connections between the tale and the historical situation of the main narrative of the film.

Certain of these connections are quite explicit: for example, when Lene recounts how the robber tells the girl to find his house in the woods—"And so that you will find the way, I will spread ashes for you"—she and Anna come upon the factory, and the camera pans slowly, ominously up the length of a very tall smokestack; the mention of ashes and the obviously emphasized shot of a smokestack

[55] Sanders-Brahms, interview in Renate Möhrmann, *Die Frau mit der Kamera*, p. 156.

can readily be interpreted as allusions to concentration camps, allusions reinforced by the prominent oven door at the base of the
furnace once the two enter the factory, combined with Lene's first
recitation of the tale's refrain: "Turn back, turn back, young bride,
you are in a house of murderers!" (p. 93).

This refrain, repeated throughout the tale, stands not only as a
warning for the girl in the tale but also as a warning—admittedly
one that comes too late—for Lene, whose story is quite similar, as a
woman whom the audience first encounters as a "young bride," a
woman who also finds herself in a "house of murderers": Nazi Germany, symbolized visually in the fairy tale sequence by a smokestack and an oven. Hans, the man who marries Lene, is not like the
men who eat the flesh of young girls in the fairy tale. In fact, he is
portrayed sympathetically for most of the film; nonetheless, he becomes part of a war machine (against his will, but without his resistance) that does consume people. Indeed, it spews him out a very
different person from the sensitive young man he had been.

The question of gender is obviously one that lurks not far beneath
the surface of the fairy tale, which speaks to ancient fears of women
in societies where decisions about their bodies and lives are made
in dealings between men, dealings in which they have no part. In
Lene's experience, the historical forces that determine her life make
a soldier of her husband, involving him in a war in which he becomes the enemy of women and children; the war creates a situation
in which women and children are controlled by competing armies.
Even in the armies who fight to defeat fascism, there are men who
act like soldiers in any conquering army—as Lene explains her rape
to Anna, "It's the right of the victor, little girl. They take possessions
and women" (p. 96). In the fairy-tale sequence, Sanders-Brahms in-
dicts war and the patriarchal types of male socialization upon which
it depends, and she demonstrates its consequences for women.

She also suggests a strategy of resistance. The girl in the tale is
saved with the help of the old woman, who is apparently a servant
of the robbers but who takes pity on her and reveals to her the true
story of the robbers' reign of terror, as it were; then she hides her,
and the girl herself sees that the old woman is not lying. Later, the
girl is able to see justice done for the crimes against women by telling the story again, cleverly disguising it as a dream until the last
moment, when she produces tangible proof—the severed finger of
the woman whose murder she witnessed. The girl is saved by the
old woman's taking pity on her, but the girl herself exercises a more
effective solidarity. She manages to see that the robbers are stopped

from further acts of violence against women, and she does so by telling *publicly* what she has seen.

The emphasis in the tale is on sharing knowledge, on voicing a warning, on telling one's story, and on providing proof: a modern reading informed by feminism would interpret the tale as an appeal to women to share knowledge of their history by recording it and gathering evidence. To take control of one's story, one must put it into words, one must tell it. The young girl in the tale takes control of the horror she has witnessed by telling it again, and through her clever control of the telling of the story, she traps the perpetrator of the horror. Helma Sanders-Brahms cannot claim to have achieved such results by telling the story of her mother's life, but the parallel between the fairy tale and the project of her film is clear.[56]

"My mother. I learned to be silent, you said. From you I learned to speak" (p. 112). Thus does Sanders-Brahms's voice-over address the first close-up of the character representing her mother. Beyond the obvious meaning of the statement, it can also be read as self-reflexive with regard to the making of the film: the forces of history, operating on many levels (some more, some less "private"), have affected Lene's life in such a way that she, like so many women before her, has become silent. But her story is not lost, because her daughter has chosen to articulate it; indeed, Sanders-Brahms "comes to speech" herself in trying to understand her mother's story. Through the telling of the disappointments and horrors that silenced her mother, she gains some control of that part of women's history, and she takes a step to ensure that its lessons (by no means only for women) are not lost. The story—and the history—she tells represent an active intervention in history, one that has an unhidden agenda for the present: a feminist and a pacifist one.

Sanders-Brahms's intervention as the subject who constructs the film is foregrounded by various distantiation techniques: her voice-over, the intersplicing of documentary footage with the constructed fiction, uses of music and the sound track, choice of actors, editing, use of the mirror motif, the opening Brecht poem, the fairy-tale sequence. All these devices interrupt or comment on the melodrama

---

[56] It is for this reason that I disagree with Bammer's interpretation of the fairy-tale sequence as depicting women outside history and powerless to intervene against the historical evils that affect and victimize them ("Through a Daughter's Eyes," pp. 106–8). The young woman in the story intervenes—and has an effect—by telling the story; this must also relate to the film director's telling of the story she chooses. For another interpretation of the fairy-tale sequence, see Barbara Hyams's sensitive, close reading, "Is the Apolitical Woman at Peace?: A Reading of the Fairy Tale in *Germany, Pale Mother*," *Wide Angle* 10, no. 3 (1988), pp. 41–51.

of the fiction, underscoring that the latter is not simply "happening" but rather is constructed from a certain perspective.

Trauerarbeit or *Mystification?*

It is always objectionable when history is trivialized to serve as a mere backdrop for a melodramatic plot (in Hollywood films, most often a love story), but when the history so misrepresented is that of the Third Reich and the Second World War, it is much more troubling—even more so if the filmmaker who chooses to treat this history in such a manner is German. The melodrama in Sanders-Brahms's film does not center so much around the male–female love story, since that is quite soon displaced by Hans's removal from the home; it revolves more around the mother–daughter relationship, which of course structures more than the melodrama in the film.

> The daughter's version of the mother's story, with its emphasis on the psychological experience of merging and of irrevocable loss, is nowhere more problematic than in this film, where the relationship in its idyllic phase is played out against the background of wartime Germany. The film confines the mother to the realm of the emotional and psychological; her liberation from the domestic sphere only enables her to become a heroic, full time nurturer. . . . This vision of women in war is most troublesome in a film which fails to enact in any detail the impact of World War II on women who were *not* middle class, German, unengaged in political resistance, or, I need hardly add, gentile.[57]

The above is Seiter's formulation of the problems she sees in Sanders-Brahms's film, which she considers an illustration of "the problem with all forms of feminism which mythologize the mother."[58] Does the film efface the historical reality of fascism and the war in a mystifying idealization of the mother–child symbiosis? Or can it be classified as a *Trauerarbeit*, a "work of mourning" that attempts to come to terms both with Sanders-Brahms's relationship to her mother and with a murderous period in German history? As critic Christian Bauer asked, "May this luxurious attempt to come to terms with childhood also be considered a process of working through collective experience?" The question was phrased in light of many of the negative reactions the film received in West Ger-

---

[57] Seiter, "Women's History," pp. 571–72.
[58] Ibid., p. 572.

many. I agree with Bauer's conclusion that the two projects do coincide.[59]

The film is in any event not silent about the plight of nongentile
women. It depicts Lene in a decidedly unfavorable light in this regard when she closes the shutters on the abduction of her classmate
Rahel Bernstein. The second instance where the plight of the Jews
is thematized is when Lene is embroidering her new blouse to wear
for Hans's return on leave. So intent is she on finishing this project
with the red thread she had bought at Duckstein's that she listens
without comprehending when her sister tells her that the Duck-
steins, being Jews, are "gone" ("weg"). She goes to their shop and
finds it boarded up, but an old woman in the building lets her in to
rummage through what is left; the red she seeks is not there, but the
old woman convinces her to make do with blue, bidding her farewell with a "Heil Hitler!" Lene's exclusive interest in a "private"
dream—pleasing Hans—causes her implication in the Nazi expropriation of the Jews. It is on a small scale perhaps, but her relationship to their plight has changed: initially unwilling to help (or even
to look), she now actively participates in the expropriation of the
Jews. And here too, the violence of the society around her is revisited upon her in a small way when the fruit of her plunder, the em-
broidered blouse, is ripped off her by her husband, whose attitude
toward women and sex is changing even as he tries to resist the socialization toward them that is typical of the soldier.

The complicity of Sanders-Brahms's parents in the crimes of fascism is thematized in the film, as is the fact that they were not engaged in political resistance. As she described her project, it was to
tell the story not of the "protagonists" of this history but rather of
those who made them possible, those who voted for Hitler, and
those who did not even do that but who also did not protest or leave
or go underground. The story deals with those who simply tried to
ignore the politics of the time, who wanted refuge in the private
realm of "love, marriage, a child" (p. 9). This is how she depicts her
parents, and they are shown to participate in the crimes of the era.

Does the film uncritically glorify the mother–child relationship?

[59] Bauer, cited above in note 26. In general, the reaction to the film was negative, as
Seiter reports (p. 7), citing Janet Maslin's review, " 'Germany, Pale Mother' set in the
Nazi era," *New York Times*, 18 March 1984, and *Variety*, 21 March 1984, as examples
of the American reception. Olav Münzberg (one of the film's defenders) summarized
the negative reception in West Germany, analyzing it in terms of "defensive reactions." See Münzberg, "Schaudern vor der 'bleichen Mutter,' " *Medium* 10, no. 7
(1980), pp. 34–57. The French reception was much more favorable: the film won first
prize at the 1980 Women's Film Festival in Sceaux.

Lene's ambivalence toward her role as mother is certainly depicted. Her difficulty carrying her child and possessions on the bridge into Berlin is clear, as is her exasperation with the child. She agrees with Hans when, concerned that breast-feeding the child is draining her, he warns her "But she's eating you up." She explains her singing and dancing with the child not as an expression of idyllic happiness but as a survival mechanism as things get ever worse: "I'm telling you, the harder it comes, the more I sing to her. Not just for the child, either. For myself."

Nor is her caring for the child merely shown as emotional, psychological nurturing, with no indication of any other activity. The skills she develops during their wandering have to do with concrete, economic survival: she is willing to take clothing from corpses, she finds shelter for her child, she deals on the black market; she is also seen helping to rebuild the ruined city, in a montage where she and her sister and daughter, passing bricks, appear to be helping a large group of Trümmerfrauen, the famed "women of the rubble," who are captured on some famous documentary footage.

The time during the war appears glorified from only two perspectives: that of the child, which is understandable, and that of the grown-up daughter, who remembers how active her mother was during the war and how paralyzed she became afterwards. There is, however, no escaping this latter perspective; it is a historical reality that, though life was hard toward the end of the war for German women, they played a greater role outside the home than they were to play a few years after the war. This is a moment in history that Sanders-Brahms's film attempts to explore, and rightly so.[60]

In depicting the "house of murderers," it is suggested that German fascism, war, militarism, and patriarchy are somehow related. The horror of the war is not glossed over, nor is it shown as "separate" from the experience of women. On the contrary, it is precisely in the middle of the film, when Lene is surviving outside the home and traveling with her daughter, that the documentary record confronts the fiction with footage showing the results of the fascists' war. This is the proof, as it were, that the horrors of war that shaped her moth-

---

[60] Seiter, citing Leila Rupp, questions the idea that wars "liberate" women, since the wartime mobilization of women is always exceptional. "Women's History," p. 572. But this is, on the one hand, precisely what the film shows: once the war is over, Lene is forced back into the home. And on the other hand, to ignore the special role modern war has played in disrupting the traditional family, and the function the memories of experiences during wartime have served in mobilizing women (and gays and lesbians, and other minorities, for that matter), is to ignore some significant history.

er's story were real, not a dream. Just as the girl in the fairy tale can disprove her refrain—"it was only a dream" (p. 96)—by producing the severed finger of the murdered woman, so Sanders-Brahms produces archival footage that provides "physical proof" of the destruction brought about by the war the fascists began.[61]

RE-PRESENTING HISTORY: *THE SUBJECTIVE FACTOR* BY HELKE SANDER

> I ask myself, what kind of world are you bringing children into? We are by now at an age where we are responsible for what's happening. And that is a realization that was made during the student movement. . . . For this is the decisive point: intervention, not refusal.[62]

Helke Sander, in a 1981 interview in connection with her film *The Subjective Factor* (*Der subjektive Faktor*, 1980), emphasized active intervention in historical struggles, a position that in many ways reflects the project of feminism as a whole: that women enter the political realm as active subjects, making and writing their own history. It is also a position that motivates both Anni, the autobiographical protagonist of the film, and Sander herself, who made this film that chronicles the origins of the West German women's movement within the student movement of the late 1960s.

An interesting aspect of Sander's statement is the emphasis on the student movement as a *positive* tradition—this from the director of a film quite critical of that movement, a film that gave some critics another chance to defame it.[63] But *The Subjective Factor* depicts both the women's movement and the student movement as parts of a common oppositional struggle that is shown as still necessary in the 1980s. The critique of the male-dominated student movement that informed the women's movement, and is presented in the film, is itself a contribution to an ongoing common struggle; Sander made the film in order "that the lessons of our experience not be lost," in

[61] This interpretation of the severed finger as "physical proof" was first suggested to me in a lecture given by Anton Kaes in his course on New German Cinema at the University of California, Berkeley, in the spring of 1983. See also Kaes, *Deutschland-bilder*, p. 121.

[62] Helke Sander, in an interview with Gudula Lorez, "Einmischung statt Verweigerung," *die tageszeitung* (West Berlin), 20 July 1981, p. 9 (originally "aus der überregionalen Ausgabe des TIP").

[63] For example, Manfred Delling, "Terror in Chile, Elend in der Küche," *Deutsches Allgemeines Sonntagsblatt*, 28 June 1981; and the review in the column "Ponkie sieht fern" in the *Abend-Zeitung* (Munich), 18/19 April 1981.

order to counter conservative and/or primarily male-oriented histories of the student movement.[64] The act of remembering is both
"subjective" and "political," to combine two problematic terms so
often used in opposition in discussions about West Germany since
the 1960s; it can occur only from a specific position within a specific
set of attitudes toward what is being remembered.

Hence the "subjective factor." Such a title is heavy with all sorts
of associations within the discursive field of West Germany in the
late 1970s and the early 1980s—the literary phenomenon "New
Subjectivity," for instance, often (mis-)perceived by critics as
merely melancholic Innerlichkeit, inwardness and narcissistic self-
absorption. Such associations are especially inappropriate in connection with Sander's film. It is most certainly informed by the feminist principle that the personal sphere is an important locus of political struggle and development. As Sander commented on the
film's reception: "An often-heard, angrily waged attack on the film
begins with the words: for me it was all completely different. Exactly. That's my point of departure. I want to hammer at it for so
long until the meaning of that sentence is understood. I connect it
with the question of how we learn history, and what if anything we
learn from it."[65]

Some reviewers were disappointed by the film: "What dominates
here is rather coolness and distance. The subjective factor doesn't
appear at all. . . . Everything moves very orderly, via the head."[66]
The "subjective factor" at work in the film has much to do with the
conviction that in both art and politics discourse should not mas-
querade as "objective," but that the "subject of the enunciation," be
it filmmaker or political theorist, be foregrounded. The film does indeed remain somewhat cool, in line with the conviction that the
process of representing history—even history experienced directly,
even autobiographical experience—cannot be separated from the
"end product," and that the temptation of simple, uncritical solu-

[64] Sander, "Es gibt viel Falsches im Wahren," an interview with Karsten Witte, in
"der subjektive faktor," a promotional program for film's opening in West Berlin at
the Filmbühne am Steinplatz, 19 June 1981.

[65] Sander, "der subjektive faktor, vertrackt," a pamphlet published by Basis-Film-
Verleih (West Berlin, 1981), p. 5.

[66] Malte Ludin, "Geschichtsunterricht," rev. of the film in Frankfurter Rundschau,
10 July 1981. Norbert Jochum also found the film too cerebral, oriented toward ideas
and not images, in his review, "Das Gesicht der Ereignisse," Die Zeit, 3 July 1981, p.
34. Thomas Thieringer and Heiko R. Blum mention inaccessibility as a problem, but
in general they write favorably about the film. Thieringer, "Zeit-Collage," Süddeutsche Zeitung, 18 July 1981, and Blum, "Die 'neue Frau.' Helke Sanders neuer
Film Der subjektive Faktor," Rheinische Post, 27 March 1982.

tions must be resisted. "The longing for simple solutions creates new tragedies," says Sander, as the narrator, toward the end of her film. She is as skeptical of such solutions in art as in politics.

The View from the Kitchen

In telling the story of the origins of the West German women's movement from the viewpoint of a woman who, like Sander herself, participated in those beginnings, Sander was motivated in part by her awareness that "official" histories had been mostly silent on the activities of earlier generations of women. When Sander became politically active in the 1960s, she herself had not been aware of these earlier efforts: "I didn't know at the time that there had already been a women's movement, and yet I had done well in history and was fairly educated. When I became aware of it, the unequivocal authority of the concepts I had learned crumbled. History was suddenly no longer 'objective' at all."[67]

The critical perspective that facilitated her loss of faith in the dominant version of German "history" resulted in part from her politicization in the student movement. But when the same critical outlook was applied to the social conventions governing her own role as a woman, she found most of her male comrades in the movement to be blind to the ideological nature of that positioning—as blind as the "official" history taught in schools had been to political efforts by women in the past.

This insensitivity on the part of male activists is depicted most effectively in the film when the character Anni waits for a chance to speak at an SDS strategy discussion on the campaign against the Springer press; she wants to make the point that a good deal of the manipulation exerted in the Springer publications had to do with women, depicted as pinups or addressed as frugal housewives. After waiting patiently for some time, she is told by one of the men to go to the kitchen. There she will find another woman, Annemarie, who is interested in such issues.[68] Anni thus finds herself relegated to the kitchen, to the traditional "feminine" realm, the private realm, apart from the discourse of politics and history that men control.

The subsequent scene, where Anni and Annemarie meet in the kitchen, represents a turning point in the film: this is the first scene

[67] Sander, "Es gibt viel Falsches."

[68] See Sander's discussion of the actual incident that inspired this scene in "vertrackt," pp. 10–12. The man who told her to go to the kitchen was Peter Schneider. Sander says that Schneider was generally more sympathetic than other male activists, and that the intention of his remark had been sympathetic as well.

in which there is any prolonged contact between women, without men around. After this point in the film, Anni is seen ever more frequently with women, whereas at the beginning, she was almost always with men (who were "enlightening" her). Anni and Anne-marie decide to call all the women they know to meet and discuss issues relevant to their problems as women, the beginning thus of the "Action Committee for the Liberation of Women" (Aktionsrat zur Befreiung der Frau),[69] the focus of Anni's political activity throughout most of the rest of the film. It is in this kitchen that Anni and Annemarie begin their efforts at uniting and empowering the women for whom the kitchen had symbolized powerlessness and isolation; it is where they plan their intervention in the "public" discourse from which they have been excluded.

To do so, they must expose the contradictions in the ideological dichotomy between a public, male sphere and a private, female sphere, "ideological divisions," as Judith Mayne writes, "which mask profound links."[70] The dichotomy of the public and private is of course closely associated with the rise of capitalism, but it is also the basis for what Kaja Silverman calls the "continuity between the discourse of capitalism and the student left on the question of woman."[71] This is the first contradiction they must expose—a con-tradiction so aptly symbolized in Sander's film by male leftists send-ing Anni to the kitchen.

That locale is central to the ideology of a private, female realm—central indeed within the traditional three-part definition of a wom-an's role in Germany: *Kinder, Küche, Kirche*—"children, kitchen, church." In the film, the kitchen becomes a motif used to depict var-ious contradictions of the public/private dichotomy. It is the central locus of interaction within the collective household, the *Wohnge-meinschaft* on which in turn the narrative is centered for that strand of the plot dealing with the years 1967 through 1970. Within the "private" space represented by the residence of the collective, the kitchen is obviously the most "public" place. It is here that disagree-ments among the sharing of household duties are most evident in the piles of dirty dishes that Anni finds a breach of collective pol-icy—a conflict that housemate Matthias personalizes by calling

[69] The *Aktionsrat* was the name of the actual group of women within the SDS who first banded together, and Sander was one of the founding members. See above, Chap-ter 1.

[70] Mayne, "Female Narration, Women's Cinema," p. 160.

[71] Kaja Silverman, "Helke Sander and the Will to Change," *Discourse*, no. 6 (1983), p. 20; cf. also Craig Owens on the "fundamentally patriarchal bias" of Marxism: Owens, "The Discourse of Others," pp. 62–63.

Anni "anally fixated" for her reaction. It is in the kitchen that a large meal prepared by Till and shared by the group represents the most harmonious moment in the collective living experiment.[72] It is also there that Anni observes the contradiction between Matthias "the socialist," with his copy of Habermas's *Theory and Praxis*, and Matthias whose "praxis" includes mailing his laundry home to his mother.

Near the end of the film, the collective household—and the student movement—have been disintegrating. This is apparent in the final sequence set in the collective's apartment. All harmony has disappeared: ex-household members Till and Annemarie, both now members of a terrorist cell, have reappeared in the apartment, and Till holds a gun. He orders Anni about, and, when the doorbell rings, he commands that she go to the kitchen. "Till's relegation of Anni to the kitchen indicates that feminism has no more to gain from terrorism than orthodox Marxism."[73] Silverman bases this conclusion on one line by Till in a short and rather puzzling scene; but in a film in which the kitchen is such an important motif, its mention cannot be ignored.

The significance—and irony—of Till's mention of the kitchen is all the greater when Till's own association with the kitchen is taken into account. He is a man who is almost always associated with the preparation of food in the film: when he is first mentioned, Annemarie tells Anni that he is moving into the apartment with her, adding that he makes breakfast—a boon to the collective (and apparently somewhat of a rare catch as a boyfriend). In the group meal mentioned above, which he has prepared, he wears an apron; and after having moved out of the household, he returns to claim an item he has left behind: a large pot. Beyond the association with work traditionally devalued as "women's work," he is also depicted as being concerned about the needs of Anni's son Andres. Till understands the child's needs for tenderness and for household duties that interest him and give him a sense of participating in the collective on more of an equal basis with the adults. Whereas Matthias shows the child documentary footage from Vietnam as a way of encouraging him to do his chores with the correct amount of solidarity, Till teaches Andres to help in the kitchen with the preparation of food, which the child obviously enjoys.

That it is the otherwise sympathetic Till who winds up on what

[72] In this scene, Jörn is convinced to eat with the group by Anni's son Andres, and the group, happy about having overcome Jörn's (unexplained) resistance, discusses sharing Anni's expenses with regard to Andres.

[73] Silverman, "Helke Sander," p. 26.

Anni calls the *Holzweg*—the "wrong track," terrorism—is a contradiction typical of the characters in the film and an indication of their complexity.[74] An interesting comparison can be made between Till and Matthias, whose political theory is so often contradicted by his personal praxis, but in a manner almost the opposite from that of Till. As a socialist, Matthias has a certain theoretical belief in the equality of women, and it motivates the experiment in group living that the film follows from 1967 through 1970: his concern for Anni as a single, working mother is cited by the narrator as the impulse for the founding of the collective household. But in the practical matters of everyday household life, he is the most resistant to change and unable to see how the dialectical analysis of which he is so fond might be applied to his own attitudes. He calls Anni "anally fixated" for complaining about dirty dishes, and he sends his dirty laundry home to his mother; he is the one who laughs most defensively at the idea that a group of women have met together, separately from the men ("What! Only women?"). When he does extend his theoretical knowledge to the situation within the household, it is only to educate someone else, Andres, and in a manner most removed from the concrete situation at hand: he explains household responsibilities via the struggle in Vietnam.

Matthias's theoretical "enlightenment" (the association with Habermas, for instance) contrasts thus with his "unenlightened" praxis at the level of personal interactions and the "private" realm of reproduction (e.g., the dirty laundry). Till's sensitivity and constructive engagement in those latter areas are in turn contrasted with his political development. The film depicts his move into terrorism as a dead end, a mistake that is indeed a major factor in the disintegration of the collective household—as well as the student movement as a whole.

It is precisely the parallel between the situation within the collective household and the movement as a whole through which Sander is able to make a statement that bridges the gap between the focus on the "private" sphere of household interactions and the "external" history of the movement with its meetings, rallies, and demonstrations in the streets. The latter level of the narrative depends most on the documentary footage Sander incorporates into her film, providing a counterpoint to the fictional scenes, which focus mostly on the collective household. Sander's critique in turn is not focused

---

[74] Such complexity refutes the assertion that Sander creates two-dimensional male characters, as was claimed for example by Uta Berg-Ganschow, "Geschichte eines Nebenwiderspruchs," *Filme*, no. 9 (June 1981), p. 58.

solely on the "personal politics" of the men in the student movement; the political strategies and attitudes that characterized the male activists in their attempts to influence the public sphere in West Germany are also the object of critical investigation. As mentioned above, Till is portrayed as personally sympathetic, but his move toward terrorism is shown as a mistake.

"Comrades, your public events are unbearable," write Anni and her two women colleagues while composing a leaflet underneath the bleachers that (through clever montage) seem to be those upon which the cheering men sit shouting "Ho, Ho, Ho Chi Minh!" This chant is led by Rudi Dutschke and Peter Weiss, captured in a piece of documentary footage. "It's as though we left our identities at home": the women are fed up with the mass ritual, the pseudo-revolutionary rhetoric and bravado that characterize many of the events the male activists organize.

What disturbs Anni and her friends is a certain male romance with such rhetoric and posturing. Immediately after the bleacher scene there is documentary footage of police using water cannons on student demonstrators.[75] The scene is defamiliarized by the use of a colored filter (a shade of orange) and fairly humorous tuba music on the sound track; this distantiation is increased by the commentary of the narrator (read by Sander herself), which presents Anni's sudden realization of a certain unity underlying the obvious polarization of the scene: "The thought occurred to me that I could view all of this under the aspect that these were all men. The idea that all of them were lovers." The contradiction between masses of men in violent, public confrontation and individual men as lovers in private settings, as well as possible parallels between the two images, undermines the traditional dichotomy of "friend versus foe," which is the normal logic of male confrontation. The narrator implies that there may be in male socialization elements that are common to both police and demonstrators, elements that are not ultimately productive for the development of a new type of politics.

The next sequence, again a mix of documentary footage that interrupts a fictional scene, would seem to pursue the same logic. When Jörn, a household member, enters the apartment, drenching wet, there are chants on the sound track that seem to be the appropriate accompaniment for the (immediately preceding) water-cannon sequence. A shot of the drenched Jörn is then followed by a medium

[75] The West Berlin police used water cannons against protesters who came to demonstrate the opening of the government's trial against Fritz Teufel, a member of the "Commune No. 1," on 28 November 1967. See Kraushaar, "Chronologie," pp. 273–74.

shot of a young man laughing, a shot from documentary footage of a similar—perhaps even the same—demonstration. The young man is also wet, laughing defiantly at having been sprayed. The next shot returns to Jörn on his bed, below the poster of his pop idol, Humphrey Bogart, a poster with which Jörn has been associated since the beginning of the film. Soon thereafter is another quick cut to documentary footage of Rudi Dutschke.

The implied association of a modern icon of masculinity, Bogart, with the hero of the West German student movement, Dutschke, and the laughing young men of the movement, underscores the romantic nature of the male role models and male bonding in the movement. In spite of their opposition to established authority, they are united with those who uphold its order by socialization as men in similarly "heroic" games and role models—and these cultural images and rituals in turn mediate their relationships with women. (It is interesting to note that women in the American protest movement came to a similar realization that men on both sides of the barricades had much in common. In 1970, for instance, feminist Robin Morgan compared the "Chicago Conspiracy" members with their enemy, establishment judge Julius Hoffman. She wrote: "*in the light of day they are all the same.*")[76]

The reading of the protest scene from a new, gendered perspective provides a guideline for interpreting the subsequent developments in the film, both inside and outside the collective household. The attraction to romantic, pseudo-revolutionary bravado and rhetoric foreshadows the deterioration of the movement into terrorist cells on the one hand and dogmatic factions squabbling over the "correct" interpretations of Marx and Lenin on the other. The men's ability to bond in a mass ritual modeled on revolutionary movements of other times and places—Vietnam, the KPD (the Communist Party of Germany) in the Weimar Republic—is interpreted by the women as "leaving one's identity at home." This characterization can also elucidate the movement toward the fetishization of praxis—as terror—on the part of some and the fetishization of theory—as dogma—by others. These developments depend on forgetting—or repressing—one's own concrete situation and history (for example, as a student with a middle-class background). The women, on the other hand, organize their activities on the basis of their own situation and needs: they establish their own child-care centers and then begin to attempt organizing the women who worked in state-

---

[76] Robin Morgan, "Goodbye to All That," in an all-women's issue of New York underground newspaper *Rat*, 9 February 1970, cited in Gitlin, *The Sixties*, p. 374.

run child-care centers. This model of activism—organizing around local, immediate issues—would prove, as I have stressed, to be the more successful model for the next decade.[77]

In terms of characters in the film, it is again Matthias who provides an early model for the tendency to enjoy the abstraction of socialist theory to the detriment of his skills in dealing with the immediate reality around him. But the faction within the movement drifting toward dogmatism is better exemplified by Uwe, the figure who laughs most loudly when Anni suggests that women might be a class. For it is Uwe who lectures Anni, at a later point when she is now his lover(!),[78] on the merits of Lenin over Bakunin while strolling through West Berlin's Botanic Gardens. When Anni brings up specific points that contradict Uwe's dogmatic generalizations, he accuses her of being too concrete: "Don't be so concretistic!" It is Uwe who feels more comfortable joining one of the new Maoist parties (the K-Parteien) than continuing his relationship with Anni, who asks so many questions and is not trusted by party members.

Just after the scene in which Anni and Uwe presumably part, she comes upon Till playing pinball in a bar. Here she tells Till that she disagrees with his political choice, calling it a dead end, but Till says hardly a word to her. Dialogue with the faction moving toward terrorism has been cut off, too. The end of Anni's relationship with Till and Uwe reflects the generalized phenomenon of fragmentation in the student movement as it degenerates into dogmatic and/or terroristic rhetoric. The next sequence further illustrates this process: at home, Anni encounters two of her housemates practicing the Morse code. They tell her: "The real revolutionaries are in jail now." She then finds Andres with a young girl who calls Anni "bourgeois" for demanding they return some things they had stolen.[79] The narrator's voice is then heard over a shot of the apartment: "The longing for simple solutions creates new tragedies."

From this point late in the film, the narrative strand following the collective household quickly comes to an end. Some documentary footage is shown; it is a demonstration of child-care workers, one of

[77] Heinz Kersten makes a similar point in his review, "Erfahrungen weitergeben," *Frankfurter Rundschau*, 16 July 1981.

[78] Anni's affair with Uwe—of all people—shows that she, too, has some contradictions. She is not idealized, as some reviewers seem to think—for example, Claudia Lenssen, "Die schwere Arbeit der Erinnerung," *Frauen und Film*, no. 29 (September 1981), pp. 41–44.

[79] In an earlier sequence, Andres had already found a box of hand grenades in a closet, which his horrified mother had then removed from the apartment.

the early organizing achievements of the new women's movement.[80] Earlier in the film, sequences of documentary footage from the 1960s had shown the heyday of the student movement. Toward the end of the film, there is much less documentary footage, and this final documentary sequence depicts the budding women's movement, which was on the rise as the student movement dissolved.

After this footage, the apartment is shown again, but as a meeting place for Anni's women's group. The next scene is that of the prostrate Jörn grieving for Sophie, with the noise of the household in obvious conflict with his mood. And the final scene in the collective household, as mentioned above, is the one in which Till orders Anni to the kitchen as he holds a gun.

The collective living experiment collapses, as does the broader student movement. What is left is a fragmented movement, terrorist cells and dogmatic sects, as well as an emergent movement of women, which seems the only hopeful strand. What does this history mean to the filmmaker who chooses to return to it ten years later? What are the coordinates of that "constellation" which contains the events of the late 1960s and the perspective of 1980, when Sander constructs her vision of the earlier period? How does the filmmaker foreground her position and interest with regard to those historical events?

Ten Years After

Sander explicitly incorporates the perspective of 1980 into the film itself. *The Subjective Factor* opens in 1980, as Anni is joined in front of the television set by her son Andres. He brings her a collection of photographs documenting the student protests of the 1960s. For himself he has bought a book of photographs documenting the recent (as of 1980) occupation by antinuclear protesters of the site of the proposed atomic reactor at Gorleben.[81] The camera focuses on the books, one partially covering the other, as both Anni and Andres begin to page through them. This image concretizes the overlap of two historical positions: the late 1960s and 1980. Anni starts to review her memory of the issues and events of the 1960s, while

---

[80] On the sound track, as the footage of the women's demonstration is shown, the song "Honolulu" is heard, with its mention of a utopian Honolulu (as opposed to the real one) in the "Land of the Amazons." This song was composed (and performed) by Valie Export and Ingrid Wiener some years after the demonstration depicted here.

[81] The book Anni receives is called *Ihr müßt diese Typen nur ins Gesicht sehen. Apo Berlin 1966–1969* (You only need to see the faces of these guys: extraparliamentary opposition in Berlin). The book Andres holds is *Republik Freies Wendland*.

Andres looks at more current issues and events, the ones that engage him in 1980. Neither position can be seen as separate from its relation to the other.

It is Andres who makes possible Anni's act of remembrance, which opens up the narrative of the years 1967 through 1970. She pauses at a picture in the book he has given her; the picture then comes to life, as it were, through a cut to documentary footage of the car pictured in the photo. This transition to the re-presentation of memory is underscored by Anni's voice-over: "That's your mother in the car." It is Andres who will provide the major clue for the viewer as to whether a sequence in the film takes place in the later 1960s or in 1980, simply by his age (and of course the fact that two different actors play him). It is ultimately Andres who provides the link to the issues of the 1980s, a link that demonstrates that the film is not merely a pessimistic treatise on the failures of the past but a critique grounded in a concern that the struggle is still as necessary as ever.

Andres appears as an adolescent three times in the film. The first is at the beginning, where his age and Anni's hair length and style become associated with the 1980 strand of the film's narrative. After the documentary sequence initiated by Anni's paging through the book, a fictional sequence opens with a shot of a little blond boy calling to Anni; the transition to 1967 is thus completed, underscored by the ensuing voice-over narration.

The next sequence where Andres appears as an adolescent is the one that could be labeled the "cockroach sequence," since it begins with an extreme close-up of a cockroach, seen from its underside as it climbs up a clear surface, presumably the transparent wall of some kind of encasement. The next shot shows seemingly gigantic cockroaches in what is actually a miniature kitchen; on a glass wall of the case that encloses this exhibit (in the aquarium at the Berlin Zoo),[82] one can see the reflection of the adolescent Andres. On the sound track one hears Anni's voice: "Did you know that we were here before, thirteen years ago?" She is thus presumably talking to Andres, as becomes clear in a subsequent shot. Next she mentions that *NASA* experiments with radioactivity have caused cockroaches to grow in size. This remark is followed immediately by Mick Jagger singing the words "Time is on my side" on the sound track, from the song of the same name. The next shot shows the same exhibit; on the glass one sees a reflection of Anni and Andres, now once again a small boy. The date is therefore thirteen years before: 1967.

[82] According to Berg-Ganschow, "Geschichte," p. 58.

Andres, filmically a sign of the 1980s, is thus once again associated thematically with nuclear issues. It is a relatively well-known hypothesis among those concerned about the arms race that cockroaches may survive a nuclear war; time is on their side, so to speak, unless Andres's (or some future) generation can prevent their inheriting the planet. This is in any case the future that, from the standpoint of 1980, Andres seems to face.

The final sequence in which Andres appears as an adolescent is a montage of still photographs. It is a nondiegetic photo essay that begins after one of the many camera pans across the posters on the wall of the collective apartment (including movie posters for Louis Malle's *Viva Maria* and Godard's *La Chinoise*). Then the montage of stills begins: the opening photograph is one of soldiers raping a woman. The camera then pans across a photo of Soviet leader Leonid Brezhnev with the Politburo, then across a photo of U.S. President Jimmy Carter with the leaders of the Western Alliance (all men, except for Great Britain's Prime Minister, the indomitable Margaret Thatcher); next one sees a photo of Carter and Helmut Schmidt standing side-by-side, followed by one of Brezhnev and East German leader Erich Honecker kissing. Then there is a still photo of a jet behind rows of bombs in v-formation, followed by a photo of a pile of skulls, identified by Silverman as the skulls of Holocaust victims.[83] The sequence is concluded by the photo of the adolescent Andres.

There are various possible interpretations of this sequence of images primarily from about 1980. An obvious one would be that the world was still very much in danger a decade after America's involvement in Vietnam and the protest movement it spawned. Superpower interventionism was still posing a threat (the reference at another point in the film to El Salvador also seems to emphasize this threat).[84] But such continuities in superpower interventionism are only one aspect of the montage. Another aspect also demands analysis: the perspective of gender. Two women are shown in the entire sequence, one a victim of the rape of soldiers, the other Prime Minister Thatcher, a woman who seems quite at home with her role as a member of one of the two dominant military blocs. She does not seem at all uncomfortable in the community of men about her, nor does she seem out of place in a montage unified thematically by images of soldiers, bombs, military alliances, and male bonding rites

[83] Silverman, "Helke Sander," p. 23.
[84] See below, note 106.

(best typified by Honecker and Brezhnev kissing). Her presence does not undermine a depiction of militarism as primarily masculine.

Nonetheless, as Silverman asserts, the film does not settle for any easy "conflation of male subjectivity" with power, militarism, and fascism.[85] For of course the last male figure in the photo montage is Andres, the child of the protagonist Anni, the child Anni declares more important to her than all the causes in the world. The association of Andres with nuclear issues suggests an interpretation of his presence at the end of the photo montage: he represents the generation that will inherit—and have to confront—the world of soldiers, Cold War leaders, bombs, and the potential for mass genocide the photo sequence depicts. Silverman suggests that in Andres can be read the hope of a different kind of man, not aligned so much with "classic male values."[86]

Sander avoids any kind of biological determinism. In the face of the situation threatening the planet, both men and women are needed, men who will resist the militaristic logic she indicates as having roots in male socialization (and certainly in patriarchy), and women who will refuse to accommodate that pervasive logic. Just as Thatcher has little quarrel with the dominant logic, so too are women shown in the film who side with the male leadership against Anni. One of the most subversive aspects of the project of feminism can certainly be seen in Sander's film: the questioning of binarism and the traditional dichotomies so basic to dominant ideologies. In seeing an underlying unity between police and students in terms of male socialization, in seeing the limitations of traditional definitions of the split between "right" and "left," in seeing the danger to the world posed by both sides of the East/West power struggle, Sander undermines standard dichotomies. Her film aligns itself with both feminism and the peace movement's search for a peaceful world order in which the hegemony of superpower blocs has been eliminated.[87]

---

[85] Silverman, "Helke Sander," p. 23.

[86] Ibid.

[87] Now, in the aftermath of 1989, when the Soviet Union loosened its hegemonic hold on East Germany and Eastern Europe, there are new questions: whether the influence of the other superpower will be lessened, and whether in post–Cold War Germany, the pacifist "Green" tendencies with which Sander's film aligns itself will be able to play a role, or whether more conservative, nationalistic forces will remain dominant. In the 1980s the peace movement in Germany (and elsewhere) seemed stymied—until Gorbachev's ascension. It is unclear whether what E. P. Thompson calls "the forces of peace and freedom, of a greenish libertarian socialism" will ultimately prevail, but he is right to assert that one major factor influencing the changes in Eastern Europe has been precisely those nonaligned forces, through redefining

Sander does not see her feminist commitment as requiring withdrawal from other oppositional struggles, nor does she see the critique of the student movement that led to the formation of the women's movement as a denunciation of the former. "The women in the film write in their leaflet—an authentic one, by the way—for the Vietnam Congress: 'Comrades, your public events are unbearable'; but that didn't keep them from participating in those events."[88] The women considered themselves part of a broader movement—as is clear from the wording of Sander's own speech to the SDS Congress in September 1968, which is cited in the film. In this speech, she appealed to the organization to take seriously the question of the role of women, warning of the waste of energy a split in the movement would entail should the men oppose women's attempts to include their concerns as part of the broader agenda of the movement.

Why the movement did indeed fragment and dissipate is one question Sander investigates, and some possible answers are implied: the (distracting) attraction of dogma and violence, for example, is depicted as a major cause. The filmmaker's interest in the demise of the movement from her perspective ten years later is in no small part to provide the oppositional movements she supports in the 1980s a chance to review the mistakes of the past and learn from them, and to arm a new generation with a history of the struggles they are continuing.

In 1981, Sander spoke of the necessity for young women to know the beginnings of the women's movement, and of the need for older activists to work through their own history ("if you don't deal with your history, it will re-emerge as destruction").[89] She warns against resignation and dogmatic factionalism and counsels activist intervention by women especially in the broader struggles of the 1980s, underscoring again the example of the women in the SDS: "They didn't perceive themselves as victims, but rather as autonomous human beings. What was most important was intervention, which is winning ground again today in the women's peace movement."[90]

The Politics of Representation

Sander's film itself can be considered an active intervention of the sort she calls for above. Its subjectivity has little to do with the self-

---

"the political art of the possible" and playing a critical part in the "ideological moment" when the "ideological field of force" we call the Cold War became unstable. Thompson, "History Turns on A New Hinge," *The Nation*, 29 January 1990, p. 121.

[88] Sander, "Einmischung," p. 9.

[89] Sander, "Es gibt viel Falsches."

[90] Sander. "Einmischung," p. 9.

absorption so often associated with resignation and melancholy during the 1970s or with the smug, self-satisfied isolation of which the alternative culture was often accused. The connection to broader social concerns, the concern with history, and a healthy "fear of simple solutions" are not only thematized in the film but indeed structure its formal discourse.

"Subjectivity for me doesn't mean feelings. The subjective factor lies rather in connecting images with sounds, in my rhythm and style of presentation, in the *form* in which images relate to other images."[91] Sander answers those critics who accused her of making a film that is too "intellectual" by stating that this was exactly her intention: "I am accused of a certain coolness. Well, I myself have produced the breaks in atmosphere in the film; they aren't artistic mistakes."[92] The charge of "naive realism" often raised against literature and film of West Germany in the 1970s is in any case problematic, but it is not a label that can be attached to the work of Helke Sander.

The rejection of easy solutions in Sander's *The Subjective Factor* extends to the manner in which the film itself is constructed. In this sense film can be aligned with the modernist project, although the feminist revision of modernism B. Ruby Rich discusses is what I would call a postmodernism, precisely for its mixture of formal experimentation and autobiographically based narrative. In any case Sander's style is quite removed from one set of attitudes toward art that were popular during the 1970s within the leftist, alternative culture of West Germany, including the women's community. Sander addressed these attitudes, which combined a distrust of theory and "formalism" with a glorification of spontaneity, at a conference on "feminine imagery" in 1977:

> But just as progressive social theory has led to a dogmatic aesthetic, that is, the equation of "social realism" with a thesis of knowledge, . . . feminism has also had the tendency to make certain aesthetic categories a measure of the aesthetic experience. Thus spontaneity, in women not so much oppressed but rather socially patronized; it has been sharply ideologized, and the form into which this spontaneity flows has been summarily declared to be art. This phenomenon is like the fact that science's being antipathetic to women has led to women's groups' showing an antipathy to theory.[93]

The glorification of "spontaneity" was of course not limited to feminists in West Germany; it was common in the counterculture

---

[91] Sander, "vertrackt," p. 2.
[92] Ibid.
[93] Sander, "Feminism and Film," p. 50.

there, where, as we have seen, there had been since the late 1960s an amorphous political grouping whose adherents called themselves *Spontis*. The political advantages and disadvantages of their program aside, the aesthetic program around "spontaneity" does lend itself to the charge of "naive realism."[94]

Instead of having the appearance of spontaneity, or any kind of realism that makes the transition from "reality" to film seem unproblematic or indeed unnoticeable, *The Subjective Factor* is obviously the result of a carefully planned juxtaposition of images and elements that clearly reveals the hand of the director. It is also a film that necessitates conscious effort on the part of the audience in reflecting upon the relation of all the disparate elements the director has assembled. The very difficulty of transmitting the "reality" of the student protest movement to film is exactly the issue that informs the film's project: what *was* the "reality" of the student movement? *Whose* reality, as the title makes clear—that remembered by Sander, a female activist who has a very distinct perspective? Or that which was "documented" by various filmmakers and journalists of the time? There is no "objective" truth to be attained about the events at issue, and personal memory is not only limited but impossible to utilize without mediation of some kind—language, narrative, fictional reenactment. Such problems are precisely what Sander foregrounds. The film's "breaks in atmosphere" are the direct result of this foregrounding.

From the very opening of the film, the movement of the camera disrupts formal conventions that help create an illusion of unmediated "reality"—the camera draws attention to its own mediation by traveling through Anni's apartment without being connected to the perspective of any character. The camera takes its time winding through the apartment before finding Anni; it does not then stop to focus on her in front of the television but rather continues in its trajectory toward the wall behind her, where it stops on a poster, and only then turns and fixes on Anni.

If it sounds from this account that the camera is somehow becoming personified, this is because the camera in Sander's film (operated by Martin Schäfer) does seem to take on a life of its own, to become a character in its own right. The camera carries on an investigation that does not completely coincide with the fictional narrative it records. The film is not merely the reenactment but an *investigation*

---

[94] Of course, to the extent that artists aspired to naiveté, it was a conscious, and thus not so naive, attempt—a point made, for example, by Jörg Drews, "Selbsterfahrung und Neue Subjektivität in der Lyrik," *Akzente* 24 (1977), p. 95.

of memory. The camera creeps down corridors, pans across walls, where it examines posters, roams up and down stairwells, through apartments, out windows, and all to a certain extent independently of the characters whose movements and perspectives would normally determine camera movement in a more conventional narrative film. For example, there is a sequence early in the film in which Anni follows Luc through a factory hall wheat-pasting posters; after they leave, Sander directs the camera to move back across a wall examining the posters, instead of having the camera follow the two characters, or concluding the shot with their departure.

Such movement independent of the psychology of the fictional characters—coupled with the frequent use of the hand-held camera, which makes the presence of a camera all the more obvious—hinders the identification by the spectator of her or his look with that of the camera, the identification that Christian Metz asserts is the basis of the psychological power of classical narrative cinema.[95] One's identification with the camera is hindered to the extent that it is obvious there is an independent subjectivity controlling the camera, mediating between the characters of the fiction and the spectator. What is seen can no longer be experienced just as a "story"; rather it is openly a discourse constructed by another subject—the filmmaker.[96]

But more fundamental to the film's disruption of conventional cinematic techniques, to its breaking of illusionistic "atmosphere," is its incorporation of documentary footage into the film, interrupting thereby the fictional narrative. As I have emphasized, this is a strategy employed by many German filmmakers since the mid-1970s, including Alexander Kluge, Jutta Brückner, and of course Helma Sanders-Brahms. It fosters a questioning of the traditional boundaries between genres that is especially relevant to the issues examined by *The Subjective Factor*: between the "objective" public record, the documentary film, and the conventional vehicle for depicting personal experience, the fiction film, which makes possible a type of "subjective" response—via psychological identification—on the part of the spectators. Kluge has written much on the theoretical implications of this mixing of genres; his project is not identical to Helke Sander's, but one can see similarities. For example, Kluge writes that "the artificial opposition of documentary and mise-en-scène" must be undermined:

[95] See Metz, *The Imaginary Signifier*, pp. 40, 45–52.
[96] See Metz, "Story/Discourse."

Mere documentation cuts off relations: nothing exists objectively without the emotions, actions and desires, that is, without the eyes and the
sense of the people involved. I have never understood why the depiction
of such acts (most of which have to be staged) is called fiction, fiction-
film. But it is equally ideological to assume that individuals could determine history. Therefore, no narrative succeeds without a certain propor-
tion of authentic material, i.e. documentation. Such use of documentation establishes a point of reference for the eyes and senses: real
conditions clear the view for the action.[97]

Sander appears to agree with Kluge to the extent that she obviously was not satisfied with exclusive use of either fictional reenactment or documentary material for her film; her investigation of those
turbulent years at the end of the 1960s combines both, and both elements—personal experience and historical documents—comment
upon and contextualize each other.[98] This is a postmodernist project
typical of what Hutcheon calls the "historiographic metafiction," in
which "documentary sources as well as the narrative form of history
come under as serious scrutiny . . . as they do in the philosophy of
history today."[99]

Helke Sander does not attempt to blend her fictional discourse
with the documentary one to the extent that Sanders-Brahms does
in *Germany, Pale Mother* (as when Lene appears to talk to the boy
in the documentary footage). Sander, like Kluge, seems more committed to foregrounding the seams of her montage. In *The Subjective
Factor*, her defamiliarization of documentary footage includes adding color, by shooting it through colored filters—red, pink, orange,
sepia. Not only does it stand apart from and thus comment on the
fiction, but also any illusion of "objectivity" it might have is undermined by the director's foregrounding of her own attitude toward
the footage. Kluge's notion of the "authenticity" of documentary
footage seems to avoid the problem of the subjectivity of the original
documentary filmmaker as well as that of the director who then
chooses to use a piece of footage and edit it into a certain place in
his or her film. With Sander this is not the case; she constantly foregrounds her own use of footage with colored filters and with Heiner
Goebbels's ironic music. For example, her commentary is fairly ev-

[97] Alexander Kluge, "On Film and the Public Sphere," trans. Thomas Y. Levin and
Miriam B. Hansen, *New German Critique*, nos. 24/25 (1981/1982), p. 206. This excerpt
is from Kluge, *Die Patriotin* (Frankfurt: Zweitausendeins, 1979).

[98] See Sander, "vertrackt," p. 2.

[99] Hutcheon, *A Poetics of Postmodernism*, p. 56. See also Elsaesser on Sander's
film, *New German Cinema*, pp. 191–93.

ident in the scene in which the police shoot water cannons at the demonstrators: she uses a colored filter, comical tuba music, and of course her own voice-over (which provides the insight that all participants on both sides were men). Heroic or tragic readings—which this footage could otherwise easily invite—are immediately undermined.

Sander's montage of various elements is typical of the Brechtian legacy she shares with Kluge. It is a juxtaposition of elements that do not fuse together but rather remain distinct and comment upon each other (or rather invite the spectator to make some kind of critical connection between them): fictional and nonfictional sequences; the overlay of voice-over, background music, and songs—both diegetic and nondiegetic[100]; the use of color filters; and shots of posters, printed pages, and book covers (e.g., Matthias's copy of *Theory and Praxis*, shown while he packs the dirty laundry to send home to his mother). All such techniques demonstrate Sander's employment of a variety of filmic codes simultaneously to interrupt the narrative, foreground the discursive commentary, suggest connections, and provoke interpretation of depicted events from a variety of perspectives.

Montage as the negation of synthesis is a central principle of modernist art. Editing various elements into a film not in order to synthesize an illusion of reality or to create an overpowering emotional "atmosphere" but rather to contrast with and comment upon each other, and thus disrupt the linearity of the narrative and open it to various critical interpretations: this strategy adds up to a modernist program for film editing. Here Sander and Kluge coincide. Where they differ is with Sander's willingness to foreground her own position in structuring the film. Kluge does not foreground his own position as the authority who assembles the various elements that the spectator in turn must then put into some kind of relationship. In his emphasis on the gap between disparate elements as the locus of meaning, dependent on the activity of the spectator who "fills" the gap, he underemphasizes his own activity as the one who structures those gaps.[101] Although he admits the privileged position of this activity, and the lopsided power relationship with regard to the

[100] For example, the "Einheitsfront" ("The United Front") and Italian leftist songs are sung by characters in the action; "Honolulu" is juxtaposed with footage of the demonstrating child-care workers. All three songs are sung by women and indicate the shift in the course of the film from traditional leftist to feminist politics.

[101] See Kluge, "On Film and the Public Sphere," p. 220. The excerpted interview is from Klaus Eder and Alexander Kluge, *Ulmer Dramaturgien: Reibungsverluste* (Munich: Hanser, 1980).

spectator in his writing on the subject, he does not foreground this asymmetry in his films.[102] His own activity is most evident in his films through the use of his voice as the narrator, but it is exactly this that is not problematized: it is a voice attached to no character, a voice that has access to the internal motivations of the characters, an ironic, humorous, but anonymous voice of authority whose position is not grounded or questioned or personalized.

B. Ruby Rich compares Kluge's use of voice-over narration in *Occasional Work of a Female Slave* (*Gelegenheitsarbeit einer Sklavin*, 1973) with that of Sander in *REDUPERS* (1977) and analyzes the difference from a feminist perspective:

> [T]he effect of the voiceover in the Sander film is utterly different, both in its effect upon the film text and upon the spectator. The most reductive explanation, and a persuasive one, focuses on the difference between Sander's utilization of a woman narrator to speak for and comment upon a woman character, whereas Kluge imposes a male voice upon a female subject. It is a fundamental and determining difference, but for formal reasons rather than simply those of gender identification. . . .
>
> The major break with Kluge's narrative model might be pinpointed in Sander's rejection of hegemony and authority as narrative qualities. . . . In Sander's films the other characters do not just share in the narrative authority; rather, the authoritarianism of narration is avoided in favor of a relationship that sounds at times more like a conversation than like any hierarchical ordering of narrative truth.[103]

In *The Subjective Factor*, the possibility that the voice-over is meant to be a monolithic instance of narrative authority is first undermined at the beginning of the film, when two voices speak for Anni. The first instance of voice-over narration is actually Anni's off-camera voice explaining the picture in the photo collection to Andres ("That's your mother in that car"); then another voice takes over the narration, the voice of Sander herself, talking in the third person about Anni. There are also examples of a more confusing use of off-camera voices; as in *REDUPERS*, off-camera voices of fictional characters often enjoy for a while the invisibility normally reserved for the narrator. This plurality of off-camera voices undoes the unique position the narrator's voice would otherwise occupy.[104] The

---

[102] Kluge, "On Film and the Public Sphere," p. 217 (*Ulmer Dramturgien*).

[103] Rich, "She Says, He Says," pp. 39–40.

[104] In one sequence, for example, Anni picks up items left by Andres on the hall carpet while being interrogated by a male voice coming from a character who is never shown. A later shot with Till does the same thing in reverse: Till is seen in Anni's

use of both first-person and third-person voices also complicates things: Helke Sander uses the third person in referring to Anni, which foregrounds the interplay between the fiction and the auto-biography in the film, problematizing any total identification be-tween Anni and Sander as narrator. But at the same time, the limi-tation of Sander's own perpective is paralleled by the general focus on one person's experience—the narrator has access to only one character's subjectivity, the one who is based on her own experi-ence. The personal nature of the investigation of the past that the narrator conducts is not concealed.

This is most strikingly demonstrated in the scene where Sander watches documentary footage of herself giving a speech to the SDS in 1968. (See the frontispiece photograph.) The sequences within the fictional narrative preceding this scene deal with Anni's strug-gles to be appointed as a delegate to an SDS conference in order to be able to voice at a national forum the concerns of the committee she and the other women have founded in West Berlin.[105] It is not only the autobiographical aspect of the film that is foregrounded in this scene. The very project of Sander's film is foregrounded as well: her examination of personal memory and public record vis-à-vis the late 1960s from her vantage point in 1980. In the sequence, one sees some documentary footage being projected onto a screen, and as elsewhere in the film, there is an overlay of the perspective of 1980 onto that of 1968.[106] Here its achievement is striking: the director herself walks in front of the screen and takes a position on the side where she watches herself, her 1980 profile encroaching on the im-

---

doorway, and Anni speaks with him, her voice remaining off-camera, her image never shown.

[105] In the film, the speech Anni wants to give is for the SDS Conference in Frankfurt in 1968. Sander herself gave a famous speech there on behalf of the women's *Aktions-rat*, but as she explains in "vertrackt" (p. 25), in the film she makes use of documen-tary footage of a speech she gave at another conference; what is heard, however, is from the Frankfurt speech. See also Harrigan, "The German Women's Movement," p. 43; and Meinhof, "Die Frauen im SDS."

[106] In another similar sequence in the film in which issues of the 1980s intrude into the narrative strand focusing on the 1960s, the point is made that Central America has replaced Vietnam as a site of intervention. As in the sequence discussed above, here too the viewer sees a film projector being readied, and then documentary footage of demonstrations in the late 1960s is projected onto a screen (the demonstrations shown took place at the corporate headquarters of the Springer press in West Berlin). At the same time, a radio news report from 1980 is heard on the sound track, pre-senting the remarks of a conservative West German politician (Heiner Geissler) in support of the military junta then controlling El Salvador. Thus, from the standpoint of 1980, with the radio reminding her of the current state of events, the filmmaker reviews personal and collective history.

age of 1968. Not only does the subject responsible for the voice-over thus abandon the privilege of invisibility; the position of the "subject of enunciation" in regard to her film is exposed. The nature of her relationship to the fiction she has created is indeed like a "conversation," as Rich puts it; she is in a dialogue with memory and history, and she does not pretend that she plays no role in this interaction. And the extent to which her role is a privileged one is not effaced but rather openly exposed.

Sander makes films that challenge and involve viewers in the process of making sense of the disparate elements that have been assembled. The process of making sense of the relationship of personal experience and history is a difficult task, one that is not merely aesthetic but political. "The longing for simple solutions" was destructive to the student movement, as is indicated by her voice-over commentary near the end of the film. Another emblematic statement voiced by the narrator in the film stresses the importance of the process of learning over the seduction of easy answers: "One exerts oneself so much to gain information that the exertion itself becomes information." It is the search for the meaning of the 1960s in relation to the struggles today that matters; there is no "objective" depiction that reveals an "answer" to the enigma of those events. The process of working through history in terms of its relation to the concrete present is a difficult one fraught with the conflicts of memory, subjectivity, differing political agendas and strategies. But it is a crucial lesson: there is nothing more political, subjective, and urgent than the representation of history. It is the urgency of the "subjective factor" that motivates historical memory in the first place.

> To articulate the past historically does not mean to recognize it "the way it really was" (Ranke). It means to seize hold of a memory as it flashes up at a moment of danger.[107]

[107] Benjamin, "Theses on the Philosophy of History," p. 255.

Conclusion

Selves
and Others

HE SAID:

Isn't it?

Isn't it just?

Isn't it just like a woman?

SHE SAID:

It takes.

It takes one.

It takes one to know one.[1]

Lost Mastery

The ability to see and hear fade away when one has lost one's sense of self.[2]

That deaf, dumb, and blind kid
Sure plays a mean pinball.[3]

In his book on Wim Wenders, Peter Buchka asserts that all Wenders's protagonists suffer from their inadequate perception of the world around them. They cannot really hear and see. They have lost their ability to perceive external reality, for they have lost their sense of self. Connected to these problems is the difficulty these characters have with language and self-expression.[4] If one looks at the Anglo-American popular culture of the late 1960s that was so influential upon Wenders, it is interesting to note a fictional character who could almost serve as an allegorical embodiment of what in Buchka's thesis is the typical Wenders character: the hero of The Who's Rock Opera *Tommy*, who literally cannot see or hear, who is called "deaf, dumb and blind."

The juxtaposition of The Who and Wenders is not as farfetched as it might seem. Alienation from the senses and from language—and the inadequate sense of self behind this alienation—is not merely typical of characters in Wenders's films. The concern with alienation from sense perception and experience, and the desperate attempt to overcome it, can be readily connected to what Michael Rutschky called *Erfahrungshunger*, or "hunger for experience," his term for the West German malaise of the 1970s. Similar states of alienation characterize Peter Schneider's *Lenz*, the protagonist of Karin Struck's *Class Love*, and Richard in Botho Strauss's *Devotion*, and they can be noted in the work of Peter Handke. Besides Wenders's films, a film like Werner Herzog's *Kaspar Hauser* is an obvious thematicization of sensory deprivation and alienation from language.[5]

---

[1] From Laurie Anderson, "It Tango." © 1982 Difficult Music.

[2] Told to Philip Winter, protagonist in Wim Wenders's *Alice in the Cities*. Quoted in Buchka, *Augen kann man nicht kaufen*, p. 81.

[3] From Peter Townsend, words and music: "Pinball Wizard." © 1969 Fabulous Music Ltd.

[4] Buchka, *Augen kann man nicht kaufen*, p. 81.

[5] The film is about the legendary Kaspar Hauser, who grew up in darkness, never learning to speak until he was discovered as an adult, when he is slowly introduced to language and "civilization" in provincial Germany in the early decades of the nineteenth century. Other films by Herzog that easily fit into this category of sensory

Nor is the phenomenon in question limited to West German culture during the 1970s. In the same decade, after all, Christopher Lasch labeled American society The Culture of Narcissism, maintaining that the contemporary American character was typified by a weak ego incapable of adequately distinguishing internal and external realities—an impoverished sense of both self and the world. As mentioned above, Fredric Jameson characterized this phenomenon in less pathological terms, choosing to place it in the context of "postmodernity": rather than speaking of weak egos, Jameson speaks of the "death of the subject," which he defines as the end of the "experience and the ideology of the unique self." This demise of the "bourgeois individual subject" can in turn be related to the rise of consumer capitalism and a postindustrial economy.[6] Craig Owens, who views this crisis of the subject more positively than Jameson does, calls it a "loss of mastery," not merely for the individual but also in terms of the cultural, economic, and political authority of the West—as well as a perceived erosion of male authority within Western societies.[7]

Postmodern culture is characterized by what Jameson calls "the effacement . . . of some key boundaries or separations, most notably the erosion of the older distinction between high culture and so-called mass or popular culture."[8] To return to popular culture, then, specifically to The Who (the group's very name capitalized on the identity crisis of its generation): how does the "deaf, dumb, and

deprivation and/or linguistic/cultural alienation would be Land of Silence and Darkness (1971) and Stroszek (1976/1977).

[6] Jameson, "Postmodernism and Consumer Society," p. 115.

[7] Owens, "The Discourse of Others," p. 67. Discussions of narcissism that problematize its being merely subsumed into a normative (and affirmative) social psychology include Alford's "Nature and Narcissism" and Kramer's subchapters "Self and Other" and "Da(bei)sein" in "/New Subjectivity/," pp. 220–36. Kramer, in analyzing Adorno, comes to the conclusion that he believed humanity was already entering a postnarcissistic age (p. 228); her (quite reasonable) conclusion is that—pace Adorno—it is "an open question" whether "existing social conditions necessarily preclude the development of selves capable of resisting destructive tendencies in society" (p. 232). In a review of Leo Braudy's book The Frenzy of Renown, Jean-Christophe Agnew suggested an interesting, gender-sensitive reading of the current discourse on narcissism (i.e., its function of ridiculing or pathologizing). He calls for an examination of the "intersection (and contradiction) between the avowedly masculine 'longing of Alexander' [i.e., the desire not merely for power but for personal recognition] and the almost equally ancient and visceral attack" on what is derided as "female vanity," of which "the contemporary critique of narcissism may be the most recent expression." Agnew, "La Pompe Perdue," The Nation, 20 September 1986, pp. 249–52.

[8] Jameson, "Postmodernism and Consumer Society," p. 112.

blind" Tommy find a way to express himself? Self-expression and self-realization come through mastery of pinball. One can see in this an apt metaphor for the attempt of youth in the 1960s to seek fulfillment in popular culture, having rejected both classical and modernist "high art" as equally institutionalized and elitist. This backlash against high culture certainly had its effect on Wenders, whose life was supposedly "saved" by rock and roll.[9] Wenders's films highlight the trappings of American mass culture and technology in West Germany (with a specific emphasis on pinball machines, as a matter of fact).[10] He makes films that have explored not only mass culture and technology but his own ambivalence about them, which he never conceals.

In the process of contextualizing the West German literary and cinematic texts of the 1970s examined in this book, I have used the concepts of postmodernity and postmodernism. Within the broad context of the postmodern condition as conceived by Jameson (negatively) and Owens (positively), the specific experience of the 1960s—the protest movements, especially the international student movement—played a significant role, as Linda Hutcheon, Andreas Huyssen, Terry Eagleton, and others have asserted.[11] The student movement represented a type of challenge (from within) to Western political and cultural hegemony, but it also represented a traumatic experience of "loss of mastery" for those who participated in it, an experience to some extent mirroring the loss sensed in the larger culture. The movement obviously failed in terms of any attempt to overturn the power structure in Western Europe and the United States. But, as I have demonstrated specifically with regard to the West German context, the traumatic experiences of the late 1960s were formative upon much of the literary and cinematic production of the years since then, leaving in their wake a cultural legacy that continues to be influential.[12]

[9] Dawson, *Wim Wenders*, p. 11.

[10] In Wenders's film adaptation of Handke's novel *The Goalie's Anxiety* (1971), for example, pinball machines form an important part of the settings through which the hero aimlessly wanders. Also the title of one of his first experimental short films, *Same Player Shoots Again* (1967), is taken from a standard message flashed on a pinball machine.

[11] See Hutcheon, *A Poetics of Postmodernism*, p. 8; Huyssen, "Mapping the Postmodern," pp. 28–33, and Terry Eagleton, *Literary Theory: An Introduction* (Minneapolis: University of Minnesota Press, 1983), pp. 141–45, 148–50.

[12] The political experience of the 1960s has also continued to exert an influence—most recently, of course, in the style of protests that rocked Eastern Europe. Its legacy includes the international ecology, feminist, and peace movements, which, while cer-

The political and cultural movements of the 1960s stood in a sense between the modern and the postmodern. They shared with earlier avant-garde movements the desire to destroy the elitist realm of art by fusing art with life; similarly, they wanted to overthrow a technocracy of elite managers by fusing individual emancipation with democratic mass politics. Nonetheless there was still an optimism about technology's ability to "master" the "reality principle," as well as a faith in rational systems for explaining the world completely and transforming it totally. Not unrelated to this theoretical hubris was an unquestioned, almost unconscious, acceptance of male domination of the movement, indeed a blindness to any ideological implications of gender.

The initial euphoria gave way to the awareness of relative powerlessness in the face of a vastly more complex and contradictory reality than the various utopian theories and avant-garde visions had conceived. It was not possible to create any easy synthesis of apparent contradictions like those between self and society, the political and the personal, reason and emotion, art and life. The ensuing resignation led to a skepticism about millennial hopes and grand systems ("master narratives," as Owens says), whether in art or in politics.[13] Activists and artists alike were chastened by the collapse of the avant-garde/pop dreams of the 1960s for "Paradise Now" (as the Living Theater expressed it). During the 1970s, there was a shift away from global manifestos and toward a focus on the local, the everyday, the immediate, the tangible, the physical, the personal, the sexual, the marginal. Language—verbal, written, and cinematic—was investigated in terms of its concrete relation to personal and physical reality.

In the early 1970s there was a general disillusionment with politics in West Germany, and especially with dogmatic schemes of historical interpretation. By the late 1970s a need had emerged to confront German history again, but it was now examined through the perspective of (reconstructed) personal experience, rather than in terms of grand conceptual systems and teleologies. What resulted was a postmodernist examination of history and subjectivity.

The "Other History"?

At the end of the twentieth century, it is too late to expect any renewed subversive energy from a modernism already defined as

tainly not dominant, are influential. (Nor have the issues that motivate these groups become any less pressing as the 1990s begin.)

[13] Owens, "The Discourse of Others," p. 65.

"high" or "classical": "If the postmodern is indeed a historical and cultural condition (however transitional or incipient), then oppositional cultural practices and strategies must be located *within* postmodernism."[14] The undermining of boundaries in postmodern art has consisted in a blending of the popular with the elite, narrative with distantiation, modernism with classical realism, the mass-produced with the "auratic," the international with the national (and local), the traditional with the contemporary. While the blurring of such boundaries in the arts runs the risk of an easy affirmation of the contradictory status quo of postindustrial society, an ahistorical eclecticism, it can also produce works in which the disparate elements provoke critical insight, illuminating rather than effacing historical change.

The troubled dialogue with history in West Germany resulted in certain works that I would place in the latter category, works by artists shaped by that history—and by their experience of the attempts at cultural revolution in the 1960s. Notable among such artists have been filmmakers like Helke Sander, Helma Sanders-Brahms, Wim Wenders, Alexander Kluge, and Rainer Werner Fassbinder. Other critics have questioned whether the treatment of history by these directors has been sufficiently critical. Both Anton Kaes and Thomas Elsaesser imply in their discussions of the "return to history" noted in West German film in the late 1970s and early 1980s that this phenomenon actually involves the *replacement* of history by the cinema, a nostalgic recycling of images that makes history "itself" vanish, as it were.[15] This analysis bears obvious similarity to Jameson's negative view of postmodernist art as nostalgia and "pastiche." But as Linda Hutcheon has argued, the recall of history in postmodern art is "neither nostalgia nor aesthetic cannibalization":

> It is true . . . that postmodern art does not offer what Jameson desires—"genuine historicity". . . . But its deliberate refusal to do so is not a naive one: what postmodernism does is to contest the very possibility of our ever being able to *know* the "ultimate objects" of the past. It teaches and enacts the recognition that the social, historical, and existential "reality" of the past is *discursive* reality when it is used as the referent of art, and so the only "genuine historicity" becomes that which would openly acknowledge its own discursive, contingent identity.[16]

[14] Huyssen, "Mapping the Postmodern," p. 29.

[15] See Kaes, *Deutschlandbilder*, pp. 207–9, and Elsaesser, *New German Cinema*, p. 278.

[16] Hutcheon, *A Poetics of Postmodernism*, p. 24.

"Genuine historicity" outside of discourse is in any case impossible to discuss—as with all modern dreams of some pure state of authenticity or objective truth outside of human language and subjectivity. On the other hand, a genuine historicity that openly acknowledges its discursive contingency is, I would assert, what one finds in the "history films" by Sander and Sanders-Brahms discussed here. They are films that "do not try to escape, but indeed foreground, the historical, social, ideological contexts" in which they originate.[17]

I have focused on history films by two women. Often the most interesting among postmodernist explorations of history have been made by artists belonging to groups marginalized or silenced by traditional histories. As Huyssen writes:

> It was especially the art, writing, film making and criticism of women and minority artists with their recuperation of buried and mutilated traditions, their emphasis on exploring forms of gender- and race-based subjectivity in aesthetic productions and experiences, and their refusal to be limited to standard canonizations, which added a whole new dimension to the critique of high modernism and to the emergence of alternative forms of culture.[18]

Demonstrating the value of what has been excluded as "marginal" has the potential to provide a key to deconstructing "the master's game." It is ultimately a binary logic that excludes; it denies contingency and context by opposing politics to art, history to subjectivity, and social reality to discourse. The deconstruction of binarism is accomplished ultimately through the recognition of difference, as opposed to the assumption of the mirror-image opposites that make up a dichotomy. Such a project is intrinsically related to that of feminism. Through the recognition of difference, there is the possibility of a type of dialogue across (and on) the boundaries ordinarily constructed as dichotomies: gender, "subject" and "object," body and mind, self and other, the political and the personal, language and experience, text and reality, fiction and documentary, present and past. That women have often been the ones to problematize such oppositions is understandable, since they have so long been relegated outside of "history," victims of some of the most ancient dichotomous thinking (but by no means the only such victims). As Hélène Cixous has written:

---

[17] Ibid., pp. 24–25.
[18] Huyssen, "Mapping the Postmodern," p. 27.

Where is she?
Activity/passivity
Sun/Moon
Culture/Nature
Day/Night

Father/Mother
Head/Heart
Intelligible/Palpable
Logos/Pathos
Form, convex, step, advance, semen, progress.
Matter, concave, ground—where steps are taken, holding and dumping
   ground
Man

———

Woman

Always the same metaphor: we follow it, it carries us, beneath all its figures, wherever discourse is organized. If we read or speak, the same thread or double braid is leading us throughout literature, philosophy, criticism, centuries of representation and reflection.[19]

Perhaps by deconstructing this system of dichotomies, what Cixous calls "the other history" can be invented.[20]

[19] Cixous and Clément, *The Newly Born Woman*, p. 63.
[20] Ibid., p. 83.

Works Consulted

(Bibliography/Filmography)

PRIMARY SOURCES

Handke, Peter. *Falsche Bewegung* [*Wrong Move*]. Frankfurt: Suhrkamp, 1975. (Text dated 1973.)

Sander, Helke. *Der subjektive Faktor* [*The Subjective Factor*]. Basis-Film, 1980. 138 min.

Sanders-Brahms, Helma. *Deutschland, bleiche Mutter* [*Germany, Pale Mother*]. 1979. 125 min. (1st version 150 min.) U.S. dist.: New Yorker Films, New York.

Schneider, Peter. *Lenz. Eine Erzählung*. West Berlin: Rotbuch, 1973.

Strauss, Botho. *Devotion*. Trans. Sophie Wilkins. New York: Farrar, Straus, and Giroux, 1979. Orig. *Die Widmung. Eine Erzählung*. Munich: Hanser, 1977. Version cited here: Munich: Deutscher Taschenbuch Verlag, 1980.

Struck, Karin. *Klassenliebe. Roman* [*Class Love*]. Frankfurt: Suhrkamp, 1973.

Wenders, Wim. *Falsche Bewegung* [*Wrong Move*]. Filmverlag der Autoren, 1974. 103 min.

SECONDARY SOURCES

Adelson, Leslie A. *Crisis of Subjectivity: Botho Strauss's Challenge to West German Prose of the 1970s*. Amsterdam: Rodopi, 1984.

———. "The Question of a Feminist Aesthetic and Karin Struck's *Klassenliebe*." In Susan L. Cocalis and Kay Goodman, eds., *Beyond the Eternal Feminine: Critical Essays on Women and German Literature*, pp. 335–49. Stuttgart: Hans-Dieter Heinz, 1982.

———. "Subjectivity Reconsidered: Botho Strauss and Contemporary West German Prose." *New German Critique*, no. 30 (1983), pp. 3–59.

Adorno, Theodor W. *Minima Moralia. Reflexionen aus dem beschädigten Leben*. 1951. Frankfurt: Suhrkamp, 1985.

———. "Rede über Lyrik und Gesellschaft." In Adorno, *Noten zur Literatur*, vol. 1, pp. 73–103. Frankfurt: Suhrkamp, 1963.

Agnew, Jean-Christophe. "La Pompe Perdue." Rev. of *The Frenzy of Renown* by Leo Braudy. *The Nation*, 20 September 1986, pp. 249–52.

Alford, C. Fred. "Nature and Narcissism: The Frankfurt School." *New German Critique*, no. 36 (1985), pp. 174–92.

Arnold, Heinz Ludwig. "Gespräch mit Peter Handke." *Text & Kritik*, 24/24a (1976), pp. 15–37.

Auty, Marty. Rev. of *Deutschland, bleiche Mutter*, dir. by Helma Sanders-Brahms. *Monthly Film Bulletin* 48, no. 570 (1981), p. 136.

Bammer, Angelika. "Through a Daughter's Eyes: Helma Sanders-Brahms' *Germany, Pale Mother*." *New German Critique*, no. 36 (1985), pp. 91–109.

Barth, John. "The Literature of Exhaustion." 1967. In Raymond Federman, ed., *Surfiction: Fiction Now . . . and Tomorrow*, pp. 19–33. Chicago: Swallow Press, 1975.

———. "The Literature of Replenishment: Postmodernist Fiction." *The Atlantic*, July 1980, pp. 65–71.

Barthes, Roland. *S/Z: An Essay*. 1970. Trans. Richard Miller. New York: Hill and Wang, 1974.

Bauer, Christian. "Auf der Suche nach verlorenen Müttern." Rev. of *Deutschland, bleiche Mutter*, dir. by Helma Sanders-Brahms. *Süddeutsche Zeitung*, 3 January 1981.

Baumgarten, Ruth. Rev. of *Der subjektive Faktor*, dir. by Helke Sander. *Monthly Film Bulletin* 50, no. 597 (1983), p. 280.

Becher, Martin Roda. "Poesie der Unglücksfälle." *Merkur* 32 (1978), pp. 625–28.

Beck, Evelyn Torton, and Biddy Martin. "Westdeutsche Frauenliteratur der siebziger Jahre." In Paul Michael Lützeler and Egon Schwarz, eds., *Deutsche Literatur in der Bundesrepublik seit 1965*, pp. 135–49. Königstein/Ts.: Athenäum, 1980.

Becker, Peter von. "Minima Moralia der achtziger Jahre. Notizen zu Botho Strauß' 'Paare Passanten' und 'Kalldewey, Farce.' " *Merkur* 36 (1982), pp. 150–60.

Beicken, Peter. " 'Neue Subjektivität': Zur Prosa der siebziger Jahre." In Paul Michael Lützeler and Egon Schwarz, eds., *Deutsche Literatur in der Bundesrepublik seit 1965*, pp. 164–81. Königstein/Ts.: Athenäum, 1980.

Beller, Manfred. "Lenz in Arkadien. Peter Schneiders Italienbild von Süden betrachtet." *Arcadia* 13 (1978-Sonderheft), pp. 91–105.

Benjamin, Walter. "Theses on the Philosophy of History." In the collection of his essays *Illuminations*, pp. 253–64. Ed. Hannah Arendt, 1955. Trans. Harry Zohn, 1968. New York: Schocken, 1969.

Berg-Ganschow, Uta. "Geschichte eines Nebenwiderspruchs." Rev. of *Der subjektive Faktor*, dir. by Helke Sander. *Filme*, no. 9 (June 1981), pp. 58–59.

Berman, Russell A. "Language and Image: Cinematic Aspects of Contemporary German Prose." In Sigrid Bauschinger, Susan L. Cocalis, and Henry A. Lea, eds., *Film und Literatur: Literarische Texte und der neue deutsche Film*, pp. 210–29. Bern: Francke, 1984.

———. "The Recipient as Spectator: West German Film and Poetry of the Seventies." *German Quarterly* 55 (1982), pp. 499–511.

Beutin, Wolfgang, et al., eds. *Deutsche Literaturgeschichte: von den Anfängen bis zur Gegenwart*. Stuttgart: Metzler, 1979; 2nd ed. 1984.

Biermann, Wolf. "Das gute Wort 'Dableiben.' " Rev. of Lenz by Peter Schneider. Spiegel, 10 December 1973, p. 142.

Bloch, Ernst. "Diskussionen über Expressionismus" and "Das Problem des Expressionismus nochmals." In Bloch, Die Kunst, Schiller zu sprechen. Frankfurt: Suhrkamp, 1969.

————. Erbschaft dieser Zeit [Heritage of Our Times]. 1935. Frankfurt: Suhrkamp, 1973.

———— et al. Aesthetics and Politics. Afterword by Frederic Jameson. Trans. ed. Ronald Taylor. London: NLB, 1977.

Blumenberg, Hans C. "Ein Brief an Lene." Rev. of Deutschland, bleiche Mutter, dir. by Helma Sanders-Brahms. Die Zeit, 10 October 1980, p. 54.

————. "Deutschlands tote Seelen." Rev. of Falsche Bewegung, dir. by Wim Wenders. Die Zeit, 21 March 1975, p. 24.

Bovenschen, Sylvia. "Is There a Feminine Aesthetic?" Trans. Beth Weckmueller. New German Critique, no. 10 (1977), pp. 111–37.

Brecht, Bertolt, script: Kuhle Wampe. Dir. Slatan Dudow. 1932. 75 min. U.S. dist.: West Glen Films, New York.

Breton, André. Manifestoes of Surrealism. 1924. Trans. Richard Seaver and Helen Lane. Ann Arbor: University of Michigan Press, 1969.

Brinkmann, Rolf Dieter, and R. R. Rygulla, eds. Acid. Neue amerikanische Szene. Darmstadt: März-Verlag, 1969.

Brückner, Jutta. Hungerjahre [Years of Hunger]. 1980. 100 min. U.S. dist.: West Glen Films, New York.

Buchka, Peter. Augen kann man nicht kaufen: Wim Wenders und seine Filme. Munich: Hanser, 1983.

Büchner, Georg. The Complete Plays. Ed. Michael Patterson. London: Methuen, 1987.

————. Lenz. 1835. In Georg Büchner: Werke und Briefe. Ed. Fritz Bergemann. Munich: Deutscher Taschenbuch Verlag, 1976.

Bullivant, Keith, ed. After the "Death" of Literature: West German Writing of the 1970s. Oxford: Berg Publishers, 1989.

Bürger, Christa, and Peter Bürger, eds. Postmoderne: Alltag, Allegorie und Avantgarde. Frankfurt: Suhrkamp, 1987.

Bürger, Peter. Theory of the Avant-Garde. Trans. Michael Shaw. Minneapolis: University of Minnesota Press, 1984. Orig. Theorie der Avantgarde. Frankfurt: Suhrkamp, 1974.

Burroughs, William S. The Adding Machine: Selected Essays. New York: Seaver, 1986.

Buselmeier, Michael. "Nach der Revolte. Die literarische Verarbeitung der Studentenbewegung." In W. Martin Lüdke, ed., Literatur und Studentenbewegung: Eine Zwischenbilanz, pp. 158–85. Opladen: Westdeutscher Verlag, 1977.

Camera Obscura 1 (1976); opening issue.

Chawaf, Chantal. "Linguistic Flesh." Trans. Yvonne Rochette-Ozzello. In Elaine Marks and Isabelle de Courtivron, eds., New French Feminisms:

An Anthology, pp. 177–78. Amherst: University of Massachusetts Press, 1980. Orig. "La chair linguistique" in *Nouvelles littéraires*, 26 May 1976.

Cixous, Hélène, and Catherine Clément. *The Newly Born Woman*. Trans. Betsy Wing. Minneapolis: University of Minnesota Press, 1986. Orig. *La Jeune Née*, 1975.

Cook, Roger. "Helke Sander's *Der subjektive Faktor*." Unpublished essay, University of California, Berkeley, 1983.

Corrigan, Timothy J. *New German Film: The Displaced Image*. Austin: University of Texas Press, 1984.

———. "The Realist Gesture in the Films of Wim Wenders: Hollywood and the New German Cinema." *Quarterly Review of Film Studies* 5 (1980), pp. 205–16.

Curtius, Mechthild. "Der 'Fall' Karin Struck—ein Stück Literaturmarkt am krassen Beispiel." *Literatur und Kritik*, no. 85 (1974), pp. 296–306.

Dawson, Jan. *Wim Wenders*. Toronto: Festival of Festivals, 1976.

de Lauretis, Theresa. *Alice Doesn't: Feminism, Semiotics, Cinema*. Bloomington: Indiana University Press, 1984.

———. *Technologies of Gender: Essays on Theory, Film and Fiction*. Bloomington: Indiana University Press, 1987.

Denkler, Horst. "Langer Marsch und kurzer Prozeß. Oppositionelle Studentenbewegung und streitbarer Staat im westdeutschen Roman der siebziger Jahre." In Wolfgang Paulsen, ed., *Der deutsche Roman und seine historischen und politischen Bedingungen*, pp. 124–44. Bern: Francke, 1977.

DiCaprio, Lisa. "Marianne and Juliane/The German Sisters: Baader-Meinhof Fictionalized." *Jump Cut*, no. 29 (1984), pp. 56–59.

Drewitz, Ingeborg. "Auf der Suche nach der Mutter." Rev. of *Die Mutter* by Karin Struck. *Merkur* 29 (1975), pp. 471–73.

Drews, Jörg. "Antwort auf Jürgen Theobaldy." *Akzente*, 24 (1977), 379–82.

———. "Selbsterfahrung und Neue Subjektivität in der Lyrik." *Akzente* 24 (1977), pp. 89–95.

Duras, Marguerite. "Smothered Creativity." Trans. Virginia Hules. In Elaine Marks and Isabelle de Courtivron, eds., *New French Feminisms: An Anthology*, pp. 111–13. Amherst: University of Massachusetts Press, 1980.

Durzak, Manfred. "Für mich ist Literatur auch eine Lebenshaltung. Gespräch mit Peter Handke." In Durzak, *Gespräche über den Roman*, pp. 314–43. Frankfurt: Suhrkamp, 1976.

———. *Peter Handke und die deutsche Gegenwartsliteratur. Narziß auf Abwegen*. Stuttgart: Kohlhammer, 1982.

——— ed. *Deutsche Gegenwartsliteratur: Ausgangspositionen und aktuelle Entwicklungen*. Stuttgart: Reclam, 1981.

Eagleton, Terry. *Literary Theory: An Introduction*. Minneapolis: University of Minnesota Press, 1983.

Eder, Klaus, and Alexander Kluge. *Ulmer Dramaturgien: Reibungsverluste*. Munich: Hanser, 1980.

Ehrenreich, Barbara. *The Hearts of Men: American Dreams and the Flight from Commitment*. Garden City, NY: Anchor, 1984.

Elsaesser, Thomas. "American Grafitti und Neuer Deutscher Film: Filme-macher zwischen Avantgarde und Postmoderne." In Andreas Huyssen and Klaus R. Scherpe, eds., *Postmoderne. Zeichen eines Kulturellen Wandels*, pp. 305–10. Reinbeck: Rowohlt, 1986.

———. *New German Cinema: A History*. New Brunswick, NJ: Rutgers University Press, 1989.

———. "Tales of Sound and Fury: Observations on the Family Melodrama." 1972. In Christine Gledhill, ed., *Home is Where the Heart is: Studies in Melodrama and the Women's Film*, pp. 43–69. London: BFI Publishing, 1987.

Enzensberger, Hans Magnus. "Commonplaces on the Newest Literature." In Enzensberger, *The Consciousness Industry: On Literature, Politics and the Media*, pp. 83–94. Trans. Michael Roloff. New York: Seabury Press, 1974.

———. "Gemeinplätze, die Neueste Literatur betreffend." *Kursbuch*, no. 15 (1968), pp. 187–97.

———. *Der Untergang der Titanic. Eine Komödie* [Sinking of the Titanic. A Poem]. Frankfurt: Suhrkamp, 1978.

———. "Zwei Randbemerkungen zum Weltuntergang." *Kursbuch*, no. 52 (1978), pp. 1–8.

Fassbinder, Rainer Werner. *Die Ehe der Maria Braun* [The Marriage of Maria Braun]. 1979. 120 min. U.S. dist.: New Yorker Films.

———. *Der Händler der vier Jahreszeiten* [The Merchant of the Four Seasons]. 1971. 89 min. U.S. dist.: New Yorker Films.

———. "I Let the Audience Feel and Think." Interview with Norbert Sparrow. *Cineaste* 8, no. 1 (1977), pp. 20–21.

Fell, John L. "The Wrong Movement." *Film Quarterly* 32 (1978–1979), pp. 49–50.

Fischer, Ludwig. "Vom Beweis der Güte des Puddings. Zu Jörg Drews' und Jürgen Theobaldys Ansichten über die neuere Lyrik." *Akzente* 24 (1977), pp. 371–79.

Flückiger, Barbara. "Filme aus dem inneren Exil: Helma Sanders-Brahms." Rev. of *Deutschland, bleiche Mutter*, dir. by Helma Sanders-Brahms. *Zoom* 34, no. 8 (1982), pp. 8–11.

Foster, Hal, ed. *The Anti-Aesthetic: Essays on Postmodern Culture*. Port Townsend, WA: Bay Press, 1983.

Franklin, James. *The New German Cinema: From Oberhausen to Hamburg*. Boston: Twayne, 1983.

Freud, Sigmund. "Zur Einführung des Narzißmus." In his *Gesammelte Schriften*, 6: 155–87. Leipzig: Internationaler Psychoanalytischer Verlag, 1925. In English: "On Narcissism: An Introduction." In John Rickman, ed., *A General Selection from the Works of Sigmund Freud*. London: Hogarth Press, 1937.

Frisch, Shelley. "The Disenchanted Image: From Goethe's *Wilhelm Meister* to Wenders' *Wrong Movement*." *Literature/Film Quarterly* 7 (1979), pp. 208–14.

Geist, Kathe. *The Cinema of Wim Wenders: From Paris, France to "Paris, Texas."* Ann Arbor: UMI Research Press, 1988.

———. "Mothers and Children in the Films of Wim Wenders." In Sandra J. Frieden et al., eds., *Gender and German Cinema.* Oxford: Berg Publishers, forthcoming.

———. "Wenders in the Cities." In Klaus Phillips, ed., *New German Filmmakers: From Oberhausen through the 1970s*, pp. 379–404. New York: Frederick Ungar, 1984.

Gerhardt, Marlis. "Wohin geht Nora? Auf der Suche nach der verlorenen Frau." *Kursbuch*, no. 47 (1977), pp. 77–89.

Gitlin, Todd. *The Sixties: Years of Hope, Days of Rage.* Toronto: Bantam, 1987.

———. *The Whole World is Watching: Mass Media in the Making and Unmaking of the New Left.* Berkeley: University of California Press, 1980.

Glaser, Hermann. *Im Packeis des Unbehagens: Eine persönliche Zwischenbilanz des Generationenkonflikts.* Berlin: J.H.W. Dietz, 1982.

Gledhill, Christine, ed. *Home Is Where the Heart Is: Studies in Melodrama and the Woman's Film.* London: BFI Publishing, 1987.

Gmünder, Ulrich. *Kritische Theorie. Horkheimer, Adorno, Marcuse, Habermas.* Stuttgart: Metzler, 1985.

Godard, Jean-Luc. *Alphaville.* 1965. 98 min. U.S. dist.: New Yorker Films.

Goltschnigg, Dietmar. *Rezeptions- und Wirkungsgeschichte Georg Büchners.* Kronberg/Ts.: Scriptor, 1975.

Grob, Norbert. *Die Formen des filmischen Blicks. Wenders: Die frühen Filme.* Munich: Filmland Presse, 1984.

Großklaus, Götz. "West-östliches Unbehagen. Literarische Gesellschaftskritik in Ulrich Plenzdorfs *Die neuen Leiden des jungen W.* und Peter Schneiders *Lenz.*" *Basis* 5 (1975), pp. 80–99.

Habermas, Jürgen. "Modernity—An Incomplete Project." Trans. Seyla Ben-Habib. In Hal Foster, ed., *The Anti-Aesthetic: Essays on Postmodern Culture*, pp. 3–15. Port Townsend, WA: Bay Press, 1983.

———. *Die neue Unübersichtlichkeit.* Frankfurt: Suhrkamp, 1985.

———. *Theorie des kommunikativen Handelns.* Frankfurt: Suhrkamp, 1981.

———, ed. *Stichworte zur "Geistigen Situation der Zeit."* 2 vols. Frankfurt: Suhrkamp, 1979.

Hage, Volker. "Das Ende der Beziehungen: Über den Zustand der Liebe in neueren Romanen und Erzählungen: Eine Bestandsaufnahme." In Michael Zeller, ed., *Aufbrüche: Abschiede. Studien zur deutschen Literatur seit 1968*, pp. 14–25. Stuttgart: Ernst Klett, 1979.

———. " 'Hauptsache, du verstehst, was ich meine.' Der Erzählton in der Lyrik." In Hage, *Der Wiederkehr des Erzählers. Neue deutsche Literatur der siebziger Jahre*, pp. 122–35. Frankfurt: Ullstein, 1982.

Handke, Peter. *Die Angst des Tormanns beim Elfmeter. Erzählung* [The Goalie's Anxiety at the Penalty Kick]. Frankfurt: Suhrkamp, 1970.

------. "Die Geborgenheit unter der Schädeldecke." *Theater Heute*, no. 12 (1973), p. 2.

------. "Ich bin ein Bewohner des Elfenbeinturms." 1967. In Handke, *Ich bin ein Bewohner des Elfenbeinturms*. Frankfurt: Suhrkamp, 1972.

------. *Der kurze Brief zum langen Abschied. Erzählung* [*Short Letter, Long Farewell*]. Frankfurt: Suhrkamp, 1972.

------. *Die linkshändige Frau* [*The Left-Handed Woman*]. Frankfurt: Suhrkamp, 1976.

------. *Die linkshändige Frau* [*The Left-Handed Woman*]. Prod. Wim Wenders. 1978. 119 min. U.S. dist.: New Yorker Films.

------. *A Moment of True Feeling*. Trans. Ralph Manheim. New York: Farrar, Straus, and Giroux, 1977. Orig. *Die Stunde der wahren Empfindung*. Frankfurt: Suhrkamp, 1975.

------. "Die Tyrannei der Systeme." *Die Zeit*, 9 January 1976.

------. *Wunschloses Unglück. Erzählung* [*A Sorrow Beyond Dreams*]. Frankfurt: Suhrkamp, 1972.

Hansen, Miriam. "Cooperative Auteur Cinema and Oppositional Public Sphere: Alexander Kluge's Contribution to *Germany in Autumn*." *New German Critique*, nos. 24–25 (1981–1982), pp. 36–56.

Harrigan, Renny. "The German Women's Movement and Ours." *Jump Cut*, no. 27 (1982), pp. 42–44.

Hartung, Harald. "Lyrik zwischen Paul Celan und Nicolas Born. Skizze einer Poetik des Gedichts in den 70er Jahren." *Praxis Deutsch* (1981-Sonderheft), pp. 4–7.

Hartung, Klaus. "Die Repression wird zum Milieu. Die Beredsamkeit linker Literatur." *Literaturmagazin*, no. 11 (1979), pp. 52–79.

------. "Versuch, die Krise der antiautoritären Bewegung wieder zur Sprache zu bringen." *Kursbuch*, no. 48 (1977), pp. 14–43.

Heimgärtner, Sabine. Rev. of *Der subjektive Faktor*, dir. by Helke Sander. *Medium* 11, no. 8 (1981), pp. 37–38.

Hermand, Jost. "Fortschritt im Rückschritt. Zur politischen Polarisierung der westdeutschen Literatur seit 1961." In Manfred Durzak, ed., *Deutsche Gegenwartsliteratur: Ausgangspositionen und aktuelle Entwicklungen*, pp. 299–313. Stuttgart: Reclam, 1981.

Hiller, Eva. "mütter und töchter: zu 'deutschland, bleiche mutter,' (helma sanders-brahms), 'hungerjahre' (jutta brückner), 'daughter rite' (michelle citron)." *Frauen und Film*, no. 24 (June 1980), pp. 29–33.

Hochhuth, Rolf. *Der Stellvertreter* [*The Deputy*]. Reinbek: Rowohlt, 1963.

Hofe, Gerhard vom, and Peter Pfaff. *Das Elend des Polyphem: Zum Thema der Subjektivität bei Thomas Bernhard, Peter Handke, Wolfgang Koeppen und Botho Strauß*. Königstein/Ts.: Athenäum, 1980.

Hofstätter, Dietrich. Rev. of *Lenz* by Peter Schneider. *Schweizer Monatshefte* 54 (1974–1975), pp. 128–33.

Hohendahl, Peter U. "Habermas' Philosophical Discourse on Modernity." *Telos*, no. 69 (1986), pp. 49–65.

Hohendahl, Peter Uwe. "Politisierung der Kunsttheorie: Zur ästhetischen Diskussion nach 1965." In Paul Michael Lützeler and Egon Schwarz, eds., *Deutsche Literatur in der Bundesrepublik seit 1965*, pp. 282–99. Königstein/Ts.: Athenäum, 1980.

Höhne, Petra. Rev. of *Deutschland, bleiche Mutter*, dir. by Helma Sanders-Brahms. *Medium* 10, no. 5 (1980), p. 37.

Hosfeld, Rolf, and Helmut Peitsch. " 'Weil uns diese Aktionen innerlich verändern, sind sie politisch.' Bemerkungen zu vier Romanen über die Studentenbewegung." *Basis* 8 (1978), pp. 92–126.

Hutcheon, Linda. *A Poetics of Postmodernism: History, Theory, Fiction.* London: Routledge, 1988.

Huyssen, Andreas. *After the Great Divide: Modernism, Mass Culture, Postmodernism.* Bloomington: Indiana University Press, 1986.

———. "Mapping the Postmodern." *New German Critique*, no. 33 (1984), pp. 5–52.

———, and Klaus R. Scherpe, eds. *Postmoderne. Zeichen eines kulturellen Wandels.* Reinbek: Rowohlt, 1986.

Hyams, Barbara. "Is the Apolitical Woman at Peace?: A Reading of the Fairy Tale in *Germany, Pale Mother*." *Wide Angle* 10, no. 3 (1988), pp. 41–51.

Iser, Wolfgang. "Die Appellstruktur des Textes." 1970. In Rainer Warning, ed., *Rezeptionsästhetik*, pp. 228–52. Munich: Wilhelm Fink, 1975. In English: "Indeterminacy and the Reader's Response in Prose Fiction." In J. Hillis Miller, ed., *Aspects of Narrative*, pp. 1–45. New York: Columbia University Press, 1971.

Jameson, Fredric. "The Politics of Theory: Ideological Positions in the Postmodernism Debate." *New German Critique*, no. 33 (1984), pp. 53–65.

———. "Postmodernism and Consumer Society." In Hal Foster, ed., *The Anti-Aesthetic: Essays on Postmodern Culture*, pp. 111–25. Port Townsend, WA: Bay Press, 1983.

Jencks, Charles. *What Is Post-Modernism?* London: Academy, 1987.

Johnson, Uwe. *Jahrestage* [*Anniversaries*]. 4 vols. Frankfurt: Suhrkamp, 1970, 1971, 1973, 1980.

Johnston, Sheila. *Wim Wenders* ("BFI Dossier No. 10"). London: British Film Institute, 1981.

Jurgensen, Manfred. *Deutsche Frauenautoren der Gegenwart.* Bern: Francke, 1983.

———. *Karin Struck: Eine Einführung.* Bern: Peter Lang, 1985.

———, ed. *Frauenliteratur. Autorinnen—Perspektiven—Konzepte.* Bern: Peter Lang, 1983.

Kaes, Anton. *Deutschlandbilder. Die Wiederkehr der Geschichte als Film.* Munich: edition text + kritik, 1987. In English: *From Hitler to Heimat: The Return of History as Film.* Cambridge, MA: Harvard University Press, 1989.

———. "History, fiction, memory: Fassbinder's *The Marriage of Maria Braun* (1979)." In Eric Rentschler, ed., *German Film and Literature: Adaptations and Transformations*, pp. 276–88. New York: Methuen, 1986.

———. "Verfremdung als Verfahren: Film und Dada." In Wolfgang Paulsen and Helmut G. Herman, eds., *Sinn aus Unsinn. Dada International*, pp. 71–83. Bern: Francke, 1982.

Kaplan, E. Ann. "The Search for the Mother/Land in Sanders-Brahms's *Germany, Pale Mother* (1980)." In Eric Rentschler, ed., *German Film and Literature: Adaptations and Transformations*, pp. 289–304. New York: Methuen, 1986.

———. *Women and Film: Both Sides of the Camera*. New York: Methuen, 1983.

———, ed. *Postmodernism and Its Discontents*. London: Verso, 1988.

Keitel, Evelyne. "Verständigungstexte—Form, Funktion, Wirkung." *German Quarterly* 56 (1983), pp. 431–55.

Keith, Vibeke Rützou. "*Kursbuch* 1965–1975: Ten Years of Social, Political and Literary Perspectives of West Germany." Ph.D. Diss., New York University, 1985.

Kittler, Friedrich. "Über die Sozialisation Wilhelm Meisters." In Gerhard Kaiser and F. Kittler, eds., *Dichtung als Sozialisationsspiel. Studien zu Goethe und Gottfried Keller*, pp. 13–124. Göttingen: Vandenhoek and Ruprecht, 1978.

Klinkowitz, Jerome, and James Knowlton. *Peter Handke and the Postmodern Transformation*. Columbia: University of Missouri Press, 1983.

Kluge, Alexander. *Abschied von gestern* [*Yesterday Girl*]. 1966. 88 min. U.S. dist.: West Glen Films, New York.

———. *Gelegenheitsarbeit einer Sklavin* [*Occasional Work of a Female Slave*]. Munich: Kairos Film, 1973. 91 min.

———. "On Film and the Public Sphere." Trans. Thomas Y. Levin and Miriam B. Hansen. *New German Critique*, nos. 24/25 (1981/1982), pp. 206–20.

———. *Die Patriotin* [*The Patriot*]. Munich: Kairos Film/Mainz: ZDF, 1979. 121 min.

———. *Die Patriotin*. Frankfurt: Zweitausendeins, 1979.

———, and Edgar Reitz. *In Gefahr und größter Not bringt der Mittelweg den Tod* [*In Danger and Deep Distress, the Middle Way Spells Certain Death*]. RK (Edgar Reitz, Alexander Kluge). 1974. 89 min.

———, and Edgar Reitz. "In Gefahr und größter Not bringt der Mittelweg den Tod." *Kursbuch*, no. 41 (1975), pp. 41–84.

———, R. W. Fassbinder, Volker Schlöndorff et al. *Deutschland im Herbst* [*Germany in Autumn*]. 1978. 124 min. U.S. dist.: New Yorker Films.

Koch, Gertrud. "Exchanging the Gaze: Re-Visioning Feminist Film Theory." *New German Critique*, no. 34 (1985), pp. 139–53.

Koebner, Thomas. "Tendenzen der deutschen Gegenwartsliteratur." *Sonderdruck* from *Kröners Taschenbuchausgabe*, vol. 405, pp. 215–50. Stuttgart: Alfred Kröner, 1984.

Kolneder-Zecher, Ulrike, ed. *Eine linke Geschichte. Ein Lesebuch zum Stück*. West Berlin: GRIPS Theater, 1980.

Koonz, Claudia. *Mothers in the Fatherland: Women, the Family and Nazi Politics.* New York: St. Martin's Press, 1987.

Kosta, Barbara. "*Deutschland, bleiche Mutter*: An addendum to history." Unpublished essay, University of California, Berkeley, 1983.

―――. "Helke Sander's *der subjektive faktor.*" Unpublished essay, University of California, Berkeley, 1983.

Kracauer, Siegfried. *From Caligari to Hitler: A Psychological History of the German Film.* 1947. Princeton, NJ: Princeton University Press, 1974.

Kramer, Karen Ruoff. "/New Subjectivity/: Third Thoughts on a Literary Discourse." Ph.D. Diss., Stanford University, 1984.

Kraushaar, Wolfgang. "Notizen zu einer Chronologie der Studentenbewegung." In Peter Mosler, *Was wir wollten, was wir wurden: Studentenrevolte—zehn Jahre danach,* pp. 249–95. Reinbek: Rowohlt, 1977.

Krechel, Ursula. "Leben in Anführungszeichen. Das Authentische in der gegenwärtigen Literatur." *Literaturmagazin,* no. 11 (1979), pp. 80–107.

Kreuzer, Helmut. "Neue Subjektivität. Zur Literatur der siebziger Jahre in der Bundesrepublik Deutschland." In Manfred Durzak, ed., *Deutsche Gegenwartsliteratur: Ausgangspositionen und aktuelle Entwicklungen,* pp. 77–106. Stuttgart: Reclam, 1981.

Kuhn, Annette. *Women's Pictures: Feminism & Cinema.* Boston: Routledge & Kegan Paul, 1982.

Künzel, Uwe. *Wim Wenders. Ein Filmbuch.* Freiburg: Dreisam-Verlag, 1981.

Kunzelmann, Dieter. "Ohne uns läuft hier gar nichts mehr." Interview in the West Berlin magazine *Zitty,* 14–27 September 1984, pp. 61–67.

Kursbuch, no. 15 (November 1968): "Tod der Literatur?"

―――, no. 35 (April 1974): "Verkehrsformen. 1. Frauen Männer Linke. Über die Schwierigkeiten ihrer Emanzipation."

―――, no. 37 (October 1974): "Verkehrsformen. 2. Emanzipation in der Gruppe und die Kosten der Solidarität."

―――, no. 48 (June 1977): "Zehn Jahre danach."

Labanyi, Peter. "When Wishing Still Helped: Peter Schneider's Left-Wing Melancholy." In Keith Bullivant, ed., *After the Death of Literature: West German Writing of the 1970s,* pp. 313–39. Oxford: Berg Publishers, 1989.

Laemmle, Peter. "Büchners Schatten. Kritische Überlegungen zur Rezeption von Peter Schneiders *Lenz.*" *Akzente* 21 (1974), pp. 469–78.

Lasch, Christopher. *The Culture of Narcissism: American Life in an Age of Diminishing Expectations.* New York: W. W. Norton and Co., 1978.

Lenssen, Claudia. "Die schwere Arbeit der Erinnerung. *Frauen und Film,* no. 29 (September 1981), pp. 41–44.

――― et al. "From Hitler to Hepburn: A Discussion of Women's Film Production and Reception." *New German Critique,* nos. 24–25 (1981–1982), pp. 172–85.

Levin, Kim. *Beyond Modernism: Essays on Art from the 70s and the 80s.* New York: Harper and Row, 1988.

Literaturmagazin. Reinbek: Rowohlt, 1974—. Of particular interest: no. 3 (1975): " 'Die Phantasie an die Macht.' Literatur als Utopie"; no. 4 (1975):

"Die Literatur nach dem Tod der Literatur. Bilanz der Politisierung"; no. 5 (1976): "Das Vergehen von Hören und Sehen. Aspekte des Kulturzerfalls"; no. 9 (1978): "Der neue Irrationalismus"; no. 11 (1979): "Schreiben oder Literatur."

Lüdke, Martin. "Der neudeutsche Literaturstreit. Beschreibung einer Misere." *Literaturmagazin*, no. 17 (1986), pp. 28–45.

Lüdke, W. Martin, ed. *Literatur und Studentenbewegung. Eine Zwischenbilanz.* Opladen: Westdeutscher Verlag, 1977.

————, ed. *Nach dem Protest. Literatur im Umbruch.* Frankfurt: Suhrkamp, 1979.

Lukács, Georg. *Die Zerstörung der Vernunft. Der Weg des Irrationalismus von Schelling bis Hitler* [*The Destruction of Reason*]. East Berlin: Aufbau, 1954.

Lützeler, Paul Michael, and Egon Schwarz, eds. *Deutsche Literatur in der Bundesrepublik seit 1965.* Königstein/Ts.: Athenäum, 1980.

Lyotard, Jean-François. "Answering the Question: What Is Postmodernism? Trans. Regis Durand. In Lyotard, *The Postmodern Condition*, pp. 71–82. Trans. Geoff Bennington and Brian Massumi. Minneapolis: University of Minnesota Press, 1984.

————. *The Postmodern Condition.* Trans. Geoff Bennington and Brian Massumi. Minneapolis: University of Minnesota Press, 1984.

Marcuse, Herbert. *One-Dimensional Man: Studies in the Ideology of Advanced Industrial Society.* Boston: Beacon Press, 1964.

Marks, Elaine, and Isabelle de Courtivron, eds. *New French Feminisms: An Anthology.* Amherst: University of Massachusetts Press, 1980.

Mason, Tim. "Frau und Familie nach 1933." In his *Zur Lage der Frauen in Deutschland. Wohlfahrt, Arbeit und Familie.* Frankfurt: Suhrkamp, 1976.

————. "Women in Germany, 1925–1940: Family, Welfare, and Work." Part I: *History Workshop*, no. 1 (1976), pp. 74–113; Part II: *History Workshop*, no. 2 (1976), pp. 5–32.

Mayer, Margit. "The German October of 1977." *New German Critique*, no. 13 (1978), pp. 155–63.

Mayne, Judith. "Female Narration, Women's Cinema." *New German Critique*, nos. 24–25 (1981–1982), pp. 155–71.

————. "Feminist Film Theory and Women at the Movies." *Profession 87* (1987), pp. 14–19.

————. "Visibility and Film Criticism." *Film Reader* 5 (1982), pp. 120–24.

Meinhof, Ulrike. "Die Frauen im SDS, oder: In eigener Sache." *Konkret* 12 (10 October 1968).

Metz, Christian. *The Imaginary Signifier: Psychoanalysis and the Cinema.* Bloomington: Indiana University Press, 1982.

————. "Story/Discourse: Notes on Two Kinds of Voyeurism." In Bill Nichols, ed., *Movies and Methods, Vol. II: An Anthology*, pp. 543–49. Berkeley: University of California Press, 1985. Orig. "Histoire/Discours" in Julia Kristeva et al., eds., *Langue, Discours, Société.* Paris: Editions du Seuil, 1975.

Michel, Karl Markus. "Ein Kranz für die Literatur. Fünf Variationen über eine These." *Kursbuch*, no. 15 (1968), pp. 169–86.

Mitscherlich, Alexander, and Margarethe Mitscherlich. *Die Unfähigkeit zu trauern. Grundlagen kollektiven Verhaltens.* Munich: Piper, 1967. In English: *The Inability to Mourn: Principles of Collective Behavior.* Trans. Beverly R. Placzek. Ann Arbor: UMI Press, 1978.

Mittman, Elizabeth. "History and Subjectivity: Differences in German and French Feminisms." Paper presented at the Women in German Conference, Portland, Oregon, October 1986.

Mixner, Manfred. *Peter Handke.* Kronberg: Athenäum, 1977.

Möhrmann, Renate. "Feministische Trends in der deutschen Gegenwartsliteratur." In Manfred Durzak, ed., *Deutsche Gegenwartsliteratur: Ausgangpositionen und aktuelle Entwicklungen*, pp. 336–58. Stuttgart: Reclam, 1981.

———. *Die Frau mit der Kamera. Filmemacherinnen in der Bundesrepublik Deutschland. Situationen, Perspektiven. Zehn exemplarische Lebensläufe.* Munich: Hanser, 1980.

Monaco, James. *The New Wave: Truffaut, Godard, Chabrol, Rohmer, Rivette.* New York: Oxford University Press, 1976.

Morris, Meaghan. *The Pirate's Fiancee: Feminism, Reading, Postmodernism.* London: Verso, 1988.

Mosler, Peter. *Was wir wollten, was wir wurden: Studentenrevolte—zehn Jahre danach.* Reinbek: Rowohlt, 1977.

Mouton, Jan. "The Absent Mother Makes an Appearance in the Films of West German Women Directors." *Women in German Yearbook* 4 (1988), pp. 69–81.

Mulvey, Laura. "Visual Pleasure and Narrative Cinema." 1975. In Gerald Mast and Marshall Cohen, eds., *Film Theory and Criticism*, pp. 803–16. 3rd ed. New York: Oxford University Press, 1985.

Münzberg, Olav. "Einige Anmerkungen zu *Deutschland bleiche Mutter* von Helma Sanders-Brahms." In a promotional pamphlet for the film. West Berlin: Basis-Film-Verleih, 1980.

———. "Schaudern vor der 'bleichen Mutter.' " *Medium* 10, no. 7 (1980), pp. 34–57.

Nägele, Rainer. "Geschichten und Geschichte. Reflexionen zum westdeutschen Roman seit 1965." In Manfred Durzak, ed., *Deutsche Gegenwartsliteratur: Ausganpositionen und aktuelle Entwicklungen*, pp. 234–51. Stuttgart: Reclam, 1981.

———, and Renate Voris. *Peter Handke.* Munich: C. H. Beck, 1978.

Newman, Charles. *The Post-Modern Aura: The Act of Fiction in an Age of Inflation.* Evanston, IL: Northwestern University Press, 1985.

Nicholson, Linda J., ed. *Feminism/Postmodernism.* London: Routledge, 1990.

Owens, Craig. "The Discourse of Others: Feminists and Postmodernism." In Hal Foster, ed., *The Anti-Aesthetic: Essays on Postmodern Culture*, pp. 57–82. Port Townsend, WA: Bay Press, 1983.

Pender, Malcolm. "Historical Awareness and Peter Schneider's *Lenz*." *German Life and Letters*, n.s., 37 (1983–1984), pp. 150–60.

Petro, Patrice. *Joyless Streets: Women and Melodramatic Representation in Weimar Germany*. Princeton, NJ: Princeton University Press, 1989.

Pflaum, Hans Günther, and Hans Helmut Prinzler. *Cinema in the Federal Republic of Germany*. Trans. Timothy Nevill. Bonn: Internationes, 1983.

Phillips, Klaus, ed. *New German Filmmakers: From Oberhausen Through the 1970s*. New York: Frederick Ungar, 1984.

Plenzdorf, Ulrich. *Die neuen Leiden des jungen W.* [*The New Sorrows of Young W.*]. 1973. Frankfurt: Suhrkamp, 1980.

Pott, Wilhelm Heinrich. "Über den fortbestehenden Widerspruch von Politik und Leben. Zur Büchner-Rezeption in Peter Schneiders Erzählung 'Lenz.' " In Ludwig Fischer, ed., *Zeitgenosse Büchner*, pp. 96–130. Stuttgart: Ernst Klett, 1979.

Pütz, Peter. *Peter Handke*. Frankfurt: Suhrkamp, 1982.

———. " 'Schläft ein Lied in allen Dingen.' " In Raimund Fellinger, ed., *Peter Handke*, pp. 177–81. Frankfurt: Suhrkamp, 1985.

Rabinbach, Anson. "Unclaimed Heritage: Ernst Bloch's *Heritage of our Times* and the Theory of Fascism." *New German Critique*, no. 11 (1977), pp. 5–21.

Reich-Ranicki, Marcel. *Entgegnung. Zur deutschen Literatur der siebziger Jahre*. "Die Angst des Dichters beim Erzählen." Rev. of *Wunschloses Unglück* by Peter Handke (1972), pp. 315–22. "Gleicht die Liebe einem Monolog?" Rev. of *Die Widmung* by Botho Strauß (1977), pp. 330–33. Stuttgart: Deutsche Verlags-Anstalt, 1979.

———. "Anmerkungen zur deutschen Literatur der siebziger Jahre." *Merkur* 33 (1979), pp. 170–79.

Rentschler, Eric, ed. *West German Film in the Course of Time: Reflections on the Twenty Years since Oberhausen*. Bedford Hills, NY: Redgrave, 1984.

———. *West German Filmmakers on Film: Visions and Voices*. New York: Holmes and Meier, 1988.

———, ed. *German Film and Literature: Adaptations and Transformations*. New York: Methuen, 1986.

Rich, B. Ruby. "She Says, He Says: The Power of the Narrator in Modernist Film Politics." *Discourse*, no. 6 (1983), pp. 31–46.

Ritter, Roman. "Die 'Neue Innerlichkeit'—von innen und außen betrachtet. (Karin Struck, Peter Handke, Rolf Dieter Brinkmann.)" *Kontext* 1 (1976), pp. 238–57.

Roberts, David. "From the 1960s to the 1970s: The Changing Contexts of German Literature." Introduction to Keith Bullivant, ed., *After the Death of Literature: West German Writing of the 1970s*, pp. vii–xxiii. Oxford: Berg Publishers, 1989.

———. "Tendenzwenden. Die sechziger und siebziger Jahre in literaturhistorischer Perspektive." *Deutsche Vierteljahresschrift* 56 (1982), pp. 290–313.

"Die Rückkehr ins Private Leben." Title of *Feuilleton* section, *Frankfurter Allgemeine Zeitung*, 31 December 1975, pp. 23–24.

Runge, Erika. *Bottroper Protokolle [Bottrop Transcripts]*. Frankfurt: Suhrkamp, 1968.

———. "Überlegungen beim Abschied von der Dokumentarliteratur." *Kontext* 1 (1976), pp. 97–119.

Rutschky, Michael. *Erfahrungshunger. Ein Essay über die siebziger Jahre [Hunger for Experience]*. 1980. Frankfurt: Fischer, 1982.

Safdie, Moshe. "Skyscrapers Shouldn't Look Down on Humanity." *New York Times*, 29 May 1988, "Arts and Leisure," pp. 30–32.

Sahlberg, Oskar. "Peter Schneiders Lenz-Figur." In Ludwig Fischer, ed., *Zeitgenosse Büchner*, pp. 131–52. Stuttgart: Ernst Klett, 1979.

Sander, Helke. *Die allseitig reduzierte Persönlichkeit—REDUPERS*. 1977. 98 min. U. S. dist.: Cinema Guild, New York.

———. "Einmischung statt Verweigerung." Interview with Gudula Lorez. *die tageszeitung* (West Berlin), 20 July 1981, p. 9. Orig. "aus der überregionalen Ausgabe des TIP."

———. "Es gibt viel Falsches im Wahren." Interview with Karsten Witte. In "der subjektive faktor," a promotional program for film's opening in West Berlin at the Filmbühne am Steinplatz, 19 June 1981.

———. "Feminism and Film." Trans. Ramona Curry. *Jump-Cut*, no. 27 (1981), pp. 49–50. Orig. a paper Sander delivered in Graz, Austria, in November 1977; it then appeared in *Frauen und Film*, no. 15 (1978), pp. 5–10.

———. "Open Forms." Interview by Marc Silberman. *Jump Cut*, no. 29 (1984), pp. 59–60.

———. "der subjektive faktor, vertrackt." Pamphlet. West Berlin: Basis-Film-Verleih, 1981.

Sanders-Brahms, Helma. *Deutschland, bleiche Mutter. Film-Erzählung*. Reinbek bei Hamburg: Rowohlt, 1980.

Sandford, John. *The New German Cinema*. New York: Da Capo Press, 1980.

Scherpe, Klaus R., and Hans-Ulrich Treichel. "Vom Überdruß leben: Sensibilität und Intellektualität als Ereignis bei Handke, Born und Strauß." *Monatshefte* 73 (1981), pp. 187–206.

Schlichting, Hans Burkhard. "Das Ungenügen der poetischen Strategien: Literatur im *Kursbuch* 1968–1976." In W. Martin Lüdke, ed., *Literatur und Studentenbewegung. Eine Zwischenbilanz*, pp. 33–63. Opladen: Westdeutscher, 1977.

Schmid, Elisabeth. "Frauenleben und -liebe. Zu den Romanen von Karin Struck." In Michael Zeller, ed., *Aufbrüche: Abschiede. Studien zur deutschen Literatur seit 1968*, pp. 83–91. Stuttgart: Ernst Klett, 1979.

Schmitt, Hans Jürgen, ed. *Die Expressionismusdebatte*. Frankfurt: Suhrkamp, 1973.

Schneider, Michael. "Fathers and Sons, Retrospectively: The Damaged Relations between Two Generations." Trans. Jamie Owen Daniel. *New German Critique*, no. 31 (1984), pp. 3–51.

————. *Den Kopf verkehrt aufgesetzt—oder die melancholische Linke. Aspekte des Kulturzerfalls in den siebziger Jahren.* Darmstadt: Luchterhand, 1981.

————. *Die lange Wut zum langen Marsch. Aufsätze zur sozialistischen Politik und Literatur.* Reinbek: Rowohlt, 1975.

————. "Von der alten Radikalität zur neuen Sensibilität." *Kursbuch*, no. 49 (1977), pp. 174–87.

Schneider, Peter. *Atempause. Versuch, meine Gedanken über Literatur und Kunst zu ordnen.* Reinbek: Rowohlt, 1977.

————. "Gespräch mit Peter Schneider." Interview by Jos Hoogeveen, Gerd Labroisse, and Dick van Stekelenburg. *Deutsche Bücher* 8 (1978), pp. 248–60.

Schröder, Waltraut. Rev. of *Lenz* by Peter Schneider. *Weimarer Beiträge* 20 (1974), pp. 128–39.

Schülein, Johann August. "Von der Studentenrevolte zur Tendenzwende oder der Rückzug ins Private. Eine sozialpsychologische Analyse." *Kursbuch*, no. 48 (1977), pp. 101–17.

Schulte-Sasse, Jochen. "Modernity and Modernism, Postmodernity and Postmodernism: Framing the Issue." *Cultural Critique* 5 (1986–1987), pp. 5–21.

Schulz-Gerstein, Christian. " 'Sie sind eine wirkliche Schriftstellerin.' " *Der Spiegel*, 23 May 1983, pp. 159–61.

Schütte, Wolfram. "*Falsche Bewegung*: Wim Wenders neuer Film nach Peter Handkes Drehbuch." *Neue Zürcher Zeitung*, 18 April 1975.

————. "Mütter, Töchter, Krieg und Terror." Rev. of *Etwas tut weh* by Recha Jungmann, *Hungerjahre* by Jutta Brückner, and *Deutschland, bleiche Mutter* by Helma Sanders-Brahms. *Frankfurter Rundschau*, 25 February 1980.

————. Review of *Lenz* by Peter Schneider. *Frankfurter Rundschau*, 13 October 1973, p. xi.

————. "Träumerei oder Weg nach Innen." Rev. of *Falsche Bewegung* by Wim Wenders. *Frankfurter Rundschau*, 25 April 1975.

Seeba, Hinrich. "Persönliches Engagement: Zur Autorenpoetik der siebziger Jahre. *Monatshefte* 73 (1981), pp. 140–54.

————. "Der Untergang der Utopie: Ein Schiffbruch in der Gegenwartsliteratur." *German Studies Review* 4 (1981), pp. 281–98.

Seiter, Ellen. "Women's History, Women's Melodrama: *Deutschland, bleiche Mutter.*" *German Quarterly* 59 (1986), pp. 569–81.

Silberman, Marc. "Cine-Feminists in West Berlin." *Quarterly Review of Film Studies* 5 (1980), pp. 217–32.

————. "From the Outside Moving In." Intro. to Special Section: "Film and Feminism in Germany Today." *Jump Cut*, no. 27 (1982), pp. 41–42.

Silverman, Kaja. "Helke Sander and the Will to Change." *Discourse*, no. 6 (1983), pp. 10–30.

Sloterdijk, Peter. *Critique of Cynical Reason.* Trans. Michael Eldred. Minneapolis: University of Minnesota Press, 1987. Orig. *Kritik der zynischen Vernunft*, 2 vols. Frankfurt: Suhrkamp, 1983.

Sloterdik, Peter. "Cynicism—The Twilight of False Consciousness." Trans. Michael Eldred and Leslie A. Adelson. *New German Critique*, no. 33 (1984), pp. 190–206.

Stefan, Verena. *Shedding*. Trans. Johanna Moore and Beth Weckmueller. New York: Daughters Publishing Co., 1978. Orig. *Häutungen*. Munich: Frauenoffensive, 1975.

Strachota, Kathryn. "Theory and Practice, or: Did Rudi Dutsche Send His Laundry Home to Mutti?" Unpublished essay on *Der subjektive Faktor*, dir. by Helke Sander, University of California, Berkeley, 1982.

Strauss, Botho. *Groß und klein* [*Big and Little*]. Munich: Hanser, 1978.

Struck, Karin. "Ist nur eine tote erotische Autorin eine gute erotische Autorin?" *Monatshefte* 75 (1983), pp. 353–57.

———. "Mädchenjahre im Schatten des Krieges." In Manfred Jurgensen, ed., *Deutsche Frauenautoren, der Gegenwart*, pp. 198–205. Bern: Franke, 1983.

Theobaldy, Jürgen. "Literaturkritik, astrologisch. Zu Jörg Drews' Aufsatz über Selbsterfahrung und Neue Subjektivität in der Lyrik," *Akzente* 24 (1977), pp. 188–91.

Theweleit, Klaus. *Male Fantasies*. Trans. Stephan Conway et al. 2 vols. Minneapolis: University of Minnesota Press, 1987. Orig. *Männerphantasien*. 2 vols. Frankfurt: Roter Stern, 1977.

Trotta, Margarethe von. *Die bleierne Zeit*. 1981. 107 min. U.S. title: *Marianne and Juliane*. U.S. dist.: New Yorker Films.

Vesper, Bernward. *Die Reise. Romanessay* [*The Journey*]. 1977. Reinbek: Rowohlt, 1983.

Vormweg, Heinrich. Rev. of *Die Mutter* by Karin Struck. *Merkur* 29 (1975), pp. 474–77.

Walser, Martin, "Berichte aus der Klassengesellschaft." Foreword to Erika Runge, *Bottroper Protokolle*, pp. 7–10. Frankfurt: Suhrkamp, 1968.

Weiss, Peter. *Die Ästhetik des Widerstands* [*The Aesthetics of Resistance*]. 3 vols. Frankfurt: Suhrkamp, 1975, 1978, 1981.

———. *Die Ermittlung* [*The Investigation*]. Frankfurt: Suhrkamp, 1965.

Wenders, Wim. *Die Angst des Tormanns beim Elfmeter* [*The Goalie's Anxiety at the Penalty Kick*]. Munich: Filmverg der Autoren, 1971. 100 min.

———. *Im Lauf der Zeit* [*Kings of the Road*]. Wim Wenders Filmproduktion. 1975–1976. 176 min.

———. *Nick's Film—Lightning over Water*. Berlin: Road Movies, 1980. 91 min.

———. *Paris, Texas*. New York: Gray City, 1984. 148 min.

———. *Summer in the City*. HFF Munich. 1970. 125 min.

Wiegenstein, Roland H. Rev. of *Lenz* by Peter Schneider. *Merkur* 28 (1974), pp. 92–94.

Winkels, Hubert. "Selbstheilung des Fragments. Zur Krise des Sinns bei Botho Strauß und Peter Handke." *Sprache im technischen Zeitalter* 85 (1983), pp. 89–92.

Wolf, Christa. *Kein Ort. Nirgends* [*No Place on Earth*]. East Berlin: Aufbau, 1979.

———. *Kindheitsmuster* [*Patterns of Childhood*]. East Berlin: Aufbau, 1976.

———. *Nachdenken über Christa T.* [*The Quest for Christa T.*]. Halle, East Germany: Mitteldeutscher Verlag, 1968. Version cited here: Neuwied [W. Ger.]: Luchterhand, 1971.

Wolff, Frank and Eberhard Windaus, eds. *Studentbewegung 1967–69. Protokolle und Materialien*. Frankfurt: Roter Stern, 1977.

Zeller, Michael, ed. *Aufbrüche: Abschiede. Studien zur deutschen Literatur seit 1968*. "Einleitung: Versuch, zehn Jahre westdeutscher Literatur in den Blick zu nehmen," pp. 5–13. "Die Zärtlichkeit der Gewalt. Zehn Bemerkungen zu Rolf Dieter Brinkmann," pp. 47–59. Stuttgart: Ernst Klett, 1979.

Zur Lippe, Rudolf. "Objektiver Faktor Subjektivität." *Kursbuch*, no. 35 (1974), pp. 1–34.

Index